T0131570

REFLECTIONS

ON
FAITH AND
17TH CENTURY
EUROPEAN-AMERICAN
COLONISTS

AS SEEN THROUGH THE LIVES

OF FOUR YOUNG

IMMIGRANTS

CARLOS R. HAMILTON JR.

WESTBOW
PRESS®
A DIVISION OF THOMAS NELSON
& ZONDERVAN

WestBow Press books may be ordered through booksellers or by contacting:

WestBow Press
A Division of Thomas Nelson & Zondervan
1663 Liberty Drive
Bloomington, IN 47403
www.westbowpress.com
844-714-3454

ISBN: 978-1-6642-9024-2 (sc)
ISBN: 978-1-6642-9025-9 (hc)
ISBN: 978-1-6642-9023-5 (e)

Library of Congress Control Number: 2023901263

Print information available on the last page.

WestBow Press rev. date: 3/21/2023

CONTENTS

PREFACE

The original motivation for the creation of this book stemmed from an awareness of four young people who came to colonial America during the seventeenth century. This information was the result of genealogical work done by previous generations of our families, but little information was available other than the dates of events in their lives and the names of their forebears and descendants. It is known that they were each in their teen years or early twenties when they left their homes in Nottinghamshire, England; Ostfriesland, Netherlands; La Rochelle, France; and the Electoral Palatinate of the Holy Roman Empire at various times during the seventeenth century. They either came alone or with members of their immediate family and sought their futures in Dorchester/Salem (Colony of Massachusetts Bay), Rensselaerwyck (Colony of New Netherland), New Rochelle (Colony of New York), and Germantown (Colony of Pennsylvania). An initial research interest in these individuals was to try to understand what was occurring in their specific homelands that motivated them and their families to make life-changing, permanent moves that would have been marked with great uncertainty. Indeed, a review of the European age of Enlightenment reveals a number of circumstances that prompted an extensive migration to the colonies from European states. An awareness of European history and circumstances during the American colonial era is essential to understanding many aspects of colonization of the New World. The reasons for the founding of the colonies were varied and reflected the needs or motivations of the authorities at a particular time. Most of the early colonies were founded with economic expectations or religious considerations, while after the English Civil Wars, political reasons were predominant. The reasons for individuals or families to emigrate were diverse and related to specific personal circumstances. An awareness of the personal concerns of ordinary individuals may enhance interest in the study of the past and the events that affected their lives. While this study is limited to the Anglo-European immigration, the historical background of homelands of African, Latino, and Asian immigrants are as important in understanding the circumstances of their many contributions to the subsequent culture of the United States of America.

One can generalize about the motivations to emigrate from European homelands by the subjects of this study as predominantly a) the desire for economic opportunity not available to them in their origins; b) security for one's self and their family; and c) freedom to worship according to their consciences. Our four individuals or their families would have claimed one or more of these motives for their immigration. These same issues seem to be behind the increasing numbers of immigrants seeking residence in the United States in more modern times. Immigration policy for the present should be based on these issues. People able and willing to contribute to their own well-being and the overall progress of society should be welcomed. In the seventeenth century, the North American colonies were considered as the most diverse culture of any location, a circumstance that continues to the present. This diversity should be recognized as a major strength of our society.

Even a superficial awareness of the sixteenth- and seventeenth-century Europe reveals the prolonged and overwhelming effect of the Protestant Reformation. This movement followed varied paths in the states of Western Europe, but in each, all aspects of life were affected by resulting warfare, governmental disruption, and social displacement. Although not the only motivation of colonial immigration, religion was a crucial factor in the early settlement of the New England colonies and important in the formation and growth of New Jersey and Pennsylvania. While the southern colonies of Virginia and the Carolinas were formed as the result of economic and political factors, religious issues would also be important in their development. A reason for the disruptive role of religion in Europe was directly related to the official acceptance of specific religious beliefs by the ruling secular authorities and the imposition of governmental powers of law enforcement, taxation, and military activity for their support.

Another goal of this study was to try to understand the activities of these four individuals and their movements during the first generation of their presence in the colonies. The initial plan was to relate a story of colonial America from the perspective of these young people who had much in common with people of the same age living at subsequent times in the history of this land. The character traits and values of these colonists and the large numbers of other immigrants would well serve individuals of any era. The sparse primary information about the lives of these four subjects rendered opinions about their subjective response to the circumstances of colonial life as speculation. Despite this hurdle, much can be learned of their character and values from the circumstances of their lives and their actions. These same traits were vital to the success of the entire colonial venture and remain key to maintaining the vitality of a society dependent on individual freedom and opportunity.

As information for this project was gathered, it became clear that there were many issues of interest and significance that were worthy of elaboration. Colonial incidents and circumstances were forebears of the development of basic aspects of the government, society, and customs that have played integral roles in the succeeding centuries. This study will reflect a number of these situations and experiences that contributed to the development of the structure of our government, the Constitution, and Bill of Rights. An awareness of the origins of these issues may help us better understand some of their intended meaning and significance to the present era.

The frontispiece of this work, a photograph from the artistic efforts of my oldest grandchild, Madeleine Hamilton, may be symbolic of this association. The reflected image of objects or concepts, although closer to the observer, are often not focused, and distortions may obscure their significance and be clarified only by examining the original source. What we can observe in today's America is a reflection of the past history of this nation that molded our culture and governance and that may be blurred by the passing of succeeding centuries. To understand these issues more clearly, it is useful to look back at the origins of our nation, seeking insight into issues we often take for granted.

The Bill of Rights of our Constitution specifies certain rights that were directly related to events in the colonial era and include the right to the free exercise of religion and the prevention of the establishment of religion by the government. Also protected are the freedom of speech, freedom of the press, the right of peaceful assembly, and the right to petition the government for redress of grievances. Other amendments include the right to bear arms and the prohibition of the quartering of troops in private homes, which relate to the English Common Law but were emphasized by the experiences of the colonists. These liberties were considered inherent rights of humankind, and their source was from the Creator—not created by government or other human inventions.

The protection of religious freedom was a legal principle that developed from our colonial heritage, and its persistence was unique at the time of our colonies. It has been the subject of interpretations that may be at variance from the intent of the original writers. Some sources that have been used to help clarify that original intent of the wording of this freedom may have had, at the time of their origin, meanings different from that subsequently used to clarify the original intent of the amendment.

An examination of the role of religious belief and worship in colonial America indicates its great importance in the culture and lives of those individuals and communities. Trying to understand this aspect of the era became one of the dominant subjects for our study. Religious freedom was a high priority for the writers of our Constitution and Bill of Rights, as the quest for this right was essential from the earliest settlements. The eventual diversity of religious beliefs and worship styles among the colonies and among the individual groups of colonists reflected the circumstances of their European origins and subsequent theological interpretations. While our four immigrants brought with them different aspects of the Reformed Protestant faith, their experiences were only a part of the range of beliefs prevalent in colonial America. The Roman Catholic, Anglican, Quaker, Jewish, Anabaptist, and other religious traditions had profound effects on the development of the colonies and our subsequent nation.

As our study of the colonial era indicated that religion was a primary factor in the settlement of some of the colonies and a significant issue in each of them as well as for our young immigrants, it is important to define what these issues include—both for the colonies as political entities and for individuals. It is useful to distinguish between the role of organized religious institutions and an individual's beliefs and understanding of their spiritual faith. These two aspects of religion are closely related, as it is usually through one's family and the organized church community that knowledge of one's religion, belief, and faith are influenced and formed. It is through these religious entities that one has a public expression of their belief.

Much has been written about the concepts of religion versus spirituality—a conversation that is outside the scope of this project. It is my understanding of the Christian faith that the two are inseparably intertwined. One can define a *religion* as referring to a specific organization or group of believers with common traditions, doctrines, creeds, and practices. The entity exists to perpetuate its particular beliefs and develop the understanding and commitment of their congregations. The term *spirituality* refers to a belief or faith that God can establish a personal relationship with an individual and be an ongoing presence in one's life. In the Christian faith, this refers to the Holy Spirit as a critical component in the understanding of a triune God. It is a concept that has some presence in nearly all religions. It is this aspect of religious faith that was certainly present in the experiences of our four immigrants and in many of those who were a part of the settlement of the North American colonies. This faith can have profound effects on one's actions, goals, and understanding of the purposes and significance of an individual and their family.

Spirituality was also a significant part of the religion of the Native Americans, whose beliefs were long established before the arrival of the Europeans. The interaction of these beliefs and those of the early settlers in Plymouth and Massachusetts Bay colonies had important effects on life in seventeenth-century New England. From the earliest European settlement in the Americas, the desire to extend the Christian faith to the native population was a high priority. The Roman Catholic Church was an integral part of the Spanish government's colonization of Mexico and South America and the colonization and exploration by France of what is now Canada.

The Virginia colony was begun primarily as an economic and political venture, but a number of the colonists were greatly influenced by their Reformed faith. The northern colonies of Plymouth and Massachusetts Bay arose primarily from religious controversies in England. The intent of some of these early colonists to evangelize the natives was slow to develop, but when it met with success, it resulted in cultural divisiveness for the Indians.

Soon after the colonists' arrival in New England, religious controversies based on their understanding of the spiritual interpretation of their faith, such as the Antinomian Controversy, would be disruptive and result in expansion of the settlements that became Connecticut, Rhode Island, and New Hampshire. The divisions of the native population based in part on religious issues would be a part of the Pequot War and the devastating King Philip's (or Metacomet's) War.

A review of the colonial period and the lives of our young immigrants made apparent the important role of religion throughout the colonies. Each of these four families experienced some degree of duress related to their religious faith in England, France, and the Palatinate. Their faith would be an important part of their lives in Massachusetts Bay, New Netherland, and other colonies. Certainly religion was not the only motivation for their immigration to the colonies, as the limited opportunities for economic and social advancement in Europe and the safety of one's self and family were also important issues, especially in late seventeenth-century France and the Palatinate.

This story describes the early history of the Virginia and Massachusetts Bay colonies in greater detail than the subsequent settlements, as the hardships and dangers that challenged them were well known to the later immigrants and important in shaping their expectations. The New World, despite its challenges and dangers, did provide compelling attractions for the beleaguered peoples of some European states. Perhaps the greatest incentive, along with the opportunity to worship according to their consciences, was the opportunity for ownership of land once one had completed a term of indenture or invested their own resources. Beginning in the seventeenth century, the ethnic, social, and religious diversity of the colonies was a major characteristic that would continue and be a feature of each colony. In some cases, the acceptance of this diversity would be a critical part of their success. The result of these various influences would be that each colony developed a distinct economy, culture, and personality, which were important factors in the eventual creation of a new nation.

A characteristic that defined these colonies and the subsequent United States was the ability of the leadership and the citizens to accept the fact of diverse interests and the necessity of compromise. We will try to follow the lives of these immigrant families and be reminded of the role of the church and their faith throughout colonial history—from the Reformed/Separatist movement in New England until the Great Awakening in the first half of the eighteenth century. The issue of slavery and its persistence throughout the era created overwhelming spiritual and social conflicts, which will be considered as they impacted every colony and religious group, including our four families. These four young people and their generations were thrust into a century of perhaps as much change and turmoil as any in modern history. We may be able to gain insights into our present experiences from the review of our past and the significance of these colonial issues to twenty-first-century America.

This project was completed only through the support and encouragement of my wife, Carolyn Burton Hamilton, and our family, who are all descendants of the subjects of the story. The advice of Dr. Frank de la Teja, Regents' professor emeritus at Texas State University and a leader of the Texas State Historical Association, was essential for the direction and progress of the work. I will long be in his debt.

PART I

REFLECTIONS ON THE LIVES AND FAMILIES OF FOUR COLONIAL INDIVIDUALS

A. INTRODUCTION

The story of the people whose descendants would eventually contribute to the founding of the United States of America began in earnest with the coming of individuals from Europe to North America in the seventeenth century. They created permanent settlements amid a diverse native civilization, which had existed for millennia and was often hostile to their presence. Most of the names of the ordinary people who became permanent residents and their extraordinary persistence and efforts are unknown to the vast numbers of their descendants who now live in this country. Those persons making the perilous sea voyage to North America to face the unknown dangers and opportunities that awaited came for specific reasons. Only rarely did they seek adventure or expect to acquire fortunes. Understanding their circumstances, motivations, and the outcomes of their efforts helps to illuminate their decisions and values, which ultimately became a part of the fabric of the United States of America. Although they may be ordinary by the standards of the social classes of Europe, or their financial position at that time, they were truly extraordinary in their ability to adapt to the circumstances of the New World and to remain devoted to their families and their faith.

The motivations that prompted this wave of immigration arose from the environment in Europe—physical, economic, geopolitical, social, and spiritual—that characterized its seventeenth century. Although many, especially young men, made the voyage as individuals, a significant number of settlers came as families or groups who had common interests and reasons for undertaking the dangerous journey and the subsequent challenges. In some cases, orphaned children or youth found a home in North American colonies as indentured servants when there was no immediate family available to provide care. In other cases, families left their European homeland because of threats to their security, often the result of their religious convictions, which were considered nonconformist and not in the favor of the ruling authorities. In most situations, there were several factors affecting the decision to immigrate, and we will try to understand some of those circumstances.

The following are the stories of four individuals and their families who were a part of the generation of Europeans who originally settled British North America. They were among the forbearers of generations that helped create the United States. Two of our subjects came with large families (Stoughton/Denman and Kolb), while the others came alone (Wyckoff) or with a small family group (Gaineau-Gano). The hardships and challenges faced in the New World changed significantly during the decades of the seventeenth century. The responses to those circumstances by these individuals and other immigrants molded their character and that of their descendants. Their responses are reflected in the America of the twenty-first century. Many of our traditions, beliefs, laws, and public policy can be traced to those early days. They are now a part of our daily lives and contribute to the unique nature of the United States.

We will meet these individuals and learn what we can about the circumstances in their European homelands and in their colonial destinations. Several factors complicate our ability to gather information in the search for answers to these questions. One of the difficulties is the identity of individuals due to variations in spelling (French origin) and customs affecting family names (Netherlands). In other cases, immigrants left their homeland under such hostile conditions that records of their identity and activities were intentionally destroyed by ruling authorities (Huguenots from La Rochelle). Another feature of the seventeenth century, which is an unfortunate problem for our research, is the lack of documentation of the maiden names of women in the available records. Their anonymity does not detract from their remarkable contributions to their family's apparently cohesive structures.

Although the available records cannot relate the feelings and expectations of our immigrants, we can imagine what they might have been from reflecting on the circumstances and challenges of their European origins and their subsequent actions and legacy in

North America. The documented information about the lives of these four individuals and their family members is often incomplete. What information was available to the present author is related in in the appendix (section IV, A–D). The attempt at historical accuracy is clouded frequently by inconsistent information concerning names, dates, and locations. Primary sources are scarce but of great interest when available. The introduction of these four individuals will require some conjecture on our part, but the additional information in sections II to IV will help support or confirm our conclusions. The validity of some information is rightly viewed with skepticism as the records of published genealogical writings about these early settlers are difficult to confirm or has been found by modern historical research to be inaccurate or falsified. The information is as accurate as can be established at this time but may be modified by future discoveries. We will be more concerned with the character and actions of our subjects, who are verified by the story of their lives and enacted on the stage of seventeenth-century America.

We will also try to understand how the beliefs and decisions of these individuals and the large numbers of their fellow immigrants shaped the America we live in the twenty-first century. Join me as we try to understand the nature and character of these seventeenth-century European immigrants, the world from which they came, and that in which they made new lives.

B. JOHN DENMAN I AND JUDITH STOUGHTON OF NOTTINGHAMSHIRE, ENGLAND

John Denman II was born in 1621 into a family with members who had served the Church of England for several generations. But they were faced with harassment due to their sympathies for the developing Reformed beliefs. Life in Nottinghamshire was made even more difficult for his family, as his father, and namesake, had died when young John II was two years old. He looked forward to being able to help care for his sister, Mary, who was his junior by only one year, and their mother, Judith, who had lost John I, her husband and his father. Later, he lost his stepfather, William Smead, to the illnesses that seemed ever present in their town. The father of his half brother, William, died before the boy had reached his second birthday. Life would have been grim for their family had it not been for the influence and legacies of the lives of his grandfathers, the Rev. Thomas Stoughton and the Rev. Francis Denman, who had helped them through these dark times.[1]

When young John was fourteen years old, he learned that his mother planned to move their family to Massachusetts Bay. His mind filled with excitement. The anticipation of a home in the colony greatly stimulated his imagination. He had heard of the dark forests and savage Indians who may lurk in their shadows, but he was confident that his uncles, Thomas, and Israel Stoughton, who had preceded them to the New World with Governor John Winthrop, would see to their safety. He knew the availability of land and adventure would be much to his liking. He hoped to someday obtain property of his own and help care for his mother and younger siblings.

Young John arrived in Boston with his mother, sister, and brother in the autumn of 1635, after a journey on the *Dorset,* which seemed to last forever, as they first sailed to Barbados in the West Indies. The rulers of England were displeased with additional people leaving for the Massachusetts Colony. The deception of travel to the island colony helped avoid any further interferences by the authorities in their itinerary. During the months of their ship's journey, babies had been born and some travelers had died. All suffered from the closeness of their quarters, the stench of the ship from the livestock that accompanied them, and the turmoil of the Atlantic's rough seas.

On arriving in Boston, they had been welcomed by their extended family and found lodging in Dorchester. There, Israel Stoughton had established a successful business and had assumed leadership positions in the community. Thomas Stoughton had also become well known

---

[1] See section IV, A appendix for further information concerning the careers and beliefs of Rev. Stoughton and Rev. Denman.

in Dorchester. But by the end of 1635, Thomas was making plans to move to the Connecticut River Valley, where fertile land and timber were abundant. John would later understand that some of the rules of the Massachusetts Bay Puritan leadership had proven to be restrictive, reminiscent of their native land, and had been an encouragement for Thomas's extended family to leave Dorchester. Shortly after their arrival in New England, the Pequot War erupted, and his uncle Israel would play an important part in the colony's response.[2]

Within two years of their arrival in Dorchester, his mother moved the family to Salem, where she felt more welcome in the church and where land would be available to them. The Salem church had been served by Roger Williams, whose controversial theology had invoked the ire of the Massachusetts Bay General Court. This resulted in his banishment from the colony, but many of his admirers remained in Salem. There was much that John did not understand about these controversies. But the families he knew were hardworking and honorable and had been forced to join Roger Williams in his new colony because of their beliefs.

John did not have much opportunity to dwell on these issues. Within two years of their move to Salem, in March 1639, his mother's life journey ended. With the help of her brother, Israel Stoughton, her estate was administered, and each of the three children was remembered in her will. John was an adult eighteen-year-old and became the heir to the property, which Judith had owned in the Salem area. His sister Mary was planning to wed Clement Maxfield, and she would live in Dorchester. Judith's youngest child, William (Smead), was twelve years old at the time of her death, and he was offered a place in the Boston household of John Pope as an apprentice. William would learn the weaver's trade, and the Pope family would

---

[2] The Pequot War and the role of Israel Stoughton are discussed in part III, B.

provide for him throughout his youth.[3] He would marry, raise a family of nine children in Dorchester, and serve in the Indian War.[4]

During those early Salem years, John had many opportunities to visit Dorchester, where he met and become attracted to a girl named Sarah. She was known as Sarah Hollander, but her family name was not certain, as her parents may have been killed during a conflict with Indians when she was a young child. Her family had come to the Connecticut Valley from New Netherland, and a family in Massachusetts Bay took Sarah in as one of their own. Dorchester had been the only home she could remember. She grew to be an attractive woman whose presence in the Dorchester church was likely a distraction for John when he often attended the services. They would marry in 1643 and make their home in Salem, where John had his property.[5] Three sons would be born to them; at last, there was another "young" John and two younger brothers, William and Philip. The boys would grow up in Salem until the family moved to Long Island with other families. Their exact route and the year of the move are unknown, but it is likely that they left Massachusetts Bay in the 1650s, near the time that John's relative, John Scudder, and family joined a group of Salem Puritans moving to Southold, a town in far eastern Long Island and part of the New Haven Colony.[6] By the early 1660s, they had relocated to the western end of the island in New Netherland; the John Denmans, the John Scudders, and their relative, Richard Betts, were all in western Long Island, and in 1662, they obtained land from the Lenape natives.[7] The Denman family lived

---

[3] William Smead and Mary Denman Maxfield would remain in Dorchester throughout their lifetimes with numerous descendants. See section IV, A appendix for further details.

[4] This was King Philip's War, beginning in June 1675, one of the critical events of seventeenth-century colonial history, and it is discussed in part III, B.

[5] The origin and identity of Sarah Hollander is not documented, but a scenario such as described is possible, as no others in New England have been found with that family name. Her marriage to John Denman at Dorchester in 1643 is well established.

[6] See IV,A John Denman and Judith Stoughton, page 155

[7] Ibid. pp. 155–57.

in Maspeth, although some references suggest that they resided in Long Island City. That name for the community was not used until the nineteenth century and encompassed the settlement of Maspeth, which was farther up Newtown Creek than the present-day location of Long Island City.[8] The location of their property and home is not definitely known, but the New York Public Library files contain a photograph of a building described as the old Denman home and locate it in the vicinity of the present-day intersection of Fifty-Sixth Street and Fifty-Fifth Drive in Queens near the vehicle-maintenance facility of the fire department of New York. That location would be in the area of the seventeenth-century community of Maspeth; it is near the present avenue of that name and the upper reaches of Newtown Creek. That river was known by the Indians as the Hohobosco and was a source of clams and fish (figure 1). The area was covered by forests, interspersed by naturally open ground with fertile soil ideal for crops, which included corn, beans, and squash. By the mid-seventeenth century, the European settlers had learned the cultivation of tobacco from the natives.

The Long Island native Indians were of the larger tribe known as the Lenni Lenape (or the Delaware, as called by the English) of the Algonquian language group. Their territory extended from the lower Hudson River to the Delaware River valleys and included western Long Island. To the west lived the Susquehanna tribe, and to the north the Mohawks, both of the Iroquoian language group who were ancient enemies of the Lenape. Long Island Sound separated them from hostile Pequot and Narragansett tribes. Early references indicate thirteen distinct tribal groups on Long Island, and those in the vicinity of Maspeth were the Carnasec and Rockaway clans, speaking the Munsee dialect of the language. These Lenape were initially receptive to the Dutch and English, perhaps because they saw them as potential allies against the Mohawks and Pequots, whose invasions prior to the arrival of the Europeans had been devastating, requiring the subdued Lenapes to pay annual tribute of "wampum

---

[8] Ibid. pp.156–57.

and dried clams."[9] By the 1660s, the Lenape began migrating to the Ohio River Valley, as the numbers of Dutch and English settlers were increasing.

Information about the life of the Denman families in Maspeth is incomplete, but they likely provided timber and produce from their property for the growing Manhattan population. It is not known if they had slaves or other laborers. The sons of John II and Sarah would reach adulthood in Maspeth and make their lives in the colonies of New York and Connecticut. Their second son, William, would not marry and would live in the family home for his lifetime. John Denman II and his wife, Sarah, died in about 1691 and were buried near their Maspeth home. Two of their sons would marry—Philip to Hasadiah Slough of Derby, Colony of New Haven, where they would live and raise six children born between 1678 and 1688. Philip was often mentioned in the records of the Derby community.[10] Three of their daughters married and raised families in the Colony of Connecticut. Records do not indicate marriages of their sons.

John Denman III lived in the Newtown area, where records indicate that he and the second generation of his Scudder cousins obtained land from the Lenape. In March 1665, he and John Scudder and Richard Betts are listed among sixty-seven freeholders in Newtown.[11] He and Mary Gano (Gaineau) of New Rochelle married in 1690 when he was forty-seven years old. Mary Gano, with her father and younger brother, Jeremiah, arrived in New York in about 1686 with other Huguenots fleeing their La Rochelle homeland after the revocation of the Edict of Nantes by French King Louis XIV in 1685.[12] Mary and John would live in Newtown and raise four sons, John IV (born 1700), William (1702), Philip (1704), and Thomas (1706), and three daughters, Martha, Mary, and Elizabeth

---

[9] NS.Prime (1845), 90–95.

[10] S. Orcutt and A. Beardsley (1880).

[11] _

[12] This event is described in greater detail in section II, "Reflections on the European Age of Enlightenment," and in the sections about Mary and the Gaineau (Gano) family.

(dates of birth are unknown). The Denman family worshipped at the Newtown Reformed Church, now known as the Elmhurst Presbyterian Church (figure 2). John III would not live to see these children reach maturity, as he died in 1713.

The transfer of New Netherland to the English, initially in 1664 and permanently in 1674, was disruptive to those owning land in Long Island, as the deeds to their property that had been negotiated directly with the Lenape natives were often not recognized by the new English authorities. A large portion of the acreage that John had claimed was taken from him. John Denman III subsequently obtained a tract in Essex County in the Colony of New Jersey when it was established as separate from New York. He and his family continued to make their home in Newtown, where he had public responsibility for roadway construction.

John's family would not move permanently until after his death in 1713. His will, a copy of which was in the office of the county clerk in Jamaica, Long Island, in the early twentieth century,[13] indicates a continuing close relationship between the Denman family and their Scudder relatives and Mary's brother, Jeremiah Gano, who lived in Newtown and never married. The Denman family remained members of the Reformed Church in Newtown, and John III was buried in that area. After selling the Long Island property, Mary and her six children moved permanently to Essex County, Colony of New Jersey.[14] These children are all mentioned in the will of John Denman III, and they and the next generation would make their homes in Elizabethtown, Westfield, and Springfield, where they worshipped at the Reformed Churches of the communities.[15] Each of the sons of John Denman and Mary Gano are buried on the respective church property of their towns. Their descendants were patriots, serving in the colonial army or state militia, and afterward

---

[13] Harris, H.N. Denman Family History; From the Earliest Authentic Records Down to the Present Time. 1913.

[14] See IV, A appendix for more detail about their family and the relatives of Judith Stoughton Denman.

[15] Ibid. Will of John Denman. page 157.

received land grants for their service. Many of the family members of the next generation moved to the Northwest Territories of Ohio and Indiana or to Virginia and Georgia. They appear to have maintained the traditions of independence, faith, and care for their families that had been passed down from the first generation of immigrants.

Additional information about the Denman families is found in section IV, A.

C. PIETER CLAESSEN WYCKOFF AND GRIETJE VAN NESS OF OSTFRIESLAND AND HOLLAND, THE NETHERLANDS

Pieter Claessen would never forget the date of March 4, as it was then that the ship *Rensselaerswyck* finally arrived at Manhattan in the New Netherland colony. He would set foot on solid ground for the first time in months. The voyage had begun in September 1636, and for the first three months, they struggled with storms and contrary winds that detoured their journey, first to Spain and then to Ilfracombe on the north shore of Devon in the Cornwall peninsula of England. The early part of their journey was tormented by the tumultuous weather and by illness that seemed to affect nearly all of the passengers. It must have been especially difficult for Annetie Barents, who gave birth on the day in early November when the severe weather damaged the ship's rudder. The baby's parents named him Storm (Albertze Van Der Zee). Even the respite in Ilfracombe was perilous, as some of the passengers went to a local tavern in early December, and Cornelis Thomasz, a smith traveling with his family, was killed by his hired helper. The "offender was carried away in the name of the king," and the ship's rudder, which had been removed by the authorities to preclude their leaving during the investigation, was returned. The adverse weather persisted, and the *Rensselaerwyck* was unable to proceed toward America until January 9, 1637, when Skipper Jan Tiepkesk Schellinger took advantage of the brisk northeasterly winds; at last they were on their way to the New World.[16]

The difficulty of the voyage helped distract Pieter's thoughts from the ambivalence he felt about making the journey. It had been less than two years since the terrible plague had swept through Marienhafe, killing his mother and father and scores of their neighbors. Over two hundred residents of their small village died from this fearsome pestilence. He was still in his teen years when they died, and with other youth who had lost their parents, he was given shelter by the local Reformed Church. Pieter Claessen was especially appreciative of the church elder, Ehme Poptes, a friend of his family who likely recommended him as a worker for the New Netherland patroonship of Killiaen van Rensselaer. Able-bodied men and youth from the province of Ostfriesland were being recruited for immigration to the Dutch lands in America. Pieter knew that the opportunity to learn about farming and eventually obtain land of his own was not likely in his home country. The prospects for his future in the Low Country were dim; a young man with no family or inheritance had little likelihood of work other than as a laborer, clerk, or soldier. The future in America was at least one that he could influence more by his efforts.

In the spring of 1636, when flowers were appearing on the Low Country fields, Pieter learned that his future would lie in the New World. He would sail to New Amsterdam and then to the outpost of Fort Orange, where a town was being built and settlers were needed to occupy and farm the territory. Pieter had only rarely been more than a few miles away from his home in the Nordin township. He had seldom glimpsed the bustling cities of the western provinces of the Netherlands and the mysterious woodland of the Teutoburg Forest to the south, which was the origin of a lively stream that became the gentle Ems River flowing to the bay near his home. The idea of traveling across the ocean and the uncertainty of what his

---

[16] Log of the Ship Rensselaerwyck on its Voyage from Amsterdam to New Netherland, September 25, 1636–April 7, 1637, from the translated by AJF Van Lear, 1908.

future would hold were causes of concern. He had heard of the dark forests in the New World and the Indians who inhabited them, but this caused excitement rather than fear in his mind.

The ship on which they had traveled was outfitted by Rensselaer, a prosperous Amsterdam diamond merchant and investor. In 1631, he had gained a concession or patroonship for land near the upper navigable limit of the Hudson River in exchange for transporting settlers and livestock to the area. Through his agents, he had obtained a tract of land from the native Indians, which was then referred to as Rensselaerwijck.[17] This was near Fort Orange, where the Dutch West India Company had established a military presence in 1624 to protect the beaver pelt trade, a highly prized source of wealth for the Dutch. Because their claim to this area was challenged by the French to the north and the English to the east, the presence of settlers would improve their claim, and farming efforts would help support the soldiers. Of the thirty-eight passengers on the ship, there were several families, a number of tradesmen, and many young people—all heading for Fort Orange on the Hudson River.[18] Most of the passengers were farmers or youth who would become laborers in the patroonship.

They had chosen an unfortunate time of the year to sail westward across the North Atlantic, as the storms and unfavorable winds made the trip an ordeal. They arrived in New Amsterdam in early March 1637, but again their timing was faulty, as the Hudson River was blocked by winter ice, which delayed their arrival at Fort Orange for another month. At last, on April 7, they reached their destination, and Pieter learned more about his future. He was assigned on April 3, 1637, to Simon Walischez, a man from Wijngaerden in the province

---

[17] The Dutch term wijk is often translated as an area, neighborhood, or territory, and it was years before one could consider any of this a town or organized settlement. Van Rensselaer never personally came to his patroonship but did spend considerable resources and efforts in promoting its success. Of other Dutch patroonships, his was the only one to achieve success, and it continued until the nineteenth century.

[18]

of Friesland.[19] Pieter was pleased that he and his new supervisor shared their native Frisian language, as did some of the other travelers. This would prove to be an asset to Pieter in ways that he could not imagine at that time. Walischez had managed property in Friesland and had seen an opportunity to obtain property in the colony that was not otherwise available to him in the Netherlands. Pieter would have a place to live and work for a term of six years on Walischez's property that had been leased to him by the patroonship. Pieter would be paid fifty guilders per year for the first three and seventy-five guilders per year for the remaining three years, when his term of indenture would be completed; he would be an adult and able to begin making a future for himself.

Rensselaerwijck gradually developed as a small village, providing a Reformed Church building and several taverns, which seemed to attract more visitors than the church. Pieter attended the Reformed Church and during his fourth year in the colony made the acquaintance of Cornelis Hendrick Van Ness, who had moved with his family from Havendyck, Holland, in 1641. Van Ness was a brewer by trade, well educated, and respected in the community, and he had been a longtime resident of Holland but a native speaker of Frisian. He was the father of a number of children, including a daughter, Grietje. Pieter's interest in the van Ness family was heightened by the attraction this young lady seemed to have for him. Van Ness was certainly aware of the industrious young man with whom he could converse in his native tongue, and despite Pieter being of a distinctly lower social class than Cornelis and his wife, Maycke Hendrieux van den Burchgraeff, he did not discourage their friendship.

Pieter completed his term of indenture in 1644, when he received his three hundred seventy-five guilders from the Rensselaer estate. He then rented a farm for his own use, which may have been the property on which he had worked for six years, as Simon Walischez's lease was canceled due to his being an "unsatisfactory tenant." Within

---

[19] The spelling of this Dutch name of Walischez is uncertain, as many versions have been used by writers, such as Walichsz, Waischez, Walichs, Walischsen, Walinschsz, and others.

the year, Grietje accepted Pieter's marriage proposal, and he would also manage farm property for his father-in-law, Cornelis van Ness. Cornelis had little farming experience and was actively engaged in managing his brewery, participating in public activities, and dealing with the contentious and autocratic director of the patroonship, Brant van Slichtenhorst. The original patroon, Killiaen van Rennselaer, died in 1643, never having visited his New Netherland holdings, which became part of his extensive estate. Patroons and their directors had become accustomed to the semiautonomy of their holdings previously granted by the more liberal Director-General Peter Minuit and had been alarmed by the aggressive dealings with the Indians by the prior director (Kieft's War). They chaffed under the administration of Peter Stuyvesant, who reestablished the legitimate authority of the West India Company in the domestic affairs of New Netherland. Van Ness was involved in lawsuits with van Slichtenhorst, which also included Pieter Claessen. They may have supported the authority of Stuyvesant over the aggressive policies of the local director. It is likely that van Ness and Pieter were known to Stuyvesant, who may have later encouraged Pieter to consider a move to the New Amsterdam area. Stuyvesant was also a native speaker of Frisian, which may have provided a bond between him and the young Pieter Claessen. Van Slichtenhorst created a major conflict with the general director by developing a town, Beverwyck, close to the military garrison of Fort Orange, contrary to the directive of Stuyvesant. This conflict would eventually result in the arrest and imprisonment of van Slichtenhorst, and conflicts may have been factors in the relocation of Pieter and Grietje from Beverwyck. The availability of land in the growing communities of Het Lange Eiland (Long Island) was certainly a consideration.

While living in Beverwyck, Grietje and Pieter were blessed with the birth of two children, Claes Pieterse (Nicholas) and Margarietje,[20]

---

[20] Dutch proper names indicated the person's social class, and the landed gentry, such as the Van Nesses, would use a family name, while others, such as Pieter, would be known as Pieter Claessen (Pieter son of Claus), and his son, Claes Pieterse (Claus son of Pieter). Claes or Claus is a contraction of Nicholas.

and by 1649, they had moved to New Amsterdam. Their next two children, Annetje and Mayken, were said to have been born in Nieuw Amsterdam and were baptized at the Reformed Dutch Church in 1650 and 1653. The residence of the family in those years is uncertain, as Pieter purchased property on May 27, 1652, in Nieuw Amersfoort (Flatlands) and may have been there soon after their move in 1649. The Manhattan church was the only one in the area where a baptism could be performed, until 1661 when new churches were formed in Flatlands and other Brooklyn locations.

Annetje and Mayken were named for Grietje's grandmother and mother, whose families provided social status and inheritance, which greatly benefitted the growing family.[21] There would be twelve children, and eleven would survive to marry and raise families of their own in New Netherland. During these early years in Nieuw Amersfoort, as Grietje was busy with her children, Pieter proved to be an effective farmer and manager. In 1655, he signed a contract to manage the cattle and farmland of Petrus Stuyvesant on his "bouwery at Amesfoort." The property was near that which Pieter had obtained between 1652 and 1658. His own bowery (or farm) included a house, the initial rooms of which are attributed to the former director general, Wouter van Twiller, built during his administration between 1633 and 1638[22] (figure 3). Van Twiller had not been a popular leader and was succeeded by William Kieft, who used military force against the local Indian tribes, alarming the Dutch settlers, especially in the New Amsterdam and Long Island areas. After Kieft was dismissed in 1647, Petrus Stuyvesant was appointed director general, and stability was restored to the colony as the rules of the West India Company were enforced.[23] A result of this was the conflict with van Slichtenhorst in Rensselaerwyck, which resulted in his arrest and deportation. As Pieter Claessen was establishing his family in Nieuw

---

[21] Wyckoff, WF and Streeter, MB. 1934, pages 9–31.

[22] See section IV, B. The house still exists as the Fidler-Wyckoff House in Brooklyn, the oldest existing structure in New York.

[23] More information concerning the leadership of New Netherland and the turmoil of its early history is considered in section III.

Amersfoort, Cornelis van Ness remained in Rensselaerwyck, serving as magistrate or councilor (raets persoon) between 1652 and 1663. His wife, Maycke Hendrieux van den Burchgraeff, died in about 1659 or 1660, and her estate was divided between her six children, including Grietje. Cornelis obtained property in New Amersfoort but primarily resided in Rennselaerwyck until his death in 1684 at the age of eighty-four years.

Pieter Claessen gained respect within the Amersfoort community, as he was named magistrate (schepen) in three separate years between 1655 and 1663. There has been much speculation about the origin of the Wyckoff name, which does not appear in any preserved record until September 1687 when Pieter Claessen Wijckoff and six of his sons are listed on "The Roll of those who have Taken the oath of allegiance in the kings County in the Province of New York the 26:27:28:29 and 30th day of September in the Third year of his Maytsh Raigne annosue Domine 1687."[24] The use of a family name was required by the English authorities when the colony was ceded to England after the Anglo-Dutch Wars. Recent study of the linguistic and geographic significance of the Wyckoff name has convincingly corrected long-held misconceptions of its origin. Pieter Claessen, when directed to adopt a family name, chose the name of an estate, the Wyckoff, near his home in Marienhafe township, Norden (Norderland province), Ostfriesland, from which he had emigrated in 1636.[25] This scholarly work speculates that Pieter's mother may have been a worker at the estate at the time of her death in 1635 (figure 4).

It is certain that Peter Claessen Wyckoff and his family were an important part of the Dutch Reformed Church in New Netherland. He is listed as one of the founders of the Dutch Reformed Church of Flatlands, which was established in 1654 under the guidance

---

[24] This oath was taken in the third year of the reign of His Majesty James II of England. Pieter Claessen Wijkoff is listed as having lived in the province for fifty-one years. His sons are all listed as natives.

[25] Wykoff, M. William. What's In A Name? History and Meaning of Wyckoff. Rochester, N.Y. 2014.

of Reverend Johannes Megapolensis, minister of the church in Manhattan. Pieter Claessen Wyckoff died June 30, 1694, at his home in Flatlands and is buried on the grounds of the church. It is said that the grave is beneath the current sanctuary building. Grietje may have lived until 1703 and is buried beside Pieter (figure 5).

The eleven married children and their families were living in Amersfoort (Flatlands), in other Long Island locations, and in various communities in New Jersey by the early 1700s. This generation married into families of Dutch origin living in the Long Island area and by the time of the American Revolution represented a sizable population. Some served in the war, and subsequent generations would spread to other states of the new nation. Many remained in the New York area, and the original farmhouse, which was occupied by descendants until the early twentieth century, is preserved as the oldest surviving structure in New York.[26]

D. MARIE GAINEAU (GANO) OF LA ROCHELLE, FRANCE

Marie Gaineau (as she was known in her home in France) was twenty-six years old when she fled to the English Colony of New York in 1686 with her father, Francis, and her younger brother Jeremie and changed her name to Gano. Their escape was fraught with danger and was an experience she would often relate to her family over the years.[27] She had expected to be married by this time in her life, but the tumultuous decade prior to their move had delayed

---

[26] See IV, C appendix.

[27] The documented information about Francis Gaineau and his family is very limited, and even their identities in the Colony of New York are problematic. Most of this confusion can be resolved and is considered in greater detail in the appendix IV, C. His fleeing from France due to the threats to the safety of his family caused by the revocation of the Edict of Nantes in 1685 resulted in the loss of his property and any documentation of his previous business activities. This narrative is based on the story told by his daughter Mary and repeated by subsequent generations. Although it cannot be historically documented, it is consistent with the social and political milieu of that time.

that possibility. Marie was the oldest child in her family and had assumed many responsibilities following the death of her mother ten years earlier, when her brother was very young. Other children in their family had also died of the maladies that caused childhood to be such a tenuous time for young lives. She had assumed motherhood roles for Jeremie and responsibilities of the household for her father, leaving little time for her personal life.

Francis Gaineau was active in the business community and the Reformed Church. As a young man, he had begun working in the years after the disastrous Siege of La Rochelle in 1627–28 that caused the death of so many in their city. Over the decades, he learned much about the business of the fur trade and gained the confidence of shippers from New France and buyers of the beaver pelts in Amsterdam and London. After the tragic loss of his wife and all but two of their children, he delegated household responsibilities to his daughter and focused his efforts on his growing business. Although he had success in his career as a merchant, the threats resulting from his adherence to the Reformed Church were a continuous challenge. His family had located in La Rochelle in previous generations due to the upheavals created by their acceptance of Calvinist theology. They and many French Christians in the Reformed Church experienced great uncertainty during the seventeenth century because of the continuous political disruption resulting from the Reformation. The devastating Wars of Religion (1562–98) had ended with the Edict of Nantes, signed by King Henry IV, which granted freedom of worship and other privileges of citizenship. The peace, however, was always tenuous, as the political leadership, since the onset of the Reformation during the reign of Francis I (1515–47), viewed the presence of a Christian faith at variance with the Roman Church to be a threat to the royal authority.[28] Henry IV was sympathetic to the Huguenots, as he had only formally returned to the Roman Church in 1589 to secure his inheritance of the monarchy. He died

---

[28] The Reformation in France was of unusual violence, which extended over the reigns of several monarchs. More details of these conflicts are described in part II.

at the hand of a fanatical Roman Catholic assassin in 1610, and his queen, Marie de Medici, acted as regent for their nine-year-old son, Louis XIII, for seven years. She attempted to sustain a policy of moderation, confirming the Edict of Nantes with its toleration for the Huguenots, but she was exiled in 1617, and hostility toward the Protestants increased.

The young Louis XIII was greatly influenced by anti-Huguenot advisers, and in 1622, a partially successful military action by the royal forces limited the Huguenots' control to the cities of Montauban and La Rochelle. These hostilities culminated in the Siege of La Rochelle in 1627, led by Cardinal Richelieu, resulting in the death of two-thirds of the thirty thousand inhabitants of the city.[29]

In the succeeding decades, tolerance of the Huguenot faith established by the Edict of Nantes was maintained, although the former independent political and military rights of the city were lost. The prosperity of La Rochelle gradually improved, but the efforts of Louis XIII to redevelop La Havre and Dieppe would eventually make them the dominant French Atlantic ports. The years from before the siege until the death of Louis XIII in 1643 were influenced by the events of the Thirty Years' War, which began in 1618 as a civil conflict in the Holy Roman Empire between Roman Catholic and Protestant estates.[30] An attempt to discourage French Protestant

---

[29] The religious aspect was not the only factor involved in the Siege of La Rochelle, and the nearly complete elimination of the local Huguenot population was not its only or even its most long-lasting result. For the prior millennium, France was not the political entity that we now recognize. The authority of the kingdom of France was often limited to the middle Seine area, including Paris and Reims. Autonomous regions, such as Lorraine (east), Picardy (north), and Normandy (west), as well as Brittany and Aquitaine each had their own unique languages, hereditary royalty, and varying degrees of political independence. It was not until Louis XIII that an effective central authority was established. The Siege of La Rochelle was a key event in ending the administrative and military autonomy of these various regions.

[30] See part II for more details of this conflict, which was of a magnitude greater than any previous European conflict and reasonably considered to be the actual first world war.

independence contributed to the intense royal response in the siege. In 1635, the religious nature of the Thirty Years' War changed with the Peace of Prague. The secular fighting continued with the involvement of Spain, Sweden, the Netherlands, and France seeking to gain territory at the expense of the Hapsburg Empires and limit the hegemony of Austria and Spain.

With the death of Louis XIII, the heir apparent to the throne was the four-year-old Louis XIV. Authority passed to a regency council led by his mother, Anne, who instilled in him the idea of absolute and divine power of the monarch. The Thirty Years' War ended in 1648, and the next decade saw a general tranquility, but the central authority in France was expanded at the expense of the regional feudal aristocracy. The burgeoning national debt and theological challenges from Calvinists and other sects, such as the Jensenites, created uncertainty. In 1661, Louis XIV, at the age of eighteen years, assumed his personal reign of a country on the verge of bankruptcy. Over the next two decades, Francis Gaineau and others in the La Rochelle business community would prosper, but the national financial burden and religious controversies were challenges to the absolute authority assumed by Louis XIV.

The hostility toward the Protestant population became severe in 1681 when the policy of dragonnades was instituted by Louis XIV and directed by his military leadership. This policy called for the quartering of troops in the households of Protestant families, resulting in the abuse of the inhabitants and a loss of their property and domestic tranquility due to the often poorly disciplined soldiers. The removal of these unwanted troops would occur only if the families recanted their Protestant beliefs. The authorities initially expected this policy to encourage emigration, which would result in the loss of their property, as their wealth would revert to the distressed royal treasury. Soon the policy was changed to prohibit emigration and required that the Huguenots convert to the Roman faith.

During the early years of the dragonnades policy, Francis Gaineau coped with what could be a desperate situation for his adult daughter

Marie and for his mercantile efforts. He likely attempted a deception of the unwelcome dragoons by presenting Marie as his wife and Jeremie as their son, but it was certain that this deception could not be successful for long. One conclusion was inescapable; remaining in France was not an option. He planned an escape from La Rochelle that would, if successful, improve the chances of their safety and a preservation of some of his financial assets. Francis had established relationships in London and Amsterdam, for which he supplied beaver pelts imported from New France for the active industry of manufacturing the highly prized headgear for the European market. These contacts were sympathetic with his plight as a member of the Reformed Church and were willing to assist him in his deception. In October 1685, the final straw fell on the back of the beleaguered camel that was the Reformed population. Louis XIV signed the Edict of Fontainebleau, which formally revoked the Edict of Nantes, ending any freedoms that had been preserved for the Calvinist Christians.

It was crucial that his escape plans not become known to the authorities who were implementing the royal mandate to coerce Huguenots to surrender their Reformed faith. Such defiance could lead to imprisonment from which others had never returned. Even Marie must not know of the details that he had devised to evade the decree. She and Jeremie would go by coach to the town of Dieppe, whose port offered a direct route to England and had a strong Reformed congregation.[31] From there, Marie and Jeremie would sail to London, and his contacts had been willing to arrange this transportation even though they were not aware of the extent of his deception or its ultimate purpose. A young woman and a youth would not attract scrutiny about their intentions, and Francis had confidence in his daughter's ability to carry out this plan. Should his own escape fail, his agents had assured him that they would see to

---

[31] The Reformed Church in Dieppe was active before the Wars of Religion began in 1562 with the Massacre of Vassy. The congregation had survived the intense persecution during the earlier reign of Henry II. In 1559, the Scottish Reformed leader John Knox served the church in Dieppe when returning to Scotland from Geneva. –

the future of Marie and Jeremie. Despite the coldness of the season and the uncertainty of sailing schedules with the westerly Atlantic winds, the execution of his plan was now at a point of no return.

Marie was alarmed by the intensity of her father's farewell as she and Jeremie boarded the coach with what seemed an unusual amount of luggage for what she thought would be a short sojourn to London. Their journey to Dieppe was uneventful, but Marie was made uneasy by the stares of the soldiers who seemed to be at every stop through Normandy. They were met by a family in Dieppe who was well known by her father and were taken to a ship captained by their son. The sailing to London was uneventful, and they were met by a gentlemanly banker who escorted them to an inn, where they were to remain until word was received from her father.

Several days passed before their father appeared at the inn, somewhat more disheveled than expected but in high spirits, representing a level of excitement that was unusual for their otherwise staid parent. Their evening meal was a celebration, and when Francis related the details of his journey, Marie was barely able to respond through her tears of amazement and relief.

Francis told Marie and Jeremie that he had worked for months to prepare for what would be the only chance he would have to escape from the tyranny and abuse of his native land and, hopefully, begin a new life for his family. He had carefully avoided revealing knowledge of his plan to anyone in La Rochelle, as none could be expected to resist authorities who would use torture or bribes to extract wanted information. On the day after saying goodbye to his children, there would be four tobacco hogshead casks of prepared beaver pelts assigned for the regular monthly shipment to London, as was the procedure for his enterprise.[32] There would be one difference.

One of the casks had been carefully altered to provide a top compartment holding enough pelts to reassure any inspector that

---

[32] The tobacco hogshead casks used in colonial times were usually forty-eight inches long and thirty inches in diameter at the head. They held about one hundred forty-five US gallons, larger than a similar wine cask of sixty-three gallons.

they represented the entire contents of the cask. Below was a space that would be occupied by the owner of the firm! He would have enough space for himself, containers of water and food to sustain him for several days, and as much coin of the realm as he could accumulate without creating suspicion of his intentions. Several staves of the cask had been altered so they could be removed to provide fresh air and a chance of escape in the event of a disaster.

The four casks had been sealed as usual and loaded in the cargo hold of the ship without delay or suspicion. The voyage to London was rough, as expected, but otherwise uneventful. Francis could only conclude that his prayer requests for the safety of his family were being answered. On their arrival in London, the stevedores were surprised when one of the hogsheads opened itself and its cargo walked away, smiling broadly!

Other than the assets on deposit in London and Amsterdam, Francis had his only worldly possessions and his children with him at the inn. For the next several weeks, he would be occupied with the closing of his fur-trading business and settling accounts with his buyers. During this interval, a number of families and individuals known from their Reformed congregation in La Rochelle made their way to London, and together they made arrangements for passage to the English Colony of New York. The political environment in London had become hostile to the Reformed Church members, and there was great unrest with the reign of James II.[33] All agreed that New York would be the best location in the American colonies for them to make new homes. He had anticipated the response of the French authorities to his escape and was not surprised when word came that his home, possessions, and remaining business had been confiscated. Sometime later, his disgust with the circumstances led him to not only disown his French citizenry but to change his name to an Anglicized version, and he stated that he would want to be known as Gano.

---

[33] Further information about the era of James II and the dominion of New England is found in part III, B.

In the spring of 1687, Francis, Marie, and Jeremie, along with other Reformed Christians from La Rochelle and elsewhere in France, sailed to New York, where they found that the political controversies seen in London had affected the colony. There was unrest caused by the political changes brought about by the reign of James II and the possibility that a Roman Catholic regime could change the religious freedoms that the colonies had enjoyed. Shortly after their arrival in New York, the Huguenots were met by Jacob Leisler, who would be instrumental in helping them establish a community in the colony. Leisler, a devout member of the Calvinist Reformed faith, was a prominent merchant, militia leader, and a judge of the admiralty court in New York.[34] Due to his sympathy for the Huguenots and their faith, he negotiated with John Pell for the purchase of 6,100 acres that had been inherited from his uncle Thomas Pell. This land became the site of their settlement named New Rochelle[35] (figure 6).

---

[34] Jacob Leisler was an important part of the turbulent history of the colony of New Netherland / New York and will be considered in part III, C. He had an established Calvinist Christian faith, which he learned from his father and grandfather, who were Reformed ministers in their homelands in Germany and the Swiss cantons. Jacob pursued a military career after the early death of his father and in 1660 came to New Netherland in the service of the Dutch West Indies Company. He brought an awareness of the bitter conflict of the Thirty Years' War and hostility of the Roman Church toward those of his faith. He soon left the military career and married in 1663 Elsje Tymens, the widow of a well-established businessman. Over the next decade, he became wealthy through the fur and tobacco trade while residing in Albany. His Reformed Church affiliation and leadership ability placed him between the Dutch establishment and the Anglican English leadership during the era of James II and the dominion of New England in 1686 and the turmoil of the Glorious Revolution in 1688, which he strongly supported.

[35] Thomas Pell (1612–1669) was an English physician and brother of mathematician John Pell, who obtained a fifty-thousand-acre tract from the Siwanoy Indian tribe in what is now Westchester County. He left his estate to his nephew, John Pell Jr. (1643–1700), who lived in the Pelham area and in 1689 sold 6,100 acres to Jacob Leisler. Leisler donated one-third of the land to the Huguenot refugees, whose names, including Gaineau, are recorded on a monument in Hudson Park in the town of New Rochelle, which they created.

Detailed information about life in their new homeland is not available, but we know that Mary Gano and John Denman III married in 1690. They lived in the Newtown area of Long Island (now known as Queens), where he had obtained land from the Lenape tribes, and they worshiped at the Newtown Reformed (Presbyterian) Church, now renamed, along with the town, as Elmhurst. Jeremiah lived in the same area, never married, and was an executor of the will of John Denman, who died in 1713. There is confusion about the date of death of Francis Gano, as he is often confused with Etienne (Stephen) Gano, who emigrated from La Rochelle in 1661 and lived in Staten Island. Both Francis and Etienne are said to have lived to the age of 103.[36] There is no evidence that Etienne ever lived in New Rochelle, but one or more of his descendants may have located to that area. Confusion due to the frequency of the name Francis and the spellings of Gaineau contribute to this uncertainty, further considered in IV, C.

We know that Mary Gano and John Denman III had seven children, three sons and one daughter who would move to the Colony of New Jersey with their mother after John's death. Those moving included John IV, born in 1700, who lived at Westfield, Essex County; William, born in 1702, in Elizabethtown; Philip, born in 1704; and Thomas, born in 1706 in Springfield, Essex County. Both Mary and John had been lifelong members of Reformed congregations, and the importance of their faith was great. This tradition appears to have been shared by subsequent generations of their family. Further information is available about these families and is related in section IV, C.[37]

---

[36] The UK Office of National Statistics, as quoted in the Mayo Clinic Proceedings, 94:110–24 (January 2019), indicates that survivorship in persons born in 1851 or earlier rarely exceeded ninety years and none were recorded over one hundred years. The likelihood of two individuals born in or before the seventeenth century, both named Gaineau (Gano) and living in the Colony of New York, is vanishingly low.

[37] Harris, Harriet N. *t* Available from Forgotten Books' Classic Reprint Series.

E. JOHANNES KOLB OF THE ELECTORAL PALATINATE, GERMANY (HRE)

In the autumn of 1707, a ship from Amsterdam arrived at the Port of Philadelphia in the Colony of Pennsylvania with four brothers, Johannes, Martin, Jacob, and Heinrich Kolb. They were in their early twenties and eager to establish new lives in British North America. The Kolb brothers had been encouraged to emigrate from their home in Wolfsheim in the Electoral Palatinate by their maternal grandfather, Peter Schumacher Sr., who knew of the war-related hardships that existed in the Rhineland and the opportunity to obtain land and live peacefully in Pennsylvania. Schumacher had been a Mennonite until adopting the Quaker faith. He lived in Kriegsheim and in 1685, with his son, Peter Jr. and three daughters, Mary, Frances, and Gertrude, immigrated to the Pennsylvania colony with a group of German Quakers. His fifth child, Agnes, had married Dielman Kolb Sr. and lived in Wolfsheim, where they were the parents of Johannes and his three brothers.[38]

Life in the Palatinate had been difficult for the Kolb and Schumacher families for as long as any could remember. An earlier generation of their families had moved there to escape the hostility in the Swiss cantons and Holy Roman Empire estates toward their Anabaptist (Swiss Brethren) beliefs. They were able to live in the Palatinate without fear, although the authorities viewed members of their faith with suspicion. During the Thirty Years' War, many Protestants had fled the invading armies for the principality of Transylvania,[39] and the family names of Schumacher and Kolb were among those who returned to their homes at the end of the war

---

[38] Different references date the arrival of some brothers in 1707 and others in 1709 but agree that by 1709 these four were in Germantown, had obtained property, and moved to Skippack, twenty miles to the northwest. The youngest brother, Dielman Jr., came in 1714. Three older siblings, Peter, Ann, and Francis, apparently remained in the Palatinate.

[39] Transylvania was a Calvinist part of the largely Lutheran Hungary and gained full religious freedom and political autonomy from the Holy Roman Empire in the Treaty of Vienna in 1606.

in 1648. In that year, Dielman Kolb Sr. was born, and he had a relatively peaceful early life in the verdant Rhine Valley, where he would become a wine maker and active member of the Mennonite community.

He married Agnes Schumacher in 1670, and she had nine children prior to 1688. In that year, their tranquility was disrupted by the invasion of the French, who had the strongest military in Europe. These hostilities devastated their area and lasted until 1697. The invading armies, as was common practice, would pillage the farms and homes of the inhabitants. Johannes was five years old at the onset of the invasion and likely, with his brothers, had responsibilities for helping care for their livestock. Dairy cows often became pets of the family, and it must have been with horror that the children saw their animals slaughtered, their vineyards destroyed, and their home looted.[40]

There was a short respite from war in the Rhine Valley after 1697, but in 1701, the death of Charles II of Spain without an heir led to further conflict between the European kingdoms (War of Spanish Succession). There was fighting in the Palatinate between the French and forces of the Holy Roman Empire aligned with the Hapsburg kingdoms in Austria, Spain, and Italy. The Palatinate at that time was connected with Bavaria, which was supportive of the French due to their dislike of the Hapsburg hegemony. The war in the upper Rhine area of the Palatine from the cities of Speyer to Landau was intense and would have been a source of anxiety for the Mennonite Kolb family in Wolfsheim. The reports of available land, the ability to worship according to their convictions, and without the threat of

---

[40] This War of the Grand Alliance (1689–97) pitted the forces of Louis XIV against the Austrian Hapsburgs and their allies, which included the Palatinate after the League of Augsburg was formed in 1686. This league proved to be an ineffective coalition in protecting the smaller German states. The war proved little but saw the defeat of the French fleet by the British and the success of the new English king, William III. In New England, this conflict was known as King William's War and was mainly an extension of King Phillip's War between the Massachusetts English and Indian tribes (Abenaki), which were supported by the French (see part III, B).

invading armies would have been very appealing to these brothers. At the ages of twenty to twenty-six years, they had concerns about the prospects for their futures. When their mother died in 1705, they began planning their immigration. Agnes was buried in Wolfsheim, and in 1707, the Kolb brothers arrived in Pennsylvania.

On their arrival at Philadelphia, they went directly to Germantown, where they would have met their Schumacher relatives. The Kolb family members were committed to the Mennonite faith, and most of the men were either ministers or trustees of the church. In 1708, Martin, Johannes, and Jacob are listed as original members of the congregation that met in the first Mennonite meetinghouse in Germantown. By 1709, each of the brothers had property in Skippack, which was twenty miles to the west in what is now Montgomery County. Johannes signed a deed dated December 15, 1709, recording his purchase of 150 acres, and he also obtained property in Chester County. The Kolbs worshipped at the Germantown church until 1725, when the Lower Skippack Mennonite Church was built. Martin and Heinrich Kolb were listed as among the first ministers.

On June 2, 1713, a petition was submitted to the Court of Quarters Session held in Philadelphia, requesting that a road be "laid out and established to accommodate the families already settled" in the area around Skippack Creek connecting them to Germantown. Johannes, Jacob, Martin, and Heinrich Kolb were among the thirty signers of the petition. The roadway was surveyed in August and confirmed by the court in March, 1714. Construction began soon and connected Skippack continuously with Gwynedd, Chestnut Hill, and Germantown to the city of Philadelphia. This western area served by the road was in the Welsh Tract established by William Penn in 1684. It had been anticipated by the earlier Welsh settlers that the local government would use the Welsh language, but this never occurred, as it was occupied by Welsh-, English-, and German-speaking settlers.[41]

---

[41] The forty-thousand-acre Welsh Tract was west of Philadelphia in the present Montgomery, Chester, and Delaware Counties. Although the Welsh language was never used by the government, many towns retain their Welsh names in what is

The other large ethnic conclave in Pennsylvania was in the Germantown area where that language was prevalent. The tract had been created by William Penn in 1683 at the insistence of Francis Daniel Pastorius, whose leadership brought the original group of Germans in 1685 from Krefeld, including Peter Schumacher and family. They were provided the tract in Germantown, which continued to attract many Protestant immigrants from the estates of the Holy Roman Empire.

Johannes Kolb was twenty-four years old when he began living at his property in Skippack, and he would have been occupied by farming and livestock efforts and would certainly have had many contacts with his Welsh neighbors. Tradition holds that he was involved in dairy farming, but there is no documentation of his work. What is certain is that he married Sarah, they had nine children between 1720 and 1736, and they moved with a group of Welsh Baptists to the upper Pee Dee River area in the Colony of South Carolina, where they were established by 1737.[42] Although documentation is not available, the circumstantial evidence makes it nearly certain that Sarah was a part of the Welsh community. Over the next two decades, Johannes became an integral part of that Baptist group. This distinct group of Welsh immigrants came to Pennsylvania between the mid-1680s and 1701. The earlier Welsh Baptists had settled in Philadelphia county and established the first Baptist church in Pennsylvania in 1684 in the home of their pastor, Elder Thomas Dungan, in Cold Spring. In 1688, they formed the Pennepack Baptist Church, which exists to this date (figure 7).

In 1701, a group of sixteen Welsh Baptists from Pembroke and Carmarthen, South Wales, with Thomas Griffith as their minister, arrived in Philadelphia on September 8. They settled

---

now referred to as the Main Line, including Gwynedd, Marion, Narbeth, Bala Cynwyd, Radnor, and others. This should be termed the Welsh Tract.

[42] The family name of Sarah is unknown, as are the dates of her birth and of their marriage. Her identity can be implied from information that suggests she was related at least to the extended, if not the immediate, family of James James, Esq., and his wife, Sarah James.

in the Welsh-speaking area of Pennepec and affiliated with the abovementioned church. Due to an obscure difference in belief about the ordinance of laying on of hands, they remained a separate congregation and in 1703 moved to what was the *second* Welsh Tract.

This tract of thirty thousand acres was granted to William Davis, David Evans, and William Willis by William Penn on October 15, 1701, for settlers from South Wales. It was located in the southernmost area of the Pennsylvania Colony in the county of New Castle, adjacent to the Colony of Maryland. Some of the settlers came from the Radnor Township in Chester County in the first Welsh Tract. One was James James, who obtained 1,244 acres including Iron Hill and land extending to Christiana Creek, by a deed on June 27, 1702. Others obtaining land included Howel James and Philip James, who may have had some relationship to James James but were not of his immediate family. James James, Esq., and his wife, Sarah, had at least four sons, Samuel, Abel, David, and Philip, the later born in 1701.[43] These holdings of the James families were near the village of Pencader Hundred, where the Welsh Baptists moving from the Pennepack church built a meeting house in 1703 on the site of the present structure of the Welsh Tract Baptist Church (figure 8).

In 1703, the records of that church show that new members "were added to the church … by Baptism—James James, Sarah James," and nine others. At a quarterly meeting, February 4, 1716, a Confession of Faith was signed by over one hundred individuals, including James James and Sarah James. A further listing "of the names of such as have been removed from us by death" includes Sarah James, February 2, 1721.[44] Between 1734 and 1737, James James, Esq., led a group of thirty families, including his three sons, Abel, Daniel, and Philip, with their wives to the Colony of South Carolina, where they established a settlement on the Pee Dee River. Among those moving

---

[43] Scharf, Thomas J. History of Delaware, 1609–1888, Volume Two, Chapter XLVIII, Pencader Hundred, pp. 854–880.

[44] Records of the Welsh Tract Baptist Meeting, Pencader Hundred, New Castle County, Delaware, 1701–1828. In Two Parts—Part 1. Published by the Historical Society of Delaware, 1904.

from Pennsylvania was the family of Johannes Kolb, his wife, Sarah, and their nine children. Others coming from the Welsh Tract Baptist Church included "Abel Morgan, teaching elder, Thomas Evans, deacon, James James, ruling elder and nineteen others."[45]

In 1731, interest in the Carolinas was stimulated with the favorable description by Hugh Meredith in the *Pennsylvania Gazette*, published by Benjamin Franklin. The turmoil that had plagued these colonies resulted from the failure of the proprietary leadership to provide effective protection from the assaults of native Indian tribes, the Spanish from their St. Augustine location, the French in Queen Anne's War, and the ever-present threat of pirates.[46] The replacement of the government by royal authority in 1730 greatly improved the economy and security of South Carolina. The governor, Robert Johnson, sought to attract new immigration to the frontier of the colony with the availability of land and the improved bounty on naval stores. In 1734, he granted ten thousand acres on the upper reaches of the Pee Dee River to the Welsh under the leadership of James James, Esq.

Johannes Kolb was forty-nine years old when he and Sarah decided to join the families moving to what would be known as the Welsh Tract. Records indicate that they sold some property in Skippack in 1734, but it is certain that they were still in Pennsylvania in 1736, as that was the year and location of birth of their ninth and last child, Sarah. Johannes may have traveled to South Carolina as early as 1734, as by that year, he had apparently obtained at least 650 acres in a loop of the Pee Dee River later known as Welsh Neck. Johannes, Sarah, their nine children, and livestock would be at their new home by 1737. He would operate a ferry and likely a

---

[45] James James, Esq., was so titled due to his service as a justice of the peace in Pennsylvania. In November 1735, when the families "were removed to Carolina and recommended by a letter to ye Church of Christ in Charles Town or elsewhere in South Carolina, or they might constitute themselves into a Church." From John W. Jordan, . Volume 2 of 3, 1911.

[46] This war from 1702 to 1713 was the colonial aspect of the War of Spanish Succession that had encouraged the Kolb brothers to immigrate to Pennsylvania.

mill at that site. This mill would have been used in the harvest of the abundant long-leaf pines that dominated the area. This resource supplied wealth from the naval stores industry, which was a labor-intensive activity that would have involved slaves.

James James died the year following the move, and his sons and their families would remain for generations as part of the Welsh Neck Baptist Church. One of the sons, Philip James, born in 1701 in Pennepack, Pennsylvania, was ordained on April 4, 1743 and served as the first minister of the church. Philip's daughter, Ann James, married Peter Kolb, a son of Johannes and Sarah, and they had six children, including a son, Abel Kolb, who served with distinction in the American War for Independence as a colonel and commander of the Patriot forces in the upper Pee Dee area under the command of General Francis Marion.

It is likely that a factor in persuading James James, Esq., and some of the families accompanying him to the Pee Dee region was the issue of slavery, which was more acceptable in Carolina than it would have been in the Mennonite community in Pennsylvania. It is known that James James and his sons brought slaves from the Welsh Tract to South Carolina. It is likely that Johannes and Sarah Kolb also owned slaves, and since this was strongly opposed by their Mennonite relatives, it may have been an incentive for their family to relocate. The Mennonites had been in the forefront of opposing the institution of slavery, and later the Quakers became staunch abolitionists. (See section IV, E, appendix, "Antislavery Resolution of the Germantown Mennonites, February 18, 1688.")

The 1730s was the time of the religious movement known as the First Great Awakening, and this clearly had effects on worship in the Welsh Neck Baptist Church. It also had effects on the relationships with the slaves whose involvement, especially with the Baptist and Methodist congregations, would change over the subsequent decades. Slaves began to take more active roles in worship in the churches as the message of spiritual equality was increasingly accepted. Many leaders of the revival efforts encouraged the education of the slaves so that they would be able to read and study the Bible. Extensive information about the Welsh Neck Baptist Church is available, and the records indicate that many slaves were admitted to full membership in the congregation. Two generations later, a slave known as Abraham, the property of the grandson and granddaughter of Johannes Kolb and Rev. Philip James (Col. Abel Kolb and Ann James Kolb), was captured by the British during the American War of Independence and assigned to tasks that would have required him to be literate. After the war, he returned to the Kolb household and his own family, when he likely could have escaped his slave condition had he so chosen.

Records indicate that the nine children of Johannes and Sarah Kolb married and raised families in South Carolina in the Welsh Neck area, which would eventually be near the town of Society Hill in Marlborough County. The area of their homesite is now the subject of extensive archeologic study, and a report of this exploration describes "the extensive familial connection 'Old Mr. Kolb' had with so many of the Pee Dee Region's earliest families. In many ways he is a type of 'Adam' for the area."[47]

---

[47] Information from Chris Judge, former staff archeologist for the Department of Natural Resources Heritage Trust Program and professor at the University of South Carolina-Lancaster.

PART II

REFLECTIONS ON THE EUROPEAN AGE OF ENLIGHTENMENT

A. EUROPE FROM THE REFORMATION TO THE AGE OF ENLIGHTENMENT (AND CHAOS)

The early decades of the seventeenth century in Europe are often referred to as the Age of Reason, and the period is described as the Age of Enlightenment. That century, which began with the close of the Elizabethan era, would experience vast changes in many aspects of life for the English-speaking world and all of Europe. We often view this time from the perspective of the artistic, scientific, and literary accomplishments that remain such a presence in our own times. Not all Europeans would have had this idealized view of their era as one of enlightenment; the reality of European life would cause great numbers to try to establish their lives in the unknown areas of North America with its uncertainties.

The 1600s would see the continuing works of Shakespeare, the King James Version of the Holy Bible, and writings of Milton, Pope, and others. It was the age of the Dutch masters—Rembrandt, Vermeer, Rubens, and others who influenced artistic styles throughout Europe. On the European continent, the century would replace Renaissance musical styles with the new baroque sounds of Monteverdi and Corelli and the later works of Vivaldi, Bach, and Handel. In England, the Renaissance music of Thomas Tallis and William Byrd would be replaced by the baroque style of Henry Purcell and others. It was the time of the Spanish Golden Age, with the art of Velazquez and El Greco and the literature of Cervantes, Lope de Vega, and Pedro Calderon establishing standards of excellence.

In the early years of the century, Francis Bacon defined what is now referred to as the scientific method of scholarship, which greatly changed philosophical and educational perspectives. Bacon drew upon the writings of Petrus Ramus (1515–72), a French humanist scholar who challenged the long-held educational principles of scholasticism and sought to apply the teachings of Aristotle and Cicero to the preparation of students for further studies in theology, medicine, or jurisprudence. The use of observation and experimentation to evaluate hypotheses began to replace the scholastic perspective of academic activity and led to modern approaches to scientific and intellectual endeavors. These new approaches were refined by Jan Amos Comenius, a Czech scholar (1592–1670) who laid the groundwork for and who is considered the father of modern educational traditions.

An example of this scientific method was the proof of the circulation of blood by William Harvey (1572–1657), who published his observations and conclusions in 1628. For more than fifteen hundred years, physicians and scholars, following the precepts of scholasticism, had accepted the view of human physiology of the ancient Greeks, which held that blood was one of the four "humors" (black bile, yellow bile, phlegm, and blood), the excess or deficiency of which was a cause of human disease and different personality types (i.e., melancholic, choleric, phlegmatic, or sanguine).[48] The concept that blood had a continuous, unidirectional circuit through the body propelled by the heart was suspected by Harvey from his observation of the flow of blood in the veins of the forearm and the presence of valves that assured the flow was only toward the heart. It took another two hundred years for these observations to significantly impact medical practice and for the observations of Claude Bernard and Louis Pasteur in the nineteenth century to begin freeing experimental medicine from philosophical and theological burdens.

One of the early proponents for the replacement of scholasticism by observation and experimentation was Rene Descartes (1596–1650), who supported and extended the ideas of Francis Bacon. His attempt to replace the Aristotelian concepts with reason and investigation put him at odds with the religious and academic hierarchy and would emphasize a growing conflict between scientific thought and theological dogma.

The microscopic discoveries of Van Leeuwenhoek and the astronomical observations of Kepler and Galileo contributed to

---

[48] These descriptions of personality types are not widely used today but refer (in order) as expressions of sadness and depression, bad temper and irritability, reduced emotional response, or optimism.

a changed perception of the universe. Galileo died in 1642, the year of the birth of Isaac Newton, who would further define mathematics and the scientific process. His understanding of mechanics would eventually lead to the technology that made the Industrial Revolution a reality. In England, the writings of John Milton, John Locke, and others would define the basis of new ideas of government and the inherent rights of people. Toward the end of this Age of Enlightenment, the preeminent French political philosopher Montesquieu would define in his *The Spirit of the Law* the idea of the importance of government based on a written constitution, defining a balanced separation of governmental powers. These ideas would forever change the world and lead eventually to the United States of America.

The extraordinary movement of individuals and families that occurred during the seventeenth century has been considered by Professor Bernard Bailyn to be one of the most significant events in the history of the Western world. His descriptions of that era suggest that the typical individual or family that sought life across the Atlantic would likely have had perspectives of the opportunities available to them in Europe that were less optimistic than the present-day perception of that era. Many Europeans would have considered it a time of high expectations but limited options and would have perceived it as an age of famine, pestilence, and war. These three scourges were closely related and directly caused the early presence of the fourth apocalyptic horseman—death. Birth rates were high, but only about one half of the newborns would reach maturity, and their subsequent life expectancy by present-day standards was limited.

The population of Europe was growing, but the Industrial Revolution with expanded employment opportunities was still in the future. The high rate of unemployment caused many to move to urban areas from their rural origins. Agricultural production was further reduced by the effects of the so-called little ice age during the middle decades of the seventeenth and eighteenth centuries. Limited nutrition and the crowding of the urban centers contributed the greatest threats to the European population, which were the repeated epidemics of plague. This scourge, which appeared in Europe in 1346, was known as the black death. By the time this pandemic subsided in 1353, over one-third of the population or about 25,000,000 people had died from the disease. The year 1353 was not the end of the devastation. Between that year and the close of the seventeenth century, there were ninety-seven years of plague epidemic in Europe, and the periods from 1602 to 1611 and 1623 to 1640 were particularly severe in the British Isles, the Low Countries, France, and the German states. Estimates of total deaths from the disease are as high as fifty million Europeans.

Those surviving had no understanding of the cause of the plague or how to best respond to its presence. What was certain, however, were the effects of the scourge on virtually every circumstance of their lives. The loss of manpower from the pandemics would create reverberations throughout the spiritual, economic, social, and governmental aspects of European life. It was widely held that the plague was a divine punishment for the sin of the people, and the inability of organized religion to influence this devastation shook the foundations of what had been the most substantial pillar of society for the prior millennium. It is not accurate to ascribe the Protestant Reformation to this alone, but there can be little question that the plague set the stage for changes in spiritual beliefs that had become an integral part of the European culture. The ramifications of this Reformation would be the basis of many of the changes affecting the lives of the people.

The population reduction caused by the plague had profound effects on the economy of the continent. The loss of available manpower prompted the collapse of the manorial system, as the increased value of one's labor encouraged mass movement from rural areas to the cities and contributed to reduced agricultural production. The fewer numbers of farm workers and the effects of unseasonably cold weather were factors in famines that afflicted Europe. Devastating famines were endured in one or more Western European countries in at least fifty-six years of the seventeenth century, resulting in up to five million deaths. The political system that was thought to be responsible for providing necessities for the people came under unexpected stress. The mutual identity of the church and the secular government contributed to a changed opinion in the minds of the population of both institutions.

The other apocalyptic threat was the pervasive presence of warfare during the latter sixteenth and seventeenth centuries. These conflicts were not only numerous and prolonged but affected the civilian population to a greater extent than previous wars, which had been usually fought between kings with their armies, often for control of territory claimed by birth or marriage. In this era, religion became a principal cause of conflict, and the devastation of the civilian population was greater than ever previously experienced. Few wars can match the intensity of the French Wars of Religion between 1562 and 1598. These wars were marked by atrocities committed by both the Calvinist French Huguenots and the Roman Catholic French national leadership, such as the St. Bartholomew's Day massacre, ordered by King Charles IX. This event in the summer of 1572 lasted several weeks, resulting in the death of thousands of prominent Protestant leaders in Paris and up to thirty thousand Huguenots across France. One of the victims of this massacre was the influential Protestant scholar and educational reformer Petrus Ramus, who was killed on August 24, 1572. These religious wars continued until 1598 when the Edict of Nantes was affirmed by the French King Henry IV.

This edict would provide a tenuous security for the prosperous Huguenot minority until its revocation in 1685 by Louis XIV. This resulted in an exodus of most of the surviving Protestants from France, with many seeking homes in North America, as noted in the experiences of Francis Gaineau and his daughter Marie in section I, D.

Another intense conflict was the Eighty Years' War (1568–1648) with the Netherland provinces, aided by the Protestant English and the French Huguenots, fighting the Spanish Hapsburg armies over the future of the Spanish Netherlands. It is estimated that this war resulted in between 230,000 and two million casualties, including civilians. A concurrent war in Ireland (Nine Years' War) was also primarily motivated by the Catholic-Protestant conflict, causing 130,000 deaths, mainly from associated famine and disease.

These wars were relatively benign when compared to the devastation resulting from the Thirty Years' War (1618–1648) that was fought in the Central European German states of the Holy Roman Empire a century following the beginning of the Reformation. The war was caused by the impact of the Reformation sweeping through these states and affecting nearly all of Europe. Estimates of the war casualties from combat, famine, and disease range from three to over eleven million persons. The territorial ambitions of Spain, France, Sweden, and Denmark contributed to the intensity of the conflicts. One cannot understand the basis of this devastation without an appreciation for the nature and significance of the Protestant Reformation, an upheaval in the European religious life that began in earnest in the early sixteenth century.

The groundwork for the events leading to this momentous situation had been long developing. Several factors that contributed to this cataclysm were the greater availability of translations of the Holy Bible from Latin into the languages of the people, the use of printing methods that distributed writings more widely, and the role of the Roman Catholic Church in the secular government of European countries. The religion of the monarch was the only recognized or permitted religion according to the widely accepted principle of *cuius regio, eius religio* (whose realm, his religion). It was the church that provided many of the social services that we associate with public life, such as education, hospitals, and the documentation of births (baptisms), marriages, and deaths. Just as the secular government was dominated by a monarch with varying degrees of influence from the governed, so was the religion dominated by the pope and the edicts of the Roman Church.

Theological controversies had for centuries challenged the Christian faith, and divisive issues concerning the nature of the Trinity had appeared very early in the Christian era when the Christian faith was defined as including individuals accepting the Nicene or Apostle's Creeds, which enunciate the belief in the triune God and the divinity of Jesus Christ. Those controversies arising in the later Middle Ages and Renaissance years involved the role of the

Gospel and the church hierarchy in the determination of theological issues. An early group of dissenters was the Waldensians, founded by Peter Waldes in Lyon, France, in the 1170s. Waldes translated the New Testament into the vernacular Franco-Provencal language, then spoken in eastern France, northwestern Italy, and parts of western Switzerland. This language is still spoken by a small number of people in the Aosta Valley region of northwestern Italy. This translation of scripture from Latin made it accessible to a majority of the people of the area, and the Waldensians' beliefs became widespread. The Roman Church declared them heretical, and by the early 1200s, the followers became the objects of persecution. The belief that aroused the greatest opposition from the established church was likely the doctrine of the universal priesthood of believers. The Waldensians also rejected the involvement of their leaders in public offices and held that the traditions of holy water, avoidance of certain foods, the supposed relics of saints, and the transubstantiation of the elements of communion were superstitions. Remnants of this group of believers survived persecution and in 1532 affiliated with the German and Swiss Reformed Church. In more recent times, the Waldensian Evangelical Church merged with the Italian Methodist Church and are members of the World Methodist Council. The influence of the Waldensians on the subsequent Calvinist and Anabaptist movements will be evident.

An important forerunner of the Reformation was John Wycliffe (1320–1384), who completed his translation of the Vulgate Latin Bible into vernacular English, known as the Wycliffe Bible near the end of his life. He had opposed the influence of papal authority on secular affairs and favored biblically centered reforms during his career as master of Baliol College, Oxford, and minister in various churches in England. He favored the supremacy of biblical teachings over papal authority, which created controversies lasting long after his death.

Wycliffe had great influence on the Czech Jan Hus, master at Charles University in Prague and a priest living from 1369 until his martyrdom in 1415. Hus had translated and supported the positions of Wycliffe, which opposed many of the actions and customs of the hierarchy of the Roman Church. His teachings were widely accepted in Bohemia and influenced Martin Luther over one hundred years later. After the execution of Hus by the church authorities, Bohemia and the adjacent area of Germany were ravaged by the Hussite Wars (1419–1431). Hus's followers divided into factions which continued to fight until 1434 when the Basel Compacts, accepted by the Roman Church, permitted the presence of a reformed church in Bohemia and Moravia. When the Lutheran Reformation began a century later, a majority of the Czech people were following the teachings of Jan Hus (Moravian Brethren Church).

The beginning of the Protestant Reformation is often dated to 1517 when Martin Luther, according to legend, nailed his *Ninety-Five Theses* to the door of the All Saints' Church in Wittenberg, Germany. Such an event, although firmly established in tradition, likely did not actually occur, but the Reformation can be dated to October 31, 1517, when Luther sent a copy of the *Theses* to his bishop. By the next January, this had been printed in German and widely distributed throughout much of Europe. His objections to some of the Roman Catholic theology and practice clearly fell on fertile ground, and his writings and teachings in Wittenberg attracted great attention. Luther's breach with Rome was fully established by late 1520, as he stated that popes did not have the exclusive right to interpret scripture and that popes and church councils could not be considered infallible. In 1521, he was declared an outlaw, and his supporters provided security for him in the Wartburg Castle in Eisenach. Here, for the next year, he would translate the New Testament into German and publish numerous criticisms of the theology of the Roman Church. Luther's persecution led followers in Wittenberg to violence, but he firmly opposed that response. This violence was a prelude to radicalization of many, which led to the German Peasants' War of 1524–25.

Luther's teaching spread throughout the German states over the next twenty years, despite the ruling of its illegality at the Diet of Worms in 1521. The adoption of this faith by the secular leaders of some states, such as Saxony, Hesse, and the Palatinate, resulted in overt warfare with Roman Catholic states in 1546–47, and hostilities persisted until the Peace of Augsburg was established with Holy Roman Emperor Charles V in 1555. This edict allowed the rulers of German principalities to choose between Roman Catholicism and Lutheranism as the official faith of their realm. It did not accept the Reformed Calvinist or Anabaptist beliefs, and this official intolerance would ultimately contribute to the Thirty Years' War (1618–1648). As Luther was beginning his work, there was religious unrest in the cantons of the Old Swiss Confederacy, in many German states, and in Bohemia. Several theologians active in this era proposed new biblical interpretations that would differ from those of Martin Luther and from one another but would eventually lead to the formation of congregations that would be known as the Reformed Church and Anabaptists. The Bohemian philosopher and writer of the Hussite movement Peter Chelcicky (1390–1460) was an early proponent of the separation of ecclesiastical matters from the secular government. He opposed the use of force in resolving spiritual issues and taught that Christians should refuse military service and public office. A German contemporary of Martin Luther was Thomas Muntzer (1489–1525), who joined Luther in Wittenberg in 1518, but soon their disagreements became severe. Muntzer was an instigator of the German Peasants' War and was executed after being captured during that uprising.[49] Among his theological positions was the rejection of the significance of infant baptism. He is often identified with the Anabaptists, but unlike most of them, he did not share their pacifist beliefs. The Anabaptist movement was the source of the Baptist faith

---

[49] Thomas Muntzer and the Peasants' War (1524–25) should not be confused with the Munster Rebellion (1532–35), although both were associated with the Anabaptist movement. The German Peasants' War was a widespread revolution based on social and economic factors, although the broader Protestant Reformation played an important role. Over one hundred thousand peasants died in their poorly planned military efforts. The Munster Rebellion took place in the German city of that name and involved a small number of radical millennialists. After their defeat, the Anabaptist leaders adopted more pacifist beliefs.

brought to the colonies from England and Wales. As it has particular significance for Johannes Kolb and his family, it will be further considered in section II, C.

Another reformer that rejected the use of violence in the name of religion and also rejected infant baptism was Andreas Karlstadt (1486–1541), who had significant influences on the Lutheran, Calvinist, and subsequent Anabaptist traditions. Karlstadt earned a doctorate in theology from the University of Wittenberg and was the chairman of theology before becoming chancellor of the university. In 1512, Martin Luther received his doctorate in theology from Chancellor Karlstadt, joined the faculty of the university, and began developing his convictions that would separate him from the beliefs of the Roman Church. During these years, Karlstadt pursued doctorates in canon and civil law in Rome, where he became disillusioned by what he saw as corruption and spiritual distortions supported by the church hierarchy. Both he and Luther were excommunicated by the pope in 1521.

Karlstadt returned to Germany and began instituting reforms in the sacraments of communion, spoke in favor of clerical matrimony, opposed the presence of art and statues in the sanctuary, and rejected the custom of infant baptism. His beliefs were considered radical, and he became estranged from Luther, but during the Peasants' War, Karlstadt was sheltered and protected by Luther. Karlstadt opposed the veneration of Mary, which created concern in the 1530s for his safety. He moved to the Swiss Confederation, where his beliefs were supported by the Lutheran Martin Bucer as well as Huldrych Zwingli and John Calvin of the Reformed Church.

Although the reformation influences of Luther and Calvin are well known in the present era, there were a number of other influential scholars who contributed to this movement that would result in theological, cultural, and governmental changes affecting much of Europe. One of the earliest of these scholars was Erasmus of Rotterdam, a Dutch humanist, priest, and theologian (1466–1536). Much of his academic activity took place in Paris and England where, during the reign of Henry VIII, he influenced many leading

English thinkers. He possibly planted the seed of separation from the Roman Church that would so greatly affect the English monarchy. His scholarship in Latin and Greek contributed to improving the available biblical translations and created an awareness of deviations from scriptural teachings in the beliefs and customs of the Roman Church. His scholarly criticism became an important reference for the growing Reformation movement.

Among the thought leaders of this movement were Johannes Oecolampadius (1482–1531), Balthasar Hubmaier (1480–1528), Hulrych Zwingli (1484–1531), and Andreas Karlstadt. These individuals were prominent in the evolving religious environment of the Swiss Confederation, especially in the university cities of Basel and Zurich. Zwingli was the most prominent of the early Reformed theologians, but with the arrival in 1533 of John Calvin (1509–1564) from France, the leadership of the Reformed Church in the Swiss cantons began to change. Calvin would dominate the Reformation in France, the Low Countries, and the British Isles. Various scholars and theologians shared many beliefs, but their differences on some issues were strong, and frequent disputations or debates between them would be held. As the leadership of the canton or kingdom in which they resided would arbitrate the outcome of these disputations, the resolution of the issues would have the effect of law in the area.

Calvin, known as Jehan Cauvin in his French homeland, was a precocious student of Latin and Greek and educated in the humanist tradition of classical studies. He would have been familiar with Erasmus, known as the Prince of Humanists, who criticized the Roman Church for its clerical abuses and also refined the available translations of the New Testament. In 1533, Calvin had a life-changing religious experience, aligned himself with other scholars critical of the Roman Church, and emphasized its need for reform. He was forced to leave France, and he moved to the Swiss city of Basel, where the Reformation was becoming established. He assumed pastoral duties as well as published his *Institutes of the Christian Religion* in Geneva in 1536. This work would be expanded and republished throughout his lifetime and would define the theology and practice of the Reformed Church, impacting the Christian faith throughout Europe.

The beliefs and theology of the Calvinist Reformed movement have impacted the beliefs of all denominations of protestant and evangelical Christianity to the present age. The departure from the centuries of belief and custom promulgated by the Roman Church was extensive, but the Reformed and Lutheran churches of the sixteenth and seventeenth centuries maintained a similarity to the Roman Church in their identity with the ruling secular government. This was clearly evident in the German states and in the Swiss cantons where either the Church of Rome, the Lutheran church, or the new Reformed Church were the exclusively permitted form of worship. Tolerance of different beliefs in these political jurisdictions was not permitted, and there was not a clear distinction between religious heretics and political traitors or anarchists. Those persisting in the disallowed beliefs and worship were subject to persecution, including death in the German, Swiss, and French jurisdictions. Those persons and their families who were less outspoken in their beliefs may have been deprived of their possessions and driven from their homeland. The forbears of the Kolb and Schumacher family in our story were likely a part of this exodus.

Holland and the German Electoral Palatine became early sanctuaries for threatened believers. The paths by which these two states became havens for Reformation Christians is of interest and important in understanding the devastating wars that were to mark the seventeenth century in Europe. Much of the conflict was due to the hegemony of the Spanish Hapsburg family, through a series of marriages, over Austria, Luxembourg, the Netherlands, and the Spanish empire. By the latter sixteenth century, the Seventeen Provinces (Netherlands) was under the dominion of Philip II of Spain, who imposed a strict conformity to the Roman Catholic Church. The Netherlands was remote from the center of political power in Spain and subjected to heavy taxation, which added to their unrest. Components of the Reformation had flourished in the Netherlands, including the Lutheran movement, the Reformed teachings of Calvin, and the Anabaptists of Menno Simons. Philip II's intense opposition to the Protestant movements contributed to the beginning of the Eighty Years' War in 1568, which was a revolt led by the Dutch leader William, Prince of Orange. By 1581, the Hapsburg armies had been defeated and the Republic of the Seven United Netherlands established. Holland, during a truce lasting until 1620, would provide sanctuary for persecuted religious groups from England and German principalities. Among them were the subsequent English Pilgrims and Baptists.

The electoral Palatinate was a German principality of the Holy Roman Empire that dated from the tenth century. It spanned the upper Rhine River, including part of Alsace to the west and the capital cities of Heidelberg and Mannheim to the east. In the mid-fourteenth century, it was designated as an electorate, indicating that its leader would be a voter to elect the emperor of the Holy Roman Empire. In 1618, Frederick V became elector of the Palatinate, and as a Calvinist, he gave the Protestants a majority of the electors of the Holy Roman Empire.

The previous year, the impending succession of Matthias, the Holy Roman emperor and king of Bavaria who would die without an heir, had become an issue. The Protestant nobility rejected the heir apparent, his nearest male relative, Ferdinand II, the crown prince of Bohemia and archduke of Austria, who was a staunch Catholic. They wanted the Calvinist Frederick V to assume the throne. His acceptance in 1619 contributed to the Thirty Years' War that would be disastrous for the Palatinate. The Spanish wanted the emperor to remain a member of the Hapsburg family and were also eager to reclaim the Netherlands. Their army was based in northern Italy, and the Palatinate was directly on their invasion path to the Netherlands, hence the ensuing Thirty Years' War would devastate that area and profoundly influence the forbears of our Kolb brothers.

Frederick V was ousted by the Austrian army led by Ferdinand II at the Battle of White Mountain, and the Palatinate was occupied by the Spanish and Bavarian troops. The fleeing survivors sought refuge in Protestant territories, including Holland and the Transylvania area of Hungary, which had adopted the first legal guarantee of religious freedom in Europe.

When the Thirty Years' War ended with the Peace of Westphalia in 1648, Central Europe was demolished and the population greatly diminished by famine and disease. The Palatine elector, Karl Ludwig, or Charles I Louis as he was known in England,[50] called for the survivors to rebuild his ravished land and welcomed those of all faiths, including Anabaptists. One of the first groups to return from Transylvania included family names of Schumacher, Kolb, and others who resettled in Wolfsheim, Kriegsheim, and other Palatinate towns. Among them were the forebears of Johannes Kolb and his brothers.

The Anabaptists' numbers in the Palatinate increased in 1671–2 when Swiss persecution peaked, but this tranquility was to be interrupted by the invasion of the army of Louis XIV of France in October 1688. This began the nine-year War of the Grand Alliance, which involved major European powers and spread to their colonies, including North America, where it was known as King William's War. The prolonged conflict failed to resolve the key issue of the possible merger of the French and Spanish empires under a Bourbon ruler and led to the War of Spanish Succession (1701–1714) also affecting the Palatinate. The hostility of Louis XIV toward Protestants continued unabated after his Revocation of the Edict of Nantes in 1685 and would cause many Palatinate Germans and French Huguenots to immigrate to North America. Among those fleeing their French homeland were Francis Gaineau and his children, who left behind most of their property as they sought new lives in the English Colony of New York. It is also not surprising that Johannes Kolb and his three brothers left the Palatinate in 1707 and came to Germantown, Colony of Pennsylvania, where freedom of one's worship was assured and invading armies were not a threat.

Just as the Palatinate provided sanctuary for the Protestant Reformation adherents from France, the Swiss Cantons, and German

---

[50] Charles I Louis was a son of Elizabeth Stuart and Frederick V, grandson of James I and nephew of Charles I of England, but he was unable to obtain English support for the Protestant cause in the war.

principalities in the sixteenth century, so did Holland receive many Non-Conformists from Britain. The victory of the Netherlands Protestants in the Eighty Years' War and the succeeding truce would make Holland a haven for refugees of the tumultuous religious and political climate in England in the early decades of the seventeenth century. Reformed and Separatist believers from England would find safety in the Netherlands, where some would be influenced by Anabaptist theology (see section II, C and appendix IV, H for further explanation).

B. THE REFORMATION AND TURMOIL IN ENGLAND

The Reformation came to England by a very different route than to other European lands, as it began in the political rather than the ecclesiastical arena. European monarchs had, from the time of Charlemagne, reinforced their authority by obtaining the blessings of the church for their reign, and that source of divine authority was the pope of the church in Rome. The first break in that chain of authority can be attributed to Henry VIII, who dissolved the ties between the English Crown and the pope in 1533 and created what would become the Anglican Church.

There was no reason to infer any ecclesiastical reason for the dissolution of the ties to the Roman Church other than the presumed authority of the pope over the actions of the English monarch. In fact, Pope Leo X in 1521 had conferred on Henry the title of Defender of the Faith for his affirmation of the supremacy of the pope in the face of the reforming ideals of the excommunicated Martin Luther. Henry remained committed to all other teachings and rituals of the Roman Church. This action, however, did represent a complete break in the relationship between the Roman Church and the English secular government. Political conflict between the English monarch and the pope had occurred many centuries earlier in the reign of Henry II and in the fourteenth century during the reign of Edward III, but the breach occurring in 1533–4 was a dissolution of ties that had been established since AD 597 when Augustine (Austin) the Apostle of the English, sent by Pope Gregory I, baptized the Anglo-Saxon King Ethelbert of Kent and thousands of his subjects. The principal seat (Bishop's See) of the English church, established with papal authority, was at Canterbury, the capital of the kingdom of Kent (see section IV, H, Church of St. Peter upon Cornhill and Celtic/Welsh Church History).

The issue that led to this breach in 1533 was the inability of Henry to produce a male heir by his wife, Catherine of Aragon, which was thought necessary to secure the continuity of the Tudor dynasty. Her only surviving child was a daughter, Mary, and with Catherine's age and history of multiple miscarriages, Henry believed that a new wife would be necessary. An annulment of their marriage would be required for any subsequent children from another wife to have legitimacy and a claim to the crown. He contended that as Catherine had been previously married to his deceased older brother, Arthur, the marriage could be annulled based on scripture in the Old Testament book of Leviticus (20:21), which seemed to prohibit this circumstance. Henry's dilemma became complicated, as he was enamored by a younger Anne Boleyn, who was attractive, well educated, and socially skillful, and in 1533, her pregnancy made the quest for the annulment a critical issue. The resolution of these issues reveals some of the most intense political maneuvering that can be imagined in both secular and ecclesiastical spheres. They involved the highest offices in the land and with results that could be fatal.

Three names dominated his reign, the first being Thomas Wolsey, who became the most powerful political figure within five years of the accession of Henry to the throne. Wolsey was the archbishop of York and became the lord chancellor, the king's top adviser, before being named a cardinal of the church. He was unable, however, to convince Pope Clement VII to annul Henry's marriage, likely due to political pressure from Charles V, the Holy Roman emperor and nephew of Catherine of Aragon. Wolsey lost his political position due to his failed effort and died when en route to the Tower of London to face charges of treason and certain execution.

The second dominant political figure was a younger protégé of Wolsey's, Thomas Cromwell, who had long been an influential member of the pro-Reformation faction in Parliament. Cromwell promoted parliamentary support for the declaration of Henry as the sole head of the church and the breaking of ties to Rome by prohibiting appeal of these ecclesiastical decisions to the courts in Rome. With these political maneuvers, the marriage to Catherine was declared illegal, and Parliament ruled that the decision could not be challenged. Henry VIII and Anne Boleyn were married in January, and in September, she gave birth to a daughter, Elizabeth. Henry named Thomas Cromwell his chief minister and appointed him royal vicegerent and vicar-general, delegating him with full authority over the church of which Henry was the head.

Over the next three years, Anne, who had few friends either at court or in the public, failed to produce a male heir, and her disagreements with Henry over church matters and an unrestrained temper led him to seek an end to the marriage. With the assistance of Cromwell, she was found guilty of adultery, and she, her brother, and four others were executed in May 1536. Within two weeks after the marriage to Anne was declared invalid, Henry married Jane Seymour, who in 1537 produced a son who would become King Edward VI in 1547 when nine years old. Shortly after her only pregnancy, Jane died of puerperal fever, and her death was a cause of great grief for Henry.

The third individual to play a critical role in the English Reformation was Thomas Cranmer, who was appointed archbishop of Canterbury. Prior to becoming the top cleric in the new Anglican church, Cranmer had established ties to the developing Reformed movement and to the Lutherans when he was the English ambassador to the court of the Holy Roman emperor in Germany. Henry VIII's break with the authority of Rome was intensely controversial in England but did have significant support from the public, Parliament, and clergy. The seeds of what would become the Reformation movement had been planted in England by the influences of John Wycliffe (1320–84) and Erasmus of Rotterdam (1466–1536), and the issues raised by Luther, Calvin, and others were widely known. In October 1532, Cranmer was appointed archbishop of Canterbury, and he worked closely with Cromwell in ruling that Henry's marriage to Catherine was illegal. Over the next decade, Cranmer would promote Reformed and Lutheran positions within the church, but significant conservative opposition seeking to maintain close ties with Rome had Henry's approval. The king, however, personally supported Cranmer, who in 1544 produced the Book of Common Prayer, which, with the backing of Parliament defined the future of the Anglican Church.

Meanwhile, all did not go well for Thomas Cromwell, who urged Henry to take a Protestant, Anne of Cleves, as his wife following the death of Jane Seymour. This relationship proved unsuccessful, and Cromwell fell out of favor; his many enemies urged the House of Lords to approve accusations against him of treason and other crimes. He was executed without a trial in July 1540. Henry subsequently regretted having lost such an effective and faithful servant.

When Henry died in 1547, his will designated his daughters, Mary and Elizabeth, to the line of succession following Edward. The young Edward VI, through the efforts of his uncle, Edward Seymour, regent and controller of the Privy Council, was able to promote the English Reformation, including the publishing of the Book of Common Prayer in 1549. The death of Edward VI from tuberculosis in 1553 led to the tumultuous reign of Mary, which was an era of havoc for those not adhering to the Roman faith.

Her goal of perpetuating a Catholic Tudor dynasty in England was not achieved, as her marriage to the Spanish prince Philip, a staunch Catholic, was not only unhappy but produced no heirs. Her attempted restoration of the ties to Rome lacked widespread public support. The execution of many Protestant leaders assured her place as one of the most disliked monarchs in English history and the designation as *Bloody Mary*. Among those who were martyred was Thomas Cranmer, who had effectively led the English Reformation and included both Lutheran and Reformed practices in Anglican church worship. After prolonged persecution, he was burned at the stake in 1556, but his efforts would provide the basis for the rejuvenated Church of England. The reign of Queen Mary I saw many Reformation-minded English flee their homeland, seeking sanctuary in Holland, where they were further exposed to the more radical views of Reformed Calvinists and Anabaptists. After Mary's death in 1558, many of those Protestants returned to their homes with beliefs and expectations that were expressed with evangelical zeal, causing conflict and turmoil within the reestablished Anglican congregations. Those returning provided the seeds that grew to become the Puritan, Baptist, and other Separatist movements.

Elizabeth I deserves the admiration of subsequent generations for her response to succession as monarch of the land. Her greatest challenge was to establish the confidence of the people in the ability of a young woman to deal effectively with extreme obstacles that in other European nations had led to genocidal civil conflicts. She immediately stated that she would count on thoughtful and trusted advisers in the decision-making process, and her first important effort was to try to heal the religious divisions that resulted from actions of her Tudor predecessors. Within her first year as monarch, Parliament passed two bills that would constitute the Elizabethan Religious Settlement in 1559. The Act of Supremacy would reestablish the separation of the Church of England from Rome and affirm Elizabeth and her successors as the supreme governor (head) of the church.

The companion Act of Uniformity was soon approved by Parliament, which was no longer controlled by conservative, pro-papal members. This reestablished the Book of Common Prayer and defined theological parameters that would be the hallmarks of Anglican belief. The positions of the Anglican Church would be clarified by the Thirty-Nine Articles, which would reflect Elizabeth's intention to follow a middle path between Roman Catholicism and the dissident Reformed Protestants. The growing number of followers of the Calvinist beliefs, identified as Puritans, were not appeased by these compromises, and many continued to express their varied opinions, much to Elizabeth's displeasure. The resulting Church of England would reflect some of the Roman Catholic influences urged by the members of the House of Lords, tempered by the increasing support for the Calvinist Reformed beliefs. These Puritan reforms would become a more severely divisive issue as the seventeenth century opened with the end of the reign of Elizabeth I in 1603. The Thirty-Nine Articles also specifically identified disagreement with the Anabaptist position that the sacrament of baptism should only involve those who had accepted the biblically defined plan of salvation and were of an age of accountability. The earlier Ten Articles of 1536 had stipulated that baptism was necessary for one to gain salvation, even for infants, clearly distinguishing them from the Anabaptist beliefs.

The enthusiasm for the changes favored by the Calvinists caused a backlash from the Anglicans. Parliament adopted the Act Against Puritans in 1593, which enforced the prior Act of Uniformity with the threat of prison for those not regularly attending the sanctioned worship services. Elizabeth I had been relatively tolerant of Puritans and other Separatists, but this was to change when James I succeeded her to the throne in 1603, as he vigorously enforced conformity. Although he was initially cheered by the English Protestants, he had a view of the monarchy that soon put him at odds with Parliament and the Calvinist clerics. These political views, developed during his reign of twenty-five years as James VI of Scotland, were described in his 1597 book, *The True Law of Free Monarchies*, in which he affirmed his belief in the divine right of kings. He considered those not adhering to the faith of which he was head as being disloyal to his rule, and many Reform-minded clergy lost their positions in the church. One such person was Rev. Thomas Stoughton Sr., the father of Judith Stoughton and grandfather of John Denman II, who was removed as rector of the Coggeshall Church in 1606 for nonconformity. As Judith and her brothers and a sister would share these religious convictions, their families were willing to join the large numbers of nonconformist Puritans who moved to the Colony of Massachusetts, seeking freedom from religious persecution and for other reasons. Judith Stoughton, mother of John Denman II, apparently had significant separatist views as she settled in Salem in the Colony of Massachusetts Bay. The church there had a separatist reputation, as Roger Williams had served as an interim pastor prior to his exile from the colony.

The low regard that James I held for Parliament soon became evident after his succession in 1603; the worsening financial condition of the government and his sympathies for Catholic Spain led to increased conflict with the House of Commons and the public. James I was faced with an enormous public debt largely due to the costly Nine Years' War with Ireland and his own spending habits. The debt increased despite the sale of extensive royal properties, and he was required to seek the support of tax funds from a reluctant Parliament. His unpopularity was enhanced by his longstanding lustful relationships with men, despite his marriage to Anne of Denmark. The most problematic of his liaisons was with George Villiers, who would be made duke of Buckingham and given numerous honors despite his providing much ill-advised consultation with James I.

On the positive side, his reign included the beginning of colonization of North America and experienced a flourishing literary and scientific environment but ended in the midst of an economic depression and plague epidemic. His son Charles I inherited the throne in 1625 and these severe problems. He also inherited a conviction of the divine right of kings and a disdain for a popularly elected Parliament, which would lead to the English Civil Wars. Religious factors also played a role in his lack of popularity. The Protestant majority was alarmed by his marriage to the Roman Catholic French princess Henrietta Maria and his lack of enthusiasm for supporting the Protestants in the Thirty Years' War in Central Europe. His response to the plight of beleaguered Huguenots at La Rochelle was to send the inept and hated duke of Buckingham in a failed foray against the Ile de Re in 1627. The lack of success for this English expedition encouraged the siege of La Rochelle by French King Louis XIII and contributed to the animosity toward Charles I by the Calvinist English. Charles also promoted ecclesiastical policies seemingly favoring Roman traditions, which further antagonized clerics with nonconformist beliefs.

The final straw for the reign of Charles I was the failure to call a Parliament for eleven years, during which he attempted to raise tax revenue without the approval of elected representatives. This may have foretold the events of one hundred thirty-four years later when the British colonies would revolt against taxation without representation. The result of Charles's policies, which were despised by both the Parliamentarians and Puritans, would be the English Civil Wars between 1642 and 1651, constituting three separate conflicts pitting these groups against Royalists. At the end of the second war in 1649, Charles I would be captured, convicted of treason, and executed. This added a new word to the English vocabulary, *regicide*, and would be viewed with alarm and disgust by much of Europe. These wars were marked by the emergence of Oliver Cromwell as an effective military and political leader and culminated in the defeat of Royalist forces then led by Charles II in 1651.

Charles II escaped to France, where he remained exiled through the nine years of the Commonwealth of England. In this time, the head of the church was assumed by Parliament and dominated by the Puritans who represented the extreme positions of the Reformed faith. The ecclesiastical organization of Presbyterianism, devised by Calvin and brought to Scotland by John Knox, was proposed as a replacement for the Anglican tradition of apostolic succession of bishops and priests. This move to make the church more democratic between 1649 and 1653 was met with resistance and intensified the public's opposition to Parliamentary rule. After 1653, Oliver Cromwell ruled the Protectorate only with the support of the army.

The war casualties and disease associated with the civil wars cost the lives of over 10 percent of the population of the British Isles by a conservative estimate and were an even higher percentage in Ireland. With the social and religious disruptions, the population welcomed the end of the Commonwealth following Oliver Cromwell's death in 1658 and the restoration of the monarchy in 1660.

Charles II returned to London from his sojourn in France to an enthusiastic welcome following the Declaration of Breda, which specified the conditions of the Restoration and required approval by Parliament. Parliament, representing both Royalists and Parliamentarians, Anglicans and Reformed Presbyterians, granted amnesty to Cromwell's supporters. The leaders of the regicide movement were not forgiven and were either executed, imprisoned, or exiled. Cromwell's body was exhumed and decapitated as a public demonstration.

Charles II reigned until 1685, during which time the Anglo-Dutch Wars were fought over competition for international trading activities and colonial claims. The second of these wars resulted in England gaining possession of the North American Dutch New Netherlands. The English navy was led by the king's brother, James, whose titles, duke of York and Albany, became the names of the former Dutch province and its major settlements. James would become monarch in 1685 upon the death of Charles II, who had no surviving legitimate children.

The circumstances of the Nonconformists, which included Reformed and other non-Anglican Protestants and Roman Catholics, did not improve during these last four decades of the seventeenth century. The Act of Uniformity 1662 required Anglican ordination for all ministers, and previous acts of Parliament excluded all Nonconformists from civil or military office, attendance at English universities, and membership in the learned professions. The reign of James II would be shortened due to the suspicion that he was overly sympathetic to the Roman Church and to his struggles with Parliament. After the Glorious Revolution of 1688, he was replaced by his Protestant daughter, Mary, and her husband, William of Orange. In 1702, they were succeeded by her sister Queen Anne, who reigned until 1714, the last of the Stuart monarchs.

The Tudor and Stuart eras of English history and the countries that we now know as Western Europe were dominated by the religious upheavals of the Reformation and its effect on the secular and political life of the realms. From a much later perspective, it is evident that the involvement of the state in the worship activities and ecclesiastical matters was a source of continual disruption in England and in many of the European countries. The idea of religious freedom, although perhaps predicted by the experience in Holland, would be delayed until the democratic experiment that was to occur in British North America. The constitutional separation of church and state would prove to be one of the most important contributions of the United States of America.

As noted, this separation of government from the influence of the Roman Church was further advanced by the Peace of Augsburg in 1555, but this was a long way from what we would consider a separation of church and state. With this background, we can more clearly understand the motivations of our four individual colonists and their families who faced these disruptions and challenges to their lives. Although the prospects of life in the relatively untamed lands of North America would be dominated by uncertainty, these fears must have seemed acceptable in light of the problems and prospects that they faced in their European homelands. Colonial life had unique challenges that could not have been predicted by the immigrant families and that would shape their views of themselves and their communities for their lives and for future generations. In fact, the Reformation in Germany, Switzerland, and in England merely transferred the union of the church and the secular government to new partners, with any pretenders being excluded from the association. The power of the government to enforce the expectations of the church would prove to be a significant factor in the flood of Europeans who would seek new homes in America in the seventeenth century.

C. MENNONITE, ENGLISH, AND WELSH BAPTISTS IN COLONIAL HISTORY

In the twenty-first century, Baptists as distinct groups of settlers in early colonial America are not widely recognized. They did contribute significantly to the early history of the colonies and had an important role in the inclusion of the cherished freedom of religion in our Bill of Rights. Baptists are not generally identified as groups of believers who adhere to a specific creed, liturgy, or hierarchy but as congregations joined in independent associations, retaining specific areas of belief, interpretation, and authority. There are, however, specific beliefs that distinguished them in the early years of the Reformation and in the English colonies. It is the contention of some more modern Welsh Baptists that their distant forbearers held some of these beliefs for centuries prior to their widespread recognition.[51] For several centuries prior to the Reformation, there were sects or theologians, as mentioned in section II, A and B, that espoused beliefs that are similar to those that later were identified as Anabaptists. Among those who expressed some of these beliefs were Peter Waldes, John Wycliffe, Jan Hus, and many others.

Two distinctive beliefs of Baptists are 1) the restriction of the sacrament of baptism to individuals over an age of accountability instead of in infancy and 2) separation of ecclesiastical and secular governance (i.e., the freedom to worship without interference from governmental authority). There was no organized group of such believers until the early 1520s when about fifteen students of the well-known Reformation theologian Huldrych Zwingli in Zurich began to develop beliefs with which their teacher disagreed. Among this group of men was Conrad Grebel, the highly educated son of a prosperous and well-connected merchant. Over several years, the group met to study the Bible and formulate their biblical interpretations and theological positions. During this time, Grebel communicated with Luther, Karlstadt, and Muntzer, but the differences in their beliefs outweighed their agreements.

The issue of infant baptism was an unresolvable conflict between the Grebel associates and Zwingli, which led to a public disputation in January 1525. The city council ruled in favor of Zwingli and infant baptism, an action that made this the law of the canton. Grebel and his associates were ordered to cease their activities or be exiled. Several days later, the group met illegally in the home of Felix Manz. George Blaurock, upon his profession of faith, was baptized by Grebel, and he then baptized the others. The first group

---

[51] These issues are described more fully in appendix IV, H.

of Anabaptists, so-called because of their prior baptism as infants, was formed.[52] They would later be known as the Swiss Brethren, and significant numbers of their followers would spread to neighboring countries due to persecution. Grebel was forced from Zurich in 1525, but during the next year, he attracted many followers in nearby cantons. After a period of imprisonment, he escaped to continue his preaching and writing but died in 1526 of the plague.

Other early Anabaptists faced torture and execution, including Manz and Blaurock, but their beliefs spread prominently in the Central European areas of Tyrol (western Austria), Moravia (Czech Republic), and southern Germany. Some of these new believers extended the idea of the separation of their spiritual lives from the influence of secular government to a literal application of the Sermon on the Mount and precluded military service, other governmental activities, and the use of public vows or oaths. These pacifist views were often viewed as anarchist by the authorities and were a cause of persecution.

Other Anabaptist followers, especially those influenced by Thomas Muntzer, were far from pacifist and were involved in the 1524–25 Great Peasants' War with the death of over one hundred thousand poorly armed and led Germans (see section II, A). The causes of this war are complex, and some historians consider it a response to the efforts of the feudal lordship to reestablish the economic structure (the manorial system) that had been ebbing since the population effects of the plague nearly two centuries earlier. As the hierarchical leadership of the numerous German estates and Swiss cantons had adopted either the Lutheran, Reformed, or Roman Catholic churches as the official religion, the Anabaptists were attracted to the peasants' revolt, although their faith was probably only a small part of the cause of the conflict.

The devastation of this war greatly increased the influence of the Anabaptist pacifist persuasion, which by 1530, through the

---

[52] The term means one who baptizes again from the Greek term (before). The Anabaptists had been baptized in infancy but were rebaptized after publicly accepting the biblical plan of salvation as they interpreted the New Testament.

efforts of Melchior Hoffman, had spread to Holland and become a significant presence. Hoffman and his peaceful followers introduced the first Anabaptist congregation in the Netherlands.[53] Their beliefs were widely received, and in 1536, they were joined by a disaffected Roman Catholic priest, Menno Simons. He soon became the most effective leader of the sect, and within a decade, the Dutch Anabaptists were known as Mennonites. This Anabaptist faith spread through the Rhine Valley both from the northern Dutch influence and from Swiss Brethren fleeing persecution in the south. By the seventeenth century, the Schumacher and Kolb families and many others were members of a well-established Mennonite religious group in the Palatinate, although they continued to face suspicion and persecution from the authorities. As noted in section I, E, the Thirty Years' War (1618–48) forced most of them to flee the advancing armies of the French and seek refuge in either the Netherlands or the province of Hungary.

As previously noted, the return of the Anabaptists to the Palatinate after the end of this war was followed by a generation of tenuous tranquility, but this was disrupted during the early lives of the Kolb brothers by the invasions of the French armies. They along with many other German-speaking Christians with Mennonite and Quaker beliefs would seek refuge in the colonies of New Jersey and Pennsylvania in the seventeenth century to preserve their spiritual freedoms.

The Anabaptist influence in Holland significantly affected the English Reformed and Separatist Protestants who fled hostility during the Tudor and Stuart eras. The ascension of James I to the English throne saw an increase in official persecution in the Anglican Church of those with Reformed beliefs. These beliefs had gained importance due to the theological influence of Cambridge University on a generation of future theologians, scholars, and church leaders. Anglican ministers such as the Rev. Thomas Stoughton and Rev. Francis Denman would find their careers in jeopardy because of their interest in this movement.

---

[53] This was in the city of Emden in East Frisia.

The desire of some to purify the Anglican Church of its Roman Catholic influences led to their being known as Puritans. Active persecution, encouraged by the Crown, forced some to escape to Holland to worship according to their consciences. Although many Puritans sought changes in the Anglican worship, others wanted to totally separate from the Church of England and form independent churches. Some so-called Separatists, such as the congregation at Scrooby Manor of one hundred followers, and their leader, John Robinson, left England in 1608 and prospered in their new home in Holland. Robinson became an important religious figure in the Dutch republic, and their numbers grew. In 1620, some of the church membership with the leadership of John Carver and William Brewster relocated to the area obtained from the Plymouth Company in the English colonial territory.[54] These Pilgrim settlers were ready to leave the Netherlands due to a desire to maintain their English heritage for the next generation, the possibility of war between Holland and Spain due to the expiration of the twenty year truce, the cultural uncertainty of remaining in a foreign land, and their desire to create a theocratic society.

Another Separatist congregation in Gainsborough, in 1607, led by John Smyth, Thomas Helwys, and John Murton also sought safety in Amsterdam. They became influenced by the believer baptism of the Anabaptists and with the principle that the church and state should be separate in governance; hence they became the first truly English Baptist church. Helwys, Smyth, and a small group returned to England in 1611, founding the first Baptist congregation in England, and faced continuous persecution. Helwys appealed to King James I concerning liberty of conscience, and he died in prison

---

[54] James I established the Virginia Company and the Plymouth Company on April 10, 1606, resulting in the Jamestown colony. There were no successful settlements in the northern area until the Pilgrims obtained their rights, which included self-government. This Plymouth Colony, with the aid of Squanto, established a treaty with the Wampanoag tribe and survived until 1691, when it was merged with the province of Massachusetts Bay.

in 1616. John Murton continued to promote the Baptist beliefs with a Calvinist influence, which became important to Roger Williams.

Another theological influence that was brought back to England from Holland by Smyth and Helwys was an Arminian version of the faith. These beliefs would shape the General Baptists of the seventeenth century and have become an important part of the theological basis for some modern-day Baptists and Methodists. These theological ideas arose from the teachings of Jacobus Arminius, a Dutch theologian who differed from the Calvinist teachings and was a prominent scholar at the University of Leiden.[55] Conflict with the Calvinists' Reformed beliefs contributed to hardships experienced by the General Baptists throughout the Cromwell years in which the Puritans and other Calvinist Separatists held the balance of political power.

The Arminian theology that influenced these newly organized Baptists would have far-reaching effects on nearly every denomination that emerged from the Reformation. These beliefs were articulated in the Five Articles of Remonstrance, which were defined by the Synod of Dort (1618–19). These five theological positions can be compared to their similar counterparts in the Calvinist view of the Christian faith:

---

[55] Jacobus Arminius was a Latinized replacement for his Dutch name, Jakob Hermanszoon, as was common in academic circles. It may be only chance that this was the name of the Germanic tribal leader at the nearby Battle of Teutoburg in 9 CE, which was the most notable defeat of the ancient Roman army and is considered one of the most decisive battles in military history. Tucker, S. 2010.

Calvinist Interpretation	*Arminian Interpretation*
1. Humans are totally separated from God by their sin and are therefore incapable of responding to Him even by faith.	1. God's grace is available to all humans even before they are aware of their need and are able to respond to Him through faith.
2. God unconditionally elects those individuals and only them, that will respond to His will without consideration of their merit.	2. God's atonement of sin is available to all humans who repent and trust in Christ for forgiveness.
3. Atonement of sin through Christ is limited and available only to the elected individuals.	3. Humans are only able to respond to God's will with the aid of the Holy Spirit.
4. God's grace, given to the elect, is an internal call that is irresistible to these humans.	4. God's grace and the Holy Spirit may be resisted and rejected by humans.
5. One cannot lose their salvation, is eternally secure in Christ and will never be tempted beyond their faith.	5. Believers are able to resist sin through grace but may be capable of forsaking God's grace by their free will.

Conflicts between Arminian and Calvinist interpretations continue in the 21st century as a source of controversy in the Baptist faith. While these distinctions may not directly affect the core beliefs, especially those that define present-day Christians, they were of profound significance to the 17th century Baptists, Puritans and others. These Arminian beliefs would become integral to the General Baptists and in the 18th century they would be refined by John Wesley and become essential to the beliefs of his Methodist tradition.

Another group of Separatists that organized in 1616 in the Southwark area of London with the leadership of Henry Jacob would give rise to the Particular Baptists that maintained more Calvinist views. These beliefs would be defined in the *London Baptist Confession of Faith A.D. 1644*, and it was this group that would have the greatest impact on the subsequent Baptist faith in the New World.

Conflicts of biblical interpretation and theological issues, which could be intense and divisive, would dominate early seventeenth-century congregations. Such departures of spiritual emphasis led to the Antinomian Controversy that was disruptive to the Puritan establishment in the Massachusetts Bay Colony. This will be considered from the religious and political perspectives in another section relating to the environment in British North America. It has been suggested that Roger Williams was closer to the Arminian than the Calvinist interpretations.

It is difficult to categorize the early Baptist congregations in the New World along General or Particular lines of belief, as each congregation remained independent in such determinations. The earliest Baptist church in Wales was of the Particular Baptist persuasion and was founded by John Myles in 1649. Myles would relocate to Swansea, Massachusetts, in 1663 and establish the fourth Baptist church in the colonies, the earlier ones being in Providence and Newport, Rhode Island, as the result of Roger Williams's colony. The next such church would be founded in Boston in 1665 but would face intense opposition from the Puritan establishment. One of their early members, Henry Dunster, was dismissed from his position as the first president of Harvard College because of his Baptist beliefs. Other members were jailed, fined, or publicly beaten because of their faith.

With the Restoration of the monarchy in 1660, the Church of England was restored as the state church under Charles II. Parliament approved the Act of Uniformity of 1662, establishing official discrimination against non-Anglican Christians (Nonconformists). Even the more liberalized environment following the Act of Toleration of 1689 was hostile to Nonconformists, as they were excluded from public education and professional associations as well as civil or military office. Some discrimination was permitted in Great Britain by law until the twentieth century.

It is not surprising that a small group of Baptists from the counties of Pembroke and Carmarthen in Wales were motivated by deep religious convictions, for which they faced persecution, "to resolve to seek their future in America." In the spring of 1701, they had constituted a church with Thomas Griffith as their minister, met at Milford Haven Waterway in Wales, embarked on the ship *James and Mary*, and landed in Philadelphia on September 8, 1701.[56] The initial group of sixteen persons was courteously treated by the earlier settlers in the William Penn colony, and they were advised to settle in the area of Pennepec, where other Welsh-speaking immigrants had settled since the mid-1680s. Their numbers grew, and they became part of the congregation of the Pennepack Baptist Church, which traced its origin to 1688 (see appendix section IV, G and gallery figure 1).

Within a year and a half of their arrival in Pennsylvania, their number had increased to thirty-seven. In 1703 they moved to the second Welsh Tract with over thirty thousand acres in Newcastle County, which had been granted by William Penn to William Davis, David Evans, and William Willis in 1701 for settlers from South Wales. This area was initially in the province of Pennsylvania, but a later boundary change placed most of their land in Delaware. On their removal to the Welsh Tract, they affiliated with the Pencader Hundred Baptist Church, now in New Castle County, Delaware.[57] Over the next thirty years, their group continued to grow in prosperity, and they established the Welsh Tract Baptist Church (gallery figure 4). Several families had become slaveholders with the demands of their growing agricultural enterprises. This likely put them at odds with others of their faith and congregation. Hence, by the mid-1730s, a number of the Welsh Baptist community were

---

[56] The church at the Welsh Tract in the county of Newcastle upon Delaware. http.//www.gpp-5grace.com/graceproclamator/pp0199welshtractchurch.htm.

[57] Gilmore, G.W. The New Schaff-Herzog Encyclopedia of Religious Knowledge, 1:467–469.

influenced by publicity concerning the availability of suitable land for farming in the Carolinas. Johannes Kolb and his wife, Sarah, and their children were in the group of settlers that moved from the Welsh Tract location to the Welsh Neck area of the Colony of South Carolina in the mid-1730s.

In May 1731, Benjamin Franklin published the accounts of Hugh Meredith in the *Pennsylvania Gazette*, which made favorable mention of these prospects. Welsh settlers had moved to the Cape Fear River area of North Carolina in 1725 but encountered hostile Indians who killed the family of a Thomas James. The continuing influx of people from Pennsylvania and other colonies had eliminated the threat of the native Indians, and many colonists with Welsh ancestry had moved into the area known as Bladen County. In the early 1730s, Robert Johnson, the royal governor of the province of South Carolina, granted ten thousand acres in the upper Pee Dee River area to more than thirty families that emigrated from the Welsh Tract to South Carolina beginning in 1735. These colonists, led by James James, Esq., and the slaves that some brought with them located to an area known as Welsh Neck, near a town later named Society Hill. James James, Esq., had served as an elder deacon in the Pencader Hundred Baptist Church and as a justice of the peace in Pennsylvania and was both prosperous and respected in the Welsh community.[58] He and his three sons, Abel, Daniel, and Philip James, and their spouses were important members of the Welsh Neck community as this South Carolina frontier area was known. It did not take long for the Welsh Baptists to form a church in their new homeland, and in 1738, the Welsh Neck Baptist Church was founded by eight families. Their first pastor was the son of James James, Esq., the Reverend Philip James, who was ordained on April 4, 1743. Philip James was born in 1701 in Pennepec, Pennsylvania, and served Welsh Neck Baptist Church until his death in 1753. The Welsh Neck Baptist Church had a far greater influence on the spiritual life of the South Carolina frontier than its small size and remote location might suggest. By the

---

[58] Jordan, J.W. "Colonial and Revolutionary Families of Pennsylvania." p.781.

end of the eighteenth century, it had served as the mother church of over thirty-five congregations in this area of westward expansion. In its early years, it preserved much of its Welsh heritage, but by 1777, it had 197 members, the majority of whom were not of direct Welsh descent.[59]

This congregation, like so many others, was greatly influenced by the First Great Awakening.[60] The evangelical zeal of this movement encouraged slaves to become full members in the church where they participated in the services, and they were encouraged to learn to read and study the Bible to further spread the Gospel to the slave population. One of the major contributions of this religious community was its association with musical practices that became such a distinctive part of evangelical Christianity. Hymn singing became a part of Baptist worship throughout the South, and some of this could be traced to the Welsh Neck influence, such as through the Saturday-morning Singing School operated by the Reverend Evan Pugh at the nearby Cashaway Baptist Church.[61]

The Welsh Baptists achieved the goals of their forbearers, dating over many centuries, to be able to worship in a fashion based on their interpretation of Holy Scripture and free of secular restriction. They and other like-minded Christians spread widely throughout the colonies and the area that would become a new nation. An important part of the Constitution of this new nation was the guarantee of a separation of the secular authority of the state and the ecclesiastical authority of scripture, the church, and its congregations.

While the persecution of Nonconformists and Separatists was a persistent feature of seventeenth-century Britain and New England, the colonies to the south were more receptive to those seeking respite from religious harassment. The middle Atlantic colonies, especially Pennsylvania, created by Charles II as a grant to William Penn, and New Jersey via a land grant to Sir George Carteret and Lord

---

[59] Johnson, L. "The Welsh in the Carolinas in the Eighteenth Century." North American Journal of Welsh Studies, Vol. 4, 1 (Winter 2004)
[60] Further described in section III, E.
[61] Ibid. p. 19.

Berkeley of Stratton by James II, were more tolerant of religious diversity. When the English assumed control of New Netherland after the second Anglo-Dutch War, the renewed hostility toward the Reformed congregations and the annulment of deeds of ownership of much of the Long Island property obtained directly from the Lenape Indians encouraged John Denman to obtain property in New Jersey with the nearing of the eighteenth century.

Our story of the Swiss Brethren/Anabaptist/Mennonite Kolb brothers included the relocation of Johannes Kolb and his family from the Colony of Pennsylvania to the banks of the Pee Dee River in the Cheraw District of South Carolina.[62] Johannes, his wife, Sarah, and their eight children were then a part of a community of Welsh Baptists. Sarah, about whom little documented information has been located, was probably from a family of Welsh, living in the Colony of Pennsylvania, and a relative of James James, Esq., a leader of the Welsh community. They made the journey from Pennsylvania to South Carolina in 1736–37 by sail with thirty-five families from the second Welsh Tract area of Penn's Colony.

---

[62] Some of the contributions of the Kolb brothers to the Mennonite Church in Pennsylvania and the role of this church in the controversy associated with slavery in the colony are described in section III, D.

PART III

REFLECTIONS ON SEVENTEENTH-CENTURY ANGLO NORTH AMERICA

A. INTRODUCTION AND THE SETTLEMENT OF THE VIRGINIA COLONY

In the sixteenth century, the kingdoms of Spain and Portugal had acquired great wealth from their possessions in the New World, and the English Crown was eager to enter the competition for this bounty of the Age of Exploration. Henry VII commissioned John Cabot (the Anglicized name of Giovanni Caboto, an Italian explorer) to seek a northerly passage to the Far East and to claim lands for England. Journeys by Cabot in 1497 and 1498 and later voyages by his son, Sebastian, in 1504 and 1508 are thought to have been the first European contact with continental North America since the Vikings. Although these explorations are poorly documented in the historical record, their description of "white bears and deer as big as horses" lends credibility to their accounts. A map published in 1500 noted the English claim to the area of North America from Newfoundland to as far south as the Chesapeake Bay. Reports of the abundance of fish in the coastal waters were an impetus for numerous fishing expeditions in the sixteenth and seventeenth centuries.

There was otherwise little significant activity concerning these northerly parts of the continent until Jacques Cartier explored the St. Lawrence River and claimed it for France in 1534–35. Thus began the fur trade with the natives, which would be a major economic boost for European nations but a significant disruption for the indigenous Indian population. In 1608 and 1609, Samuel de Champlain established Quebec City, the first permanent settlement in New France, and Henry Hudson, sailing for Holland, reached what would later be Fort Orange (a.k.a. Albany) on the river that bears his name in New Netherland. The sixteenth century saw little English interest concerning the New World with the disruptions during the reign of Henry VIII. The bringing of the Protestant Reformation and the subsequent influence of the Reformed movements would make Christianity and the different interpretations of the faith a major factor in all aspects of English life, as described in section II. It would also affect their foreign affairs, as the conflicts with

Spain would dominate the later decades of the century. The fateful Roanoke colony would be the only significant attempt at settlement of the English claims.

The end of the Elizabethan and the beginning of the Jacobean eras saw the newly formed personal union of Great Britain with serious economic challenges at home and competition abroad from aggressive European empires.[63] Public debt and unemployment were high in Britain, and taxes were an increasing burden on the population largely due to the Anglo-Spanish War (1585–1604) and the Nine Years' War (Ireland 1593–1603). The number of people moving to the cities, especially London, was increasing. Disease took a toll on the population, which nevertheless continued to increase.

An asset of the nation that had not been utilized was the vast expanse claimed in North America but not exploited or extensively explored. English investors were willing to provide leadership in seeking wealth in the New World that had enriched their foreign competitors; hence, James I of England authorized the London Company to establish colonies in Virginia and in the northern area that would become Massachusetts. Except for the short-lived Popham Colony[64] in the area of present-day Maine, there would be no English settlement in the north until the coming of the Pilgrims in 1620 and later the Puritans, for whom faith and freedom of worship were principle motivations for their settlements. In 1607, Jamestown was founded, the principal motivation being the hope of finding gold, as in the Spanish possessions, and a route to the Pacific Ocean for access to the wealth from Far East trade.

The expedition of one hundred five men and boys set sail from

[63] Queen Elizabeth I of England ruled from November 1558 to her death in March 1603. The Jacobean era dates from March 1603 when James I assumed the throne until his death in March 1625.

[64] The Popham Colony was a project of the Plymouth Company, a part of the London Company and rival of the Virginia Colony. Their second attempt successfully landed 120 men at the mouth of the Kennebec River on August 13, 1607. The colony, financed by Sir John Popham, who died in 1608, disbanded after fourteen months, and those remaining returned to England in a ship they had built.

England in December 1606, led by Captain Christopher Newport and his crew on the *Susan Constant* and two other dangerously small ships. After a tumultuous voyage of four months, they reached Puerto Rico, and on April 26, 1607, landed at Cape Henry at the junction of the Chesapeake Bay and the James River. Reconnaissance up the river encountered formidable-appearing Indians but who did not show signs of hostility. The site selected for their settlement was a peninsula about forty miles upriver from the bay and in keeping with their orders that it be defensible in the event of attack by Spanish or Dutch forces. Its other "advantage" was that no Indian settlements were nearby. Their absence was due to the many problems of the location, including the lack of available fresh water, tillable land, and large game animals for hunting and the presence of marshy areas with an abundance of disease-bearing insects! On May 14, 1607, the colonists began their establishment in the area to be known as Jamestown, and during their first month, they constructed a triangular palisade that could support cannons at the corners. Within the one-acre palisade enclosure was a structure that represented the first church in the Virginia colony.

The Anglican faith was represented on this first voyage by Rev. Robert Hunt, the chaplain of the expedition, whose career as a vicar of the church had been marred by personal problems resulting in his being relieved of his previous English parish assignment. He seemed to dutifully accept his colonial assignment, and on their arrival at Cape Henry, he gave a declaration of purpose that reflected the spiritual expectations of his Anglican superiors for the establishment of the Church of England in the colony and bringing its message to the natives.[65] Introducing the Anglican faith to the New World was a

---

[65] "We do hereby dedicate this Land, and ourselves, to reach the People within these shores with the Gospel of Jesus Christ, and to raise up Godly generations after us, and with these generations take the Kingdom of God to all the earth. May this Covenant of Dedication remain to all generations, as long as this earth remains. May all who see this Cross, remember what we have done here, and may those who come here to inhabit join us in this Covenant and in this most noble work that the Holy Scriptures may be fulfilled."

concern of the English hierarchy, in part to compete with the Roman Church influence brought by France and Spain and to fulfill the admonition to spread the Gospel throughout the world. On June 21, 1607, Rev. Hunt officiated at a service of Holy Communion, the first in the Virginia colony. Attempts to extend Christianity to the natives would show little success with the distrust and hostility generated by subsequent conflicts between the English settlers and the Indians.

Interaction with the natives was essential for the survival of the newcomers who lacked the skills and opportunity to grow or obtain needed food. In the years 1606–12, the southeastern part of the continent experienced the severest drought in seven hundred years.[66] All residents of the area had difficulty with agricultural efforts as freshwater supplies were reduced. The Indians soon lost interest in trading for food, and the colonists, led by Captain John Smith, used military action to obtain supplies required for survival of the colony. The combination of illness, warfare, and other injuries and the consumption of water from the James River that had high salinity due to the tidal flow of the river and the reduction of freshwater inflows, along with near starvation caused an alarming death rate among the colonists.

Within weeks of the completion of the Jamestown palisade, Captain Newport and his crew sailed for England, realizing that future supply trips would be critical for the survival of the colony. Newport returned in January 1608 with two ships in the First Supply voyage, bringing grain and other supplies and one hundred and twenty new colonists who also lacked the needed skills but reflected the expectations of the London Company. The desperation of the colony was confirmed, as only thirty-eight of the original settlers were still alive but in poor condition. All would have likely died had it not been for some relief from the Indians. The other ship in this supply effort was delayed until April, when it arrived with thirty new colonists but also inadequate supplies.

---

[66] Data from examination of growth rings of ancient cypress trees. Historical Archaeology 34:74-81, 2000.

Captain Newport returned to Virginia leading the Second Supply voyage in October 1608. On returning to England, he reported the catastrophic loss of life among the colonists, which included the death of Rev. Robert Hunt. The report from Jamestown indicated that Hunt had been highly regarded as a minister who had served the colony well, trying to mediate between the many factions of the quarreling leadership. The report also included writings sent by Captain John Smith, which would be published in 1608 as *A True Relation of Such Occurrences and Accidents of Noate As Hath Happened in Virginia*. This description of the hardships of the settlers and the ineptitude of the colony's leadership was widely distributed, prompting the London Company to dispatch the substantial Third Supply flotilla and plan an extensive reorganization of the colony. During these months, Smith became both the secular and military leader. He explored extensively and would report that there was no evidence of connection with the western ocean or of precious metals in the Virginia area. He personally led and dispatched other colonial leaders with soldiers to obtain food supplies from the Indians. These aggressive efforts met with limited success, and many colonists were killed in the confrontations. Smith was injured in a gunpowder accident, which would cause his return to England.[67]

In the early summer of 1609, Captain Newport with the Third Supply flotilla set sail for Virginia with nine vessels led by the flagship *Sea Venture*. Aboard was the new interim governor, Sir Thomas Gates, William Strachey, a prominent London writer, and about five hundred colonists. The flagship carried, as the replacement for Rev. Hunt, the Rev. Richard Buck along with his wife and two infant daughters. Also aboard was John Rolfe with his family, but only he would survive a nine-month interruption in Bermuda en route. Rolfe in later years would marry Pocahontas and also contribute greatly to the success of the colony with the cultivation of tobacco as a commercial crop.

The Third Supply fleet encountered a powerful Atlantic storm

---

[67] Baylin, B. pp. 15–62.

separating the lead ship and one other vessel, which were stranded on Bermuda Island and permanently damaged with the loss of most supplies. Other ships of the flotilla reached Jamestown in August and October 1609, with about three hundred colonists but only a reduced food supply resource. The Bermuda experiences of those surviving was later reported by William Strachey and widely publicized in London. This has been credited with inspiring William Shakespeare to write *The Tempest*. Captain John Smith sailed to England for treatment of his injury on a returning ship in October, and that winter would be the worst of the many difficult times for the colony.

It was not until May 1610 that Captain Newport with Gates and the Bermuda survivors reached Virginia, having built two small ships using planks from cedar trees native to Bermuda and salvage of the *Sea Venture*. What Gates and his new colonists found on arrival at Jamestown was appalling. Out of four hundred who had been sent to Virginia over the previous years, only sixty were alive but near death from starvation. Disease and hostilities had taken their toll, but actions against the settlers had ceased, as the Indians concluded that death of the remaining few was inevitable due to starvation. The reports of this "starving time" indicate that the desperate English had even resorted to consuming the flesh of the deceased in an attempt to survive.

Arriving with Gates was the Rev. Richard Buck, who gained the admiration of the colonists by ministering to the survivors with prayerful concern, respectful of their deceased members and encouraging to the living. It was immediately apparent to Gates that with the addition of new colonists to the starving remnant and with the paucity of additional supplies arriving from Bermuda, it would be necessary to return the survivors to England. Within one month, on June 10, 1610, they set sail in two makeshift vessels from the abandoned Jamestown settlement in the direction of the Chesapeake Bay and the Atlantic voyage to England.

The beleaguered colonists, within the first ten miles of their planned journey, were confronted by what many would consider a miraculous circumstance. They were intercepted by the vanguard of the fleet bringing the restructured organization of the Virginia colony that resulted from the information provided by Christopher Newport and John Smith. The fleet brought the future of the Jamestown colony, which would change in many ways. The original idea that the settlement would be a fort as a base for exploration and trading to support the quest for gold or for a passage to Asia was replaced by plans to create a permanent, productive colony. The reorganized London Company sought to recruit responsible working people with families and experiences representing useful skills and occupations. Many of the recruits were far from the company's ideal and represented Englishmen who had never been profitably employed or seemed to prefer vagrancy over labor. Up to one hundred fifty of the new colonists were former soldiers whose main experience was in plundering and savagery in the Irish and Dutch wars. Success of this new approach to the colony would require a strong leader with the authority and ability to control both the military and domestic activity. Such a leader was Thomas West, third Baron De La Warr who had extensive English military experience and the will to require the new colonists to provide the needed labor.

Conflict with the natives had continued to increase in the latter months of 1609, and by the end of 1610, one-third of the settlers had died of illness or had been killed by the Indians often after being tortured. De La Warr soon sought retribution for the colonists killed by the Indian attacks, and the new troops reacted with vengeance directed not only against the warriors but against native women and children, with destruction of their villages and fields.

The arrival of more than five hundred men, women, and children over the next year made the survival of the colony more secure. This large influx of settlers included a number of well-connected and educated adventurers who had a personal interest in the spread of the Christian faith to the Indians. Many also had strong beliefs in piety and personal responsibility, reflecting the growing Calvinist influence in England. One of them was George Thorpe, a relative of Sir Thomas Dale and a former member of Parliament who had made significant financial investments in the colony. Thorpe had an interest in converting the Indians to Christianity, and he studied and wrote about the established culture and religious views of the natives.

Another gentleman was Alexander Whitaker, MA, whose father was the master of St. John's College and Regius Professor of divinity at Cambridge, where Alexander had been a student at Trinity College, developing his strong Reformed influence. He had served as a minister in English parishes and established several churches in the expanding communities along the James River in Virginia, including Henricus, where he tried to establish a school for the Indian population.[68] He has been referred to as the "apostle of Virginia," favoring the Reformed beliefs. He wrote in 1614 that he "wished more ministers who disagreed with the Anglican hierarchy would come to Virginia where they could minister more freely."

De La Warr became ill in early 1611, and on his returning to England, Sir Thomas Dale was appointed deputy governor. Dale was an experienced military leader who, with his typical Puritan vision and strict discipline, which had been extended to the civilian population by Sir Thomas Gates, likely saved the colony. Over the next two years, they inflicted major defeats on the Powhatan, which concluded in early 1613 when Chief Powhatan's daughter, Pocahontas, was taken captive, thus ending the First Anglo-Powhatan War (1609–14). The young woman was instructed in Christianity and the English language by Whitaker at the settlement of Henricus. She developed a romantic interest in John Rolfe, and they were married in April 1614 by Rev. Richard Buck. Rolfe would become a founder of the community of Bermuda Hundred and be an early leader of promising tobacco production.

The Virginia colony and the Colony of Maryland that soon

---

[68] Henricus was the westernmost fortified settlement along the James River and was near the present site of the city of Richmond. It became known for the educational efforts of Rev. Whitaker, who served from 1611 to his accidental death in 1616. In 1618, the colony obtained a royal charter for a University of Henrico and set aside land at Henricus for its support. This effort was abandoned after the Massacre of 1622, hence Harvard College (est. 1636) rightly is known as the first higher education institution in the English colonies.

appeared in the Chesapeake Bay area would eventually have glimmers of financial success, not from a golden mineral but from the golden tobacco leaves whose cultivation would be learned from the Indians and would become a profitable commodity for the English homeland. The colonists had not been successful in growing the variety of Spanish tobacco native to Trinidad, but John Rolfe was able to produce and improve the local Chesapeake variety. By 1616, 1,250 pounds were shipped to England, increasing to sixty thousand pounds by 1620. In 1621, over one hundred thousand pounds, and by 1625, four hundred thousand pounds were shipped. The English economy had indeed found a source of "new-world gold." Financial gain from the fledgling colonies would be earned only through incredible hardships and dangers faced by the early settlers and would depend on a steady supply of laborer immigrants. This profitable production was labor-intensive, and the availability of English workers became far from adequate to compensate for the morbidity and mortality that afflicted the new residents from Europe.

The two decades following the end of the First Anglo-Powhatan War saw continuing difficulties for the colony as large numbers of ill-prepared and often unfit young people were sent from England. Malnourishment and disease took a fearsome toll on all colonists. The London Company had sent more than eight thousand people, of whom only 1,218 were alive for the census of 1625.[69] In the early decades of the colony, the English homeland was wracked by political and religious turmoil, encouraging increasing numbers of colonists as indentured servants who sought alternatives to the poverty and lack of opportunity that confronted them in England to come to Virginia and the newly developing colonies of Massachusetts, Maryland, and New Netherland. As the homeland economy improved, this demand for labor would shift to the importation of African slaves brought by Portuguese, Spanish, and Dutch merchants to the plantations of the Caribbean islands and South America.

In August 1619, the introduction of African slaves to the English

---

[69] Ibid. p. 111.

colony would eventually lead to enhancement of this production but would initiate a plague for the colonies, and later for the United States, for succeeding centuries. The first African slaves in the Virginia colony were brought to Old Point Comfort aboard a Dutch pirate ship, the *White Lion*.[70] About twenty slaves had been captured from the Spanish in the Caribbean as they were being transported between colonial sugarcane plantations. There is no evidence that either the colonists or the Dutch had arranged for this occurrence, but the pirates traded or sold the slaves for supplies that were needed for their ship. The initial Africans in Virginia were considered indentured servants, and some eventually had property of their own and became slave owners. Few Africans were brought to Virginia in the succeeding decades, as the Dutch and Portuguese slave traders found the sugar-producing areas of the Caribbean and Brazil to be more profitable destinations for their tragic human cargo. By 1650, there were about three hundred Africans in Virginia and four thousand white indentured servants. The status of the Africans began to change in the 1650s, and by 1660, the Virginia Assembly gave legal status to the practice of lifetime enslavement of Negroes, whose status was determined by the race of one's mother.[71] During and after the English Civil Wars, the number of indentured servants decreased, and by the mideighteenth century, the number of slaves in the Chesapeake area was 145,000. During the seventeenth and eighteenth centuries, the southern colonies prospered due to the profitable agricultural economy fueled by tobacco in the Middle Atlantic colonies. The naval stores industry[72] related to the vast forests

---

[70] Brown, DeNeen L. Slavery's bitter roots: In 1619, "20 And odd Negroes" arrived in Virginia. The *Washington Post*, August 24, 2018. This was originally described by John Rolfe, and later sources relate the Africans to have been brought from Angola in a Portuguese slave ship and taken by English pirates in two ships, the *White Lion* and the *Treasurer*, the latter arriving at Point Comfort several weeks later. The pirates exchanged the slaves for food and supplies.

[71] Foner, Philip. History of Black America: From Africa to the Emergence of the Cotton Kingdom. Oxford University Press, 1980.

[72] Naval stores refers to the timber for ships and pine tar, pitch, and kerosene, which were produced from the long-leaf pine trees and were essential for the

of long-leaf pine would be a source of wealth in the Carolinas in the eighteenth century as well as rice production in South Carolina. These agricultural activities required a large labor resource, and the numbers of slaves expanded significantly. There can be no question that the economic success of the English colonies was based on these agricultural activities, and the financial and manufacturing activities of the northeast were largely due to the importance of ship building, the export of agricultural products to Europe, and the import of European goods to the colonies. It is also certain that the labor of the enslaved Africans was critical to the success of each of the English colonies.

After 1614, with the end of the First Anglo-Powhatan War, the colony entered a period of lessened hostility from the Indians, and there was a large increase in the number of people sent from England, most of whom were to work as indentured servants. Many were young and in poor health. Their mortality rate was high, but so was the need for workers on the increasing number of plantations with their expanding tobacco production.

The longtime chief of the dominant Powhatan tribe died in 1618 and was replaced by his brother, Opechancanough, who began planning for a counterattack on the expanding English settlements. These new plantations encroached on Indian lands in erratic patterns, resulting in continuous contact between the two populations. This interval was relatively calm, and the English were lulled into complacency. Opechancanough used the time to rally a coalition of ten tribes and plan a massive assault that he expected to permanently limit the English to a narrowly confined coastal area.

On March 22, 1622, he carried out his plan, and Jamestown was spared only due to a last-minute warning by some "semi-Christianized Indians." The attack was otherwise a complete surprise, and about four hundred colonists were killed (a third of the population). The severity of this massacre is well described by Baylin, who concluded that "the rage against the Indians wiped out

---

English navy and merchant marine.

all thoughts of benevolence and any immediate prospect that the gospel mission would soon be renewed."[73] The Powhatans expected the English to either abandon their settlements or accept being subject to the authority of their tribe. On the contrary, the English considered this attack an unprovoked state of war and that the natives had forfeited any rights they may have claimed to the ownership of the land. Those colonists who had been most helpful to the Indians were singled out and murdered, including George Thorpe, who had attempted to personally befriend Opechancanough. This attack reinforced the belief of English survivors in the savagery and deceitfulness of their enemy. Within two months, an intermittent war of revenge began (the Second Anglo-Powhatan War), lasting until 1632 and resulting in the decimation of the native population.

This Powhatan assault would profoundly affect the colony, and the destruction of the Henricus settlement eliminated the effort to create a center for educating both the Indian and English populations. The Virginia Company had obtained a royal charter in 1618 for a university, and the First General Assembly had designated land for its support. After the massacre, these efforts vanished and would not be revived until 1693 when the College of William and Mary was established at Williamsburg. A marker on that college's first building relates its origin to the Henricus effort.

In 1624, Virginia became a royal colony, as its original charter was voided, reflecting the need for a more effective military presence and the prospect of positive economic development, which the Crown sought to more closely control. As a royal colony, the Anglican Church was the only sanctioned worship establishment and was supported by local tax revenue. As a strong Reformed influence had been established in Virginia a decade before the arrival of the *Mayflower* at Plymouth, the Anglican authority was not well received by many of the colonists. The church in Virginia suffered from the need for any local person seeking a pulpit in the colony to travel to England for ordination, as there was no bishop appointed in the

---

[73] Baylin, B. pages 100–107.

colony until 1784.[74] Worship was a more private or local activity in Virginia as the official church, attendance being required by the secular authorities never made as much of a spiritual impact as churches in other colonies. As described in another section of this story, the influences of the Great Awakening in the first half of the eighteenth century would have a profound effect on worship in Virginia.

The colonies that followed Virginia in the settlement of North America all faced the challenges of a potentially hostile native population and internal conflicts that would test their survival and growth. The colonists who were seeking opportunity for the future of their families and the freedom to worship and live according to their values brought with them very different backgrounds and experiences and dealt with unique circumstances in their colonies. Their descendants eventually created a union that would be unlike any other in history.

B. THE NEW ENGLAND COLONIES

Plymouth, Massachusetts Bay, the Connecticut Colonies, and Rhode Island–Providence Plantation

Captain John Smith, who deserves credit for the survival of the Jamestown colony during its first two years, also explored the Chesapeake Bay area before a severe injury caused him to return to England in 1609. In 1614, he led an expedition to explore and map the coast of Maine and Massachusetts Bay, and his document would be the first to use the term New England. He gave names to places that were of later prominence, including Plymouth, Cape Ann, and the Charles River. During this trip, several events occurred that deserve mention, including his leaving a lieutenant, Thomas Hunt, and crew, presumably to establish a trading presence with the natives. Hunt

---

[74] Kidd, Thomas S.page 22.

instead kidnapped a number of the local Patuxet tribe and sailed away to sell them as slaves in Spain. They, or transient fishermen, likely exposed the natives to an epidemic, which in 1616–17 devastated the population of the area. This is thought to have been small pox, measles, or leptospirosis, and it caused the death of up to 90 percent of the natives in the Massachusetts Bay area. In all of New England, the native population was reduced to perhaps 15–18,000.[75]

One of Thomas Hunt's captives, known as Squanto (Tisquantum), would play a part in the survival of the Plymouth Colony in 1620–21.[76] The Patuxet slaves were rescued by friars on their arrival in Malaga, Spain, and Squanto eventually made his way to London and back to his American homeland in 1619 on a voyage with John Smith. Squanto had learned to speak English, and it was he who greeted the Pilgrims on their arrival. He taught them how to grow the native maize (Indian corn), which would help them avoid starvation. He also taught them how to obtain the beaver pelts, which would be essential to the economic viability of the colony. The native population was not otherwise welcoming to the English, and hostile relations were the norm. The reduction in the Indian population due to the previous pestilence may have been a factor in the ability of the Pilgrims to establish their tenuous habitation in the area. They were the first of many contingents from England and elsewhere in Europe to seek homes in the New World for reasons of religion and their desire to worship without secular antagonism.

In 1623, a fishing village, sponsored by the Dorchester Company, was created at Cape Ann, but it did not prosper. In 1625, the few remaining Puritan settlers established a community under the leadership of Roger Conant close to the nearby Indian village of Naumkeag. The company was reorganized as the New England Company for a Plantation in Massachusetts Bay, and they soon were joined by John Endicott and one hundred new settlers. The town

---

[75] Vaughan, A.T. –

[76] The story of the Pilgrims and Plymouth Colony is too extensive to be repeated here and is beautifully described in Bernard Baylin's and other comprehensive publications.

was renamed Salem in 1629, and three hundred Puritans arrived in a convoy led by Rev. Francis Higginson. He had served for two decades as a highly regarded minister at a parish in Leicester, England, but his becoming a part of the Puritan movement had ended his clerical career. The company received a royal charter in 1629, and his expedition was the first to the Massachusetts Bay Colony. It seems likely that King Charles I, who vigorously opposed the Puritan faith, was unaware that his support of the colony would be used to further that cause. This was the first of the great Puritan migration, which would bring from England between 1630 and 1634 thousands who sought to escape persecution for their religious beliefs and worship. Higginson's flotilla was much better equipped than previous ventures, and substantial provisions and livestock were in their six-ship convoy. The landing in June 1629 gave them time to prepare for the coming hardships of the New England winter.

Prior to his sailing, Rev. Higginson had developed increasingly Separatist beliefs, similar to those of the earlier Pilgrims of Plymouth Colony. Before his death in 1630, he and Rev. Samuel Skelton organized the First Church of Salem, the original Puritan church in the Massachusetts Bay Colony. By 1630, the congregation had become an independent Congregational church, and in 1631, they welcomed Roger Williams as the assistant teacher minister. Roger Williams was surely one of the most interesting and controversial leaders in the colonization of New England. His life and contributions to the religious and political history of British North America and the subsequent generations have been extensively reviewed and are worthy of consideration.[77] Williams possessed exceptional intellect and charisma, which made him a highly respected and effective negotiator but would create antagonism with the colonial hierarchy.

Roger Williams was not the only thorn in the side of the Puritan establishment that in the 1630s was attempting to create a haven in which their adherents could live and worship free of the annoyance

---

[77] See section IV, I, appendix, Additional Information about Colonial Individuals, Roger Williams.

of the Anglican Church and the authority of its royal support. Challenges to the new colony were often of an internal nature, many but not all being due to different interpretations of their Puritan faith. Others were likely motivated by political or economic reasons. Many of the leading personalities of the colony were well-educated men whose abilities had advanced them in English society, but the circumstances of their birth or their Puritan faith would be limiting factors. Certainly religious issues were a principal motivation for the various Puritan ministers and their congregations to come to New England (see section IV, K, "The Praying Indians").

One of the notable ministers with a large following was Rev. John Cotton, who had become thoroughly steeped in the Puritan beliefs during his years at Cambridge, where he was known as an outstanding scholar and a talented preacher. In 1612, he became minister at Saint Botolph's Church in the Lincolnshire town of Boston, which would become a center for Puritan unrest and a prominent source of immigrants to Massachusetts Bay. His tenure at St. Botolph's is described in detail by the classic study of Emery John Battis,[78] which also relates the evolution of the spiritual life of Anne Hutchinson, who would become the sharpest thorn afflicting John Winthrop and the Massachusetts Bay leadership (see appendix section IV, J, "Anne Hutchinson").

In 1634, she came with her large extended family and her spiritual zeal aboard the ship *Griffin*. Her religious beliefs, as innocent as they may seem to modern readers, when accompanied by her keen intellect, insight, and charisma, and with her fearless and independent nature, would be disruptive to the Zion that Winthrop and his leadership were trying to develop. Anne and her followers produced the Antinomian Controversy, which would result, within three to four years of their arrival, in the banishment of Anne and her family and significant numbers of the Massachusetts Bay Colony and their congregational leaders. This small diaspora would contribute to the population of Rhode Island and New Hampshire and add

---

[78] Battis, John Emery. University of North Carolina Press, 1962.

to those that had moved to the Connecticut River Valley with Rev. Thomas Hooker. He, with many from his congregation in Newetown (Cambridge), had relocated to the western part of the colony due to the need for more land and timber and political differences with Winthrop. Among those moving to the Connecticut River Valley and what would later become a separate colony was Thomas Stoughton and his large extended family. He was an older brother of Judith Stoughton Denman. Others moved to Long Island, the eastern half of which was under the jurisdiction of Connecticut and the western half a part of the Dutch Colony of New Netherland, both with less strict religious laws and customs than Massachusetts Bay. John Denman II and a number of his extended family would make such a move by the 1650s.

Conflict with the Indian population had been a reality since the earliest settlements in New England and reached a high point in 1634 with the Pequot War and in New Netherland nine years later (Kieft's War) when Hutchinson family members would be killed. Armed defense for protection from random attacks on their homes and livestock and the importance of hunting the native animals as a source of food for their families made the response by Winthrop and the General Court following the unrest of the Antinomian Controversy particularly onerous for the men of the colony. All powder and ammunition belonging to the colony was surreptitiously removed from Boston to the Newtown and Charleston armories. The next day, agents of the court appeared at the homes of about seventy-five men of Boston and other towns who had signed a petition favoring the convicted dissidents. The court demanded the delivery of "all such guns, pistols, swords, powder, shot, & match ... in their custody, upon paine of ten pounds for every default to bee made thereof."[79] This experience perhaps confirmed in the colonial mind the fears that would lead to the Second Amendment to the United States Constitution. The right to keep and bear arms had been an implied part of the English common law as a logical extension of the

---

[79] Ibid., p. 211,

natural or God-given right of self-defense. It was later delineated in the English Bill of Rights of 1689 in response to the threats of James II to disarm nonconformist Protestants and Roman Catholics.[80] The Second Amendment to the United States Constitution may have had roots in this early colonial event and the English law adopted by Parliament and signed by William III and Mary II, the anointed coregents following the replacement of James II by the Glorious Revolution. The right to bear arms but with restrictions on the extent of this availability have a long precedent in our culture as an early attempt by itinerant fishermen and visitors to trade firearms for beaver pelts and was met with vigorous opposition by the Plymouth Pilgrims led by Miles Standish. This established a precedent for prohibition of the sale of firearms to hostile groups suspected of not having the welfare of the colonial population as a priority. These issues that continue to arise in the twenty-first century have a long precedent in our culture.

The nature and causes of the conflicts between the English and the Indians have been controversial issues for historians, almost since the seventeenth century. The descriptions of these interactions as written by the early Puritans, as expected, presented a view favorable to their intentions and methods. By the nineteenth century, the popular opinion had shifted not only in historical writings but in the general literature. An example of this is found in the writing of Herman Melville, whose classic novel *Moby Dick* uses the name *Pequod* for the ill-fated ship of Captain Ahab, whose intransigence destined it for annihilation. The name is a clear reference to the Pequot tribe that was similarly obliterated as a result of war between 1634 and 1638. This Pequot War was interpreted two hundred years later as being a racial conflict largely caused by the prejudice and intolerance of the Puritans. This view was dominant until well into the twentieth century and persists in some circles to the present. Alden T. Vaughan, professor emeritus at Columbia University,[81]

---

[80] Malcolm, J.L. Harvard University Press, pp. 94–112.
[81] Vaughan, Alden T. – Third Edition, University of Oklahoma Press, 1995.

presents "a more balanced view of this complex and sensitive area of American history in his book which is of indispensable value to any student of colonial New England."[82] He claims that it was a conflict between the European settlers with their Indian allies and the Pequot tribe, which was hostile to both native tribes and the English.

We can better evaluate the interactions between the early English settlers and the native population by considering the changing circumstances of the Indians in that time. The population of natives in eastern North America in the late sixteenth century can only be estimated, but certainly the vast area was sparsely settled. There were two major eastern linguistic groups, the Algonquian and the Iroquoian, each with many tribes and clans that spoke variations and dialects of the two languages.[83]

The former were a large population that occupied the eastern seaboard, from New Brunswick and Maine to the Massachusetts Bay area, through southern New England east of the Hudson River, Long Island, New Jersey, Delaware, eastern Pennsylvania and south to Virginia. Some of the tribal names included the Abenaki (Maine), Wampanoag, Massachusett, Pequot and Narragansett (southern New England), the Lenape or Delaware (western Long Island, New Jersey, and eastern Pennsylvania), and the Powhatan (Chesapeake Bay area and Virginia). Other Algonquian peoples, such as Potawatomi, Ojibwe, and Ottawa, lived in what is now the Midwest and Canada.

The Iroquois League was a confederacy of six nations that included the Mohawk, Onondaga, Oneida, Cayuga, Seneca, and later the Tuscarora. Other tribes of this linguistic group who were enemies of the Iroquois included the Huron, Erie, and Susquehannock. The Cherokee were of the same linguistic group but separated in their southeastern location.

The origin of the league and its migrations is uncertain, but archeological evidence suggests that by the fifteenth century, they were in what is now New York and western Pennsylvania. The

---

[82] New York Times Book Review, quoted by University of Oklahoma Press, publisher, 1995.

[83] Bailyn, B. p.17.

native legends associate their confederation to the efforts of Hiawatha and others occurring at the time of a solar eclipse (August 31, 1143). The Iroquois began expanding their territory before the coming of the English at the expense of Algonquian neighbors, as the successful growing of corn, beans, and squash had increased their population's ability to wage war.

Combat between tribes in the sparsely inhabited eastern North America had, in the past, been largely symbolic or was waged to replace numbers lost to disease or in battles. During the latter decades of the sixteenth century, the intensity of these wars increased due to the incentives of trade with European fishing expeditions and explorers that offered beads and metallic objects in exchange for beaver pelts. These objects and useful items, such as utensils, axes, and containers, were traded for the hides of beavers that were in abundance in the streams and forests throughout the region and not considered of value by the Indians. Competition for the trade routes to the Atlantic coast and the control of the habitats of the animals resulted in a decades-long conflict between tribes known as the Beaver Wars.

During the seventeenth century, permanent European settlements greatly expanded this trade, and the Iroquois and aggressive Algonquian increased their intertribal hostilities. Relations between the early English settlers and Indians in the Massachusetts Bay area were relatively peaceful for several reasons. One was the presence of Squanto and his dealings with the Wapanoag tribe, who greeted the Pilgrims at Plymouth in 1620. Another was the reduced numbers of the local tribes due to the pestilence of 1616–1617, which had not affected their western neighbor and historic enemy, the Narragansett. The effectiveness of the European weapons and the vigorous reprisals with which the Pilgrims, led by Captain Miles Standish, met even minor threats established a sense of security for the English, who were seen as allies by the Wapanoags in conflicts with the larger Narragansett and Pequot tribes. The Pilgrims and, after 1630, the Puritans dealt with the natives with fairness and generosity, largely due to their serious desire to bring the Christian faith to the natives through their charitable actions.[84]

The conflict among the native tribes was accentuated by the Pequots, the largest tribe in southern New England, who had expanded their territory into the central and southern valley of the Connecticut River. This threatened the Narragansetts and other smaller tribes that were longtime residents of the area. These natives encouraged Pilgrim and Puritan colonists to move into the area as a counter to this Pequot hegemony. By 1634, English settlers moved from several Puritan towns in the Massachusetts Bay area to new settlements of Windsor (from Dorchester), Hartford (from Newtowne), and Wethersfield (from Watertown). The English population grew with the relocation of Thomas Hooker and his congregation from Newtown to Hartford and the founding of Providence on Narragansett Bay by Roger Williams in 1636.

Conflict with the Pequot began in 1634 with the murder of an Englishman of dubious reputation, John Stone, and seven of his crew. An attempt to deal peacefully with the Pequot ended with the murder of John Oldham in the summer of 1636 while he was on a trading trip to Block Island. The Massachusetts Bay leadership sent John Endicott and ninety volunteers on a mission for "merciless revenge" in late August. They destroyed Indian property, inflicting only a few casualties on the natives at Block Island and at a coastal Pequot village. The Pequot retaliated during the fall and winter, killing some of the English defenders in the Connecticut Valley area. There was uncertainty as to the enemy being either from the Pequot or the Narragansett tribes. Roger Williams intervened, identifying the Pequot as the assailants and securing an agreement with the Narragansett for support in the conflict.

A major turn in the intensity of the war occurred in April 1637 when two hundred Pequot warriors attacked colonists at Wethersfield,

---

[84] The desire to extend the Christian faith to the native Indians was an important motivation for the Pilgrim and Puritan settlers. These evangelical efforts met some success and had effects on the tribal governance and activities, which are discussed in appendix section V, K, the Praying Indians of New England.

killing nine, including a woman and a child, and capturing two women. A total of thirty English had died in the conflicts, and the Massachusetts Bay Court ordered the enlistment of one hundred sixty men to pursue the war along with a fully alerted Connecticut population.

The war with the Pequot Indian tribe is a controversial episode in New England colonial history. Professor Alden Vaughan emphasizes that this was not an "Indian war" and that there was no suggestion of racial conflict or a clash of disparate cultures.[85] He argues that it was a war against the militant Pequots, and the English were supported by most of the other Indian tribes of the area. What fuels the arguments of those opposed to Alden's view was the intensity of the atrocity in May 1637 when Massachusetts troops led by Captain John Underhill, Connecticut troops led by Captain John Mason, and a similar number of Narragansett and Mohegan allies surrounded the Pequots at an earth-and-timber fort in Mystic, Connecticut, in what is known as the Mystic Massacre. The brush huts and timber walls were set afire, and escaping Indians were killed. The total of Pequot dead was up to six or seven hundred, and most of the survivors fled to the mercy of their longtime enemies, the Mohawks, or were hunted down by Mohegan tribesmen, led by the sachem, Uncas, and by a smaller number of the Narragansett tribe and their sachem, Miantonomo.

More than one hundred surviving Pequot warriors were attacked by fresh troops from Massachusetts, led by Captain Israel Stoughton in what is known as the Fairfield Swamp Fight. Most of the warriors were killed, and others were made prisoner and given as slaves to tribes aiding the English. Some surviving male Pequots were captured and sold as slaves in the West Indies. After the Pequot sachem, Sassacus, and forty survivors were killed by the Mohawks, the Pequot tribe ceased to exist. Israel Stoughton, the brother of Judith Stoughton Denman Smead and uncle of John Denman II, had a role in the Puritans victory, but by modern standards, it may have not been considered one of honor. He had, however, carried out his

---

[85] Vaughan, Alden T. – Chapter V. pp 122–154.

directive to annihilate the enemy, and there is no suggestion that his military activities were criticized by his peers.

The tendency to evaluate seventeenth-century history through the expectations and mores of later generations has been an ongoing challenge for those interested in that era. Those having such interests do well to maintain their focus on understanding the facts of the past situations and the purposes and expectations of those individuals and groups involved at that time. The actual participants in that era would have viewed their world and its events through eyes with a different focus than that which our perspectives can bring to the task. Our challenge is to visualize and interpret their perspectives, free of the distortions of the succeeding centuries. A possible interpretation of the causes of the Pequot War and Anglo-Powatan War in Virginia have at various times been attributed to the warlike nature and aggression of those tribes with their desire to extend hegemony over smaller, more peaceful tribes that seemed more accepting of their new English neighbors. A different view, popular in the twentieth century, has focused on the presumed desire of the Puritans in New England or the European entrepreneurs in Virginia to control land that had previously been the domain of the natives and their suspected disrespect for the natives' race and culture. While the latter interpretation may be appropriate for the Virginia experience, Alden T. Vaughan argues effectively against this view of the New England scene, and his meticulous analysis of that era may offer an alternative to those polarized viewpoints.[86] The descriptions of Vaughan and Bernard Bailyn of the culture of the natives prior to their exposure to the English newcomers may offer other speculation about the causes of these events.

A seldom mentioned small pox epidemic of 1633–1634 caused the death of four thousand of the eight thousand Pequot men, women, and children living at that time. This may have threatened the authority of the shamans (also known as the powwows or medicine men) and the sachem (chief) Sassacus. The shamans were the most respected

---

[86] Vaughan, A T. –

and feared members of the tribal hierarchy and had significant medical, political, and religious roles. The Indians were convinced that the powwows had powers of life and death, a belief that was shared by some of the Puritans who insisted that the shamans were witches and in league with Satan. The inability of tribal authorities to influence the devastation of the epidemic and the prospect of losing the authority and social control that had historically been theirs could have led them to identify a more susceptible enemy, namely the English, thereby contributing to their aggression.

One of the ultimate effects of the Pequot War was the establishment of the English as the dominant military force in New England, and lessons learned from the conflict included the value of superior European weapons and the benefit of intercolonial military cooperation. The Indian tribes were willing to make the Puritans the arbiters of intertribal disputes, especially between the Mohegan and Narragansett tribes and in other tribal conflicts that continued to threaten the peace in the region.

The forty-year interval following the Pequot War saw significant changes in the attitudes and numbers of both the Europeans and Indians and the relations between the two populations. The elimination of the hostile Pequots facilitated an expansion of the growing numbers of colonials into Connecticut, Rhode Island, and the interior of the Massachusetts Bay Colony. The number of immigrants coming from England continued to increase until the beginning of the English Civil Wars in 1642.

The internal disruptions to colonial harmony were sufficient to fully occupy the efforts of the leadership and the settlers. The chastisement of participants in the Antinomian Controversy had not ended the spiritual and social unrest besetting Puritan life in Massachusetts. It was not a small group of delusional individuals that had been affected; Battis[87] and Baylin concluded that there were 187 men and an equal number of women sympathetic to Anne Hutchinson and her beliefs (see appendix IV, J, "Anne Hutchinson

---

[87] Battis, E.J., pp. 293–344.

and the Antinomian Controversy"). Nearly all were church members, and most were freemen, merchants, or craftsmen and were well established, respectable men and women.[88] The unstable orthodoxy of their Puritan faith made it susceptible to doctrinal variations, such as those of the Baptists, Familists, and Quakers. The aggressive evangelism of the latter would have an especially disruptive influence on domestic tranquility.

If these ecclesiastical disruptions were not enough, there were additional challenges with the deteriorating economic conditions of the colony and political changes in the mother country. The shortage of access to credit and a surplus of agricultural products created financial hardships. It was hoped that an increase in manufactured products and trade, especially with colonies in the Caribbean area, would be beneficial and offset the decreasing profitability of the fur trade.

Economic development was challenged by the Puritan faith, which discouraged entrepreneurial activities and the personal accumulation of wealth. An additional threat to the colony's economic recovery was the return of many able individuals to England with the beginning of the Cromwell revolution and civil wars in 1642. Among those returning was Israel Stoughton, who would lead the Artillery Company of Boston (a borough of Lincolnshire). That port town had long been influenced by trade with Holland and was a center for Calvinist teachings and Puritan influence. Israel would not live to return to the Massachusetts colony, and many others of the "most broad-minded, innovative and imaginative minds of the younger generation" would not return to North America.[89]

Restrictive policies of the colony would be challenged by the Remonstrance of May 1646, signed by men with religious and mercantile concerns about the Puritan leadership. Among the signers was David Yale, husband of Ursula Knight (stepsister of Israel Stoughton) and mother of Elihu Yale. The General Court's response was uncompromising, and it would be another generation before a

---

[88] Bailyn, Bernard. pp. 452–465.
[89] Ibid. p. 472.

freer enterprise system could emerge from the restrictive Calvinist culture. Although Puritan colonists were beset by economic and societal problems in the decade following the Pequot War, the seeds for recovery and prosperity were being planted. Two circumstances contributed greatly to this development: first, the rapid growth of the English population due to their remarkable fertility and the high survival rate of the offspring of the initial immigrants; and, secondly, the turmoil in the English homeland that diminished the ability of the colonies to depend on external support for investment capital and military protection.

The New England recovery was largely fueled by the growth of trade between these colonies, their Caribbean counterparts, and the English homeland. New England provided, from its fertile fishing grounds and land, quantities of fish, beef, pork, grain, and timber products to Bermuda, Barbados, and other English island colonies. These products were exchanged for cotton, sugar, and tobacco, which were then transported to England in exchange for manufactured goods. This mercantile activity would expand to shipbuilding and whaling and provide wealth for the area in subsequent centuries. The interference with colonial mercantile success caused by the English Parliament's Navigation Acts of the 1660s would cause resentment, as they prohibited some of the trading practices and imposed duties and taxes without colonial consultation. This perhaps was a premonition of the hostilities that were a century in the future.

The growing population and the need for farmland and accessible sources of timber encouraged expansion to inland areas of Massachusetts, Connecticut, and the eastern portion of Long Island, which was a part of the Connecticut colony. The second generation of our Stoughton/Denman/Scudder extended family were among those who sought these new homes. It seems likely that the need for land was a significant factor in those decisions. The social and religious issues may have been involved; we know that they were involved in the Reformed churches as they moved to new locations.

In the half century following the arrival of the Pilgrims, the New England demographics changed greatly, and by the 1670s, those of

European heritage represented three-fourths of the seventy-eight thousand inhabitants. The number of Indians was about eighteen thousand—essentially unchanged from their population in 1620.[90] Losses from warfare and epidemic illnesses as well as westward migration account for the relative reduction in their numbers. There was no "frontier" separating the Indians and English, and interactions between the two populations were extensive and generally peaceful. Various tribes pledged loyalty to the English authority within which they lived; the Wampanoags to Plymouth Colony, the Narragansetts to Rhode Island, and the Mohegan to the Connecticut colonial jurisdictions. Intertribal interactions were often hostile, as they competed for trading privileges with the English, and tribal leaders were willing to accept the judicial authority and military protection of the colonies. It is likely that there was not a complete understanding of this authority, and incidents with the Indians were frequent but relatively mild. The missionary efforts of the Pilgrims, Puritans, and Roger Williams had produced surprising results, and many of these so-called praying Indians lived in towns designed by the English and had adopted some aspects of that culture (see appendix IV, K, "The Praying Indians").

A younger generation had assumed the colony's reins, and policies favoring entrepreneurship and social openness were beginning to prevail. Due to their preoccupation with religious, social, and economic issues, the colonists had little time for concern about the possibility of significant conflict with the Indians. Four decades of relative peace produced a sense of complacency that left the English unprepared for the devastating conflict that would surprise them in June 1675.

This war, known as King Philip's War (perhaps better called Metacomet's War), is regarded as a major calamity in seventeenth-century Puritan New England history. Casualties were very high but of greater significance for the smaller Indian population (40 percent) than for the English (1–5 percent). More than half of the regions

---

[90] Drake, J.D. p.16.

towns were attacked, twelve were destroyed, and relations between the English and native populations were forever changed.

Metacomet (or King Philip) was a son of Massasoit, the longtime chief of the Wampanoags, who were closely associated with the Plymouth Colony. Wamsutta and Metacomet, the sons of Massasoit, were called Alexander and Philip after the leaders of the ancient Macedonian empire. At the death of Massasoit, Alexander became chief but died under suspicious circumstances in 1662 after being arrested by the Plymouth colonists. This supported Metacomet/Philip's distrust of the English, and on becoming chief of the Wampanoag Confederacy, he began encouraging the hostility of other tribes toward the colonists. He struggled to maintain his authority with his tribe in the face of increasing military and economic reliance on the Plymouth Colony and subservience to their judicial system. He had been forced to surrender guns to the English in a new peace agreement.

An event that precipitated overt Indian hostilities resulted from information gained by the English that Metacomet was planning attacks on colonial settlements. Shortly thereafter, the informant, John Sassamon, was found dead and presumed murdered by the Wampanoags. Sassamon was a "praying Indian" who had accepted Christianity, attended Harvard College, and served as a translator for Metacomet.[91] The Plymouth Colony convicted and executed three Wampanoags in 1675 for Sassamon's murder, and shortly thereafter, in June 1675, some of the tribe attacked the isolated settlement of Swansea, killing nine colonists and destroying the town. Within the week, on June 27, a full lunar eclipse was thought by the Indians to be an omen favorable for warfare, and King Philip's War began. In the next two months, more than nine towns were attacked, including the Massachusetts Bay Colony town of Brookfield. By September 1675, the New England Confederation declared war, and the conflict soon involved all New England colonies and many of the native tribes.[92]

---

[91] For more about John Sassamon and the praying Indians, see Part V, L, appendix, "The Praying Indians of New England."

[92] Ibid. pp. 60–74.

In his assessment of the causes of King Philip's War, James Drake concludes that if "the Sassamon trial had prompted the destruction of the political world that the Indians believed they had created, the eclipse revealed to them that the means by which they should attempt to create a new one—even if they did not have a clear vision of it—it would be violent."

A notable event was the ambush of an expedition of Massachusetts Bay militia and teamsters who were bringing the fall harvest from the Connecticut River Valley. Known as the Battle of Bloody Creek, this resulted in the death of more than seventy militia men and a number of teamsters, including the eldest son of the stepbrother of John Denman II. By December 1675, the conflict had spread to the larger Narragansett tribe when the colonial militia with Mohegan allies attacked an Indian fort, killing about three hundred and destroying the fort and crops in the Great Swamp Fight. This made certain that the coming year would experience increasing violence. This attack on the Narragansetts assured their support of the Wampanoags, but Metacomet's attempt to enlist the Iroquoian Mohawk tribe in his war with the English was a serious failure. The positive relations between the Mohawks and the English governor of New York, Edmund Andros, may have persuaded them to not support their longtime enemies, the Algonquians.

In February 1676, Metacomet led more than four hundred of his allies in a raid on the remote settlement of Lancaster in the Massachusetts Bay Colony. At least fifty of the English were killed and twenty-two taken captive. One of the captives, Mary Rolandson, the wife of the town's minister, would write her memoirs several years after her ransomed release. Her descriptions would significantly influence subsequent English opinion and reflected the desperation of the colonists at that time. In early 1676, more than twenty raids would ravish towns as near as ten miles from Boston. The spring of the year saw victories of Metacomet's tribal coalition in the Plymouth Plantation and in Rhode Island, where the capital of Providence was destroyed and colonists fled to the island towns of Newport and Portsmouth.

The success of the smaller numbers of Indians in the more than twenty widely dispersed assaults reflected their effective strategies, namely their mobility in attacking without prior detection by the colonists and their ability to escape across rivers before being counterattacked. Their considerable skill with the newer flintlock muskets was also a factor. The Indians' effective use of these more accurate weapons had been gained from hunting game for their diet. The military tactics of the English were based on mass volleys from the less precise matchlock muskets, rather than accurate aiming at individual targets as in these surprise attacks.[93]

The momentum of the war began to change in early spring 1676 when a force of Connecticut colonists and a larger number of Mohegan and Niantic allies surrounded a group of Narragansetts who had attacked Sudbury, Massachusetts. Most of the Narragansetts were killed and their leader taken captive. By early April, the leader, Canonchet, was executed, and the intensity of the colonists efforts would continue to increase in the coming months. In May, a troop of one hundred fifty minimally trained colonists, led by Captain William Turner, surprised an encampment of Indians in the Connecticut River Valley. Turner was an experienced military leader but had been imprisoned eight years earlier and denied a military commission for his Baptist views. With the conflict spreading, the Massachusetts leadership could no longer afford religious intolerance, and he was given command. His troops had little interest in the cultural and religious restraints of the Puritans, took no prisoners, and more than one hundred Indians, including women and children, were killed. The withdrawing colonials were ambushed, and one-fourth of the troops, including Captain Turner, killed. The site on the river, then named Peskeopscut, was subsequently known as Turner's Falls.[94]

There was no evidence that the colonists had any ethical objections with the treatment of the Indians by the English troops. Throughout the early summer, colonists and their Mohegan allies continued to

---

[93] Ibid. pp. 125–127.
[94] Ibid. pp. 132-3.

rout groups of the Algonquian opposition, with captured fighters being executed or sold into slavery in Bermuda. Although modern military ethics would view the behavior of the English colonists with disapproval, it was well within the standards of seventeenth-century European warfare. The selling of captives into slavery was justified by the Puritans as a more humane treatment than execution and served to provide revenue for the public coffers, depleted by the cost of the war. It has been suggested that this would not have occurred if banishment of the captured Indians had been an option, as had been done with the perceived societal threats of Roger Williams and Anne Hutchinson.[95]

The colonial victories at Sudbury and Turner's Falls began a series of Puritan successes using changes in their military tactics, which led to the end of the war in southern New England by late August 1676. Instead of a defensive war, attempting to protect towns from unanticipated attacks, the colonists adopted the tactics of their enemies. By fighting alongside their praying Indian allies with what we would describe as guerrilla warfare, the English inflicted extensive damage on the tribal forces. Major John Talcott led the defeat of Narragansetts in Rhode Island, and Captain Benjamin Church the defeat of the Wampanoags at Mount Hope. With the death of Metacomet in mid-August, the war began to draw to a close. By the end of the month, Annawon, the war chief of the Pocassets, a tribe in the Wampanoag Confederacy, was captured and executed. Tuspaquin, a legendary ally of Metacomet, was also executed, and King Philip's War was over in the southern New England theater. The Iroquoian Mohawks had also joined battle against their historic Algonquian enemies, which encouraged an increasing number to seek peace and protection by surrendering to the Puritans.

The combat tactics learned from the Indians, with the leadership of Captain Church, were subsequently used successfully in the war that continued in the northern part of New England for two more years. Church played a prominent role in the conflicts with the

---

[95] Ibid. pp. 136–9.

Algonquians, which continued for decades, especially with the Abenaki tribesmen, encouraged by the French, who claimed lands to the southern boundary of Maine. Captain Church has been revered by subsequent generations as the father of the US Army Rangers. Conflicts would continue between the colonists and the Abenaki Confederacy, supported by the French, until the end of the Seven Years' War in 1763.[96] The results of combat in the French and Indian War further demonstrated the deficiency of European military tactics when engaging Indian fighters, lessons that were learned by the colonists to their benefit when later facing British troops in the American Revolution.

One of the lessons learned from the colonial experiences and confirmed repeatedly over the succeeding centuries is that military vigilance is required for the protection of societies for which complacency is a continuous threat. Complacency led to devastating attacks on the colonies of Virginia, Massachusetts, Connecticut, and New York from the local tribes that had a degree of hostility toward the unprepared colonists. The Carolina colonies had similar wars with the natives as well as repeated attacks from Spanish and French forces and pirates. More recent events, such as Pearl Harbor and the World Trade Centers attack, remind us that the quotation "vigilance is the price of peace" is an eternal truth.

Other lessons related to military strategy and preparedness were learned in the colonial period, including the necessity of having superior weaponry, as critically evident in the Pequot War when the colonists had a distinct advantage. In the mid-seventeenth century, the matchlock rifle had been replaced by the more effective flintlock rifle, with which the Indians in King Philip's War had greater

---

[96] The Seven Years' War, known in North America as the French and Indian War, was primarily between Great Britain and France with their European allies and their colonies around the world. Colonists and the British army faced French forces and their Algonquian allies. The war in North America began in 1756 when the French captured Forts Oswego and William Henry in New York and ended with their defeat in 1759 by the British, led by General James Wolfe at the Plains of Abraham with the capture of Quebec City.

experience initially. Their early success was also related to tactics that we would consider guerrilla warfare. This was adopted by the colonists and used effectively then and later in the French and Indian War and the War for Independence. Changing military technology and circumstances require adjustments in strategy to achieve desired results.

In the colonial period, a lack of awareness of the culture of the Indians hampered the ability of the colonists to interact with them effectively both in peace and war. Knowledge of other cultures and the factors that influence their motives and actions is critical, especially in the face of possible conflict. This lesson has been relearned in modern times with our experiences in Viet Nam and in the Middle East. Cultural unawareness in the colonial period was in part related to a sense of superiority by the Europeans, which on inspection was inappropriate. We need to be continuously aware of similar impressions in the present time, as disparate cultures are in such close contact and so interdependent.

Disruption due to the turmoil in the religious life, economy, and government following the death of Queen Elizabeth I had been an impetus to colonization of British North America for three decades. The conflicts between Parliament and James I, during his twenty-two-year reign, increased with the succession of his son, Charles I, leading to the English Civil Wars in 1642. During the wars and time of parliamentary rule, a number of prominent colonists returned to England, and interest in controlling the activities of the colonies by the English authorities lessened. It was during this interval that Roger Williams gained a charter for his colony with the guarantee of freedom to worship without the restraint of an official state church of either the Anglican or the Puritan persuasions. The decades witnessing the execution of Charles I, the exile of Charles II, the Commonwealth of England, and Oliver Cromwell's Protectorate eventually saw the English tire of strict Puritan rule. With Cromwell's death in 1658, the Restoration in 1660 welcomed Charles II back to the monarchy with a restructured relationship between the Crown and Parliament.

Religious and political turmoil were not the only concerns of the English homeland leading to benign neglect of the New England colonies. Internationally, they were involved in competition with the Dutch and other European realms related to mercantile issues due to their colonial presences in the Americas, Africa, India, and the Far East. These conflicts led to the First Anglo-Dutch War (1652–54), begun by Oliver Cromwell, which was a series of naval encounters that significantly changed naval battle tactics but had little effect on international trade patterns. The Second Anglo-Dutch War (1665–67) failed to improve the military position of the court of Charles II but did gain the ownership of the Dutch Colony of New Netherland for his realm. This war occurred in the same years as the Great Plague of London in which the bubonic plague killed one hundred thousand people, about one-quarter of the city's population. If that wasn't enough distraction for the English people, the Great Fire of London in September 1666 destroyed thirteen thousand homes and left one hundred thousand homeless. Many churches and other landmarks were destroyed, including St. Paul's Cathedral and the Church of St. Peter upon Cornhill.

During this era, Charles II greatly expanded the navy with the leadership of his brother James, the lord high admiral. James commanded the Royal Navy during the Second and Third Wars and in 1664 was granted control by Charles II of New Netherland, including territory between the Delaware and Connecticut Rivers. The colony and its two principal towns were renamed for James, the duke of Albany and duke of York.

Possession of the New York colony by the British became permanent when the former territories of New Netherland were ceded to England by the Treaty of Westminster in 1674. Edmund Andros, whose family had been staunch Royalists during the Civil Wars supporting Charles I and later Charles II when he was exiled in France, was appointed governor of the colony after a brief return of Dutch rule. Andros was an imperious administrator, and taxes on imports and exports, required by the duke of York, were particularly onerous to the Long Island residents.[97] In the last decade of the reign of Charles II, there was increasing conflict between the North American colonies and their mother country. The court of Charles II, chronically short of revenue, had sought to extract wealth from the mercantile efforts of the kingdom's worldwide colonies. These Navigation Acts of the 1660s were seen by the New England merchants and farmers as a taxation and an impediment to their economic recovery. England's agricultural bounty from the southern colonies was not forthcoming from the New England colonies. Furthermore, those colonies had been independently governed from their origin, and it was difficult for the Crown to exert political control. Andros, as governor of New York, was viewed with alarm by the New England colonies due to his actions with the boundaries with Connecticut and apparent lack of sympathy for the Puritans during King Philip's War. Because of the complaints about Andros that reached England, he was recalled to answer for his activities in 1681. His approval by the Crown was evidenced by his knighthood, and he was replaced in 1682 by Thomas Donegan, who continued his contentious policies.[98]

The Puritan opposition to the Church of England was another source of conflict with the Crown, whose attempts to control these colonies led to revocation of the Massachusetts Bay charter in 1684. Charles II died in 1685 without a legitimate heir (he claimed twelve illegitimate children) and was succeeded by his brother James II (also known as James VII of Scotland). The Dominion of New England was created in 1686 to facilitate control of the colonies by the Crown and extended to all territories north of the Delaware River, including the New Jersey, New York, and New England colonies. The anxiety associated with the appointment of the highly unpopular administrator, Edmund Andros, as captain general and governor in chief, was confirmed when he arrived in Boston with one hundred redcoat English soldiers. He was granted full power to make all laws and statutes for the Dominion and to assess and raise

---

[97] This tumultuous era for the colony of New York will be considered in the following section.

[98] Kammer, Michael. Colonial New York, A History. pp.98–102.

such taxes as deemed necessary, with only the advice and consent of a council of twenty-eight, also appointed by the Crown. After three generations with a degree of self-government, the English colonists were now dependent on the decrees of an individual who had no appreciation for their Puritan way of life. One of the missions for Andros was to establish the Church of England in the colonies where it had been prohibited by the Puritan leadership and to restructure the policies concerning ownership and transfer of land. Another issue during the winter of 1688–89 was renewed conflict with the Abenaki tribesmen in the north, and hundreds of militiamen were assigned to duty and commanded by the English professional soldiers rather than officers of their own choosing.[99]

During that winter, rumors of the invasion of England by William of Orange, the flight of James II to France, and the assumption of the throne by William III and Mary II reached New England. In the early spring, a company of militiamen returning from the northern wars was joined by several thousand residents of Boston, and a riot ensued. Andros and others of his leadership surrendered, and the Dominion of New England was overthrown without bloodshed. Ironically, this "First American Revolution" occurred on April 18, 1689, exactly eighty-six years before Paul Revere's ride and "the shots heard around the world" signaled the onset of the ultimate American revolutionary war.[100]

In the summer of 1688, the influential Massachusetts Puritan leader the Rev. Increase Mather and others, such as William Phips and Samuel Sewall, had gone to London to express their spiritual, governmental, and mercantile grievances about Gov. Andros and the Dominion. They were present for the angst that enveloped London with the birth of James Francis Edward Stuart to James II and his Roman Catholic wife, Mary of Modena, in June. The Catholicism of James II was not a previous concern, as the daughters by his marriage to Anne Hyde, Mary and Anne, were both Protestants and married to

---

[99] Labarre, Benjamin W. Colonial Massachusetts, A History. pp. 111–115.
[100] Ibid. p. 116.

William of Orange and Prince George of Denmark, who shared their faith. The birth of a male heir changed the expected royal succession with the likelihood of a Catholic monarch. Concerns caused by James II's advocating religious tolerance favorable to Catholics and Puritans and his antagonism of Parliament resulted in the invitation to William of Orange and Mary to come to England. This Glorious Revolution was popular with the English, and after a brief battle at Reading, James II and his family fled to France. Parliament ruled that his departure constituted abdication, and in February 1689, William III and Mary II were crowned coregents.

The new regime was willing to accept the dissolution of the Dominion of New England but did not agree to replace it with the original charters of the colonies, which had designated the Puritan faith as the only permitted church and the requirement of Puritan Church membership for full participation as a freeman. Plymouth Colony was combined with Massachusetts Bay, which was also given control of Maine but not the separated province of New Hampshire. The governor of Massachusetts would be appointed by the Crown, and a group of twenty-eight councilors would serve as an upper house of the legislature. They would be selected by the General Court, which would be elected by the vote of all adult males possessing a freehold or other property worth forty pounds sterling. This government gave new authority to the small farmers of the interior communities, and the power of the Crown was expanded, defining its veto power over the General Court and the naming of many public and military officials. The first governor, William Phips, was appointed by William III with the consultation of the Rev. Increase Mather.[101] Mather had spent three years away from his Puritan flock while successfully pursuing dissolution of the Dominion but failing to reinstate the authority of the Puritan church. During his absence, his Puritans created a crisis that would preoccupy their spiritual leader and his son, Rev. Cotton Mather for their lifetimes and have profound effects on their Puritan society.

---

[101] Ibid. pp. 115–120.

As the seventeenth century was drawing to a close, the Salem Village witchcraft trials shook the foundations of Puritan belief, changing the relationship between the church and secular government in colonial Massachusetts and reverberating throughout British North America. Religious practices in New England began changing due to this turmoil and had been facilitated by the royal mandate that the Colony of Massachusetts must accept the Anglican Church and permit the presence of other nonconformist sects. (See appendix, section V, L, "The Salem Witchcraft Trials.")

Bernard Baylin relates the remarkable expansion of the colonies into areas beyond the coastal and riverbank settlements due to the need for land to accommodate the expanding population's dependence on the productivity of the land to sustain their families and provide a source of revenue. The numbers of children and the limited amount of land made this expansion inevitable. Baylin identifies the creation of two hundred nine new townships (more than four per year) between 1660 and 1710.[102]

The extended families of descendants of John Denman II followed this pattern. John II was eighteen when his mother, Judith, died in Salem in 1639. He married Sarah Hollander, thought to be of Dutch ancestry, in 1643 in Dorchester, and they lived in Salem, where they raised three sons, John III (born 1643), Philip (born 1645), and William (born 1648). Philip married Hasadiah Slough and moved to Derby, Colony of Connecticut, in the 1660s, where they raised a large family (see part I).

John II and Sarah, with their sons, moved to Long Island prior to 1660. Their route from Salem is unknown, but they may have joined the group led by Rev. John Youngs from Salem to Southold in 1657 with their Scudder cousins (see part I, A). They soon were in western Long Island in New Netherland, where both John II and John III and their extended families (Scudder and Betts) became significant land owners. The need for land for their expanding families was likely the principal motivation for their relocation. The political effects of the

---

[102] Ibid. p. 93.

transfer of Long Island from Dutch to English rule were certainly factors in the subsequent move to New Jersey, which began after John Denman III had lost most of his property with the new English laws and regulations imposed after 1674. After his death in 1713, his wife, Mary Gano Denman, and their seven children moved permanently to Essex County, Colony of New Jersey, by 1717, where the next generation would greatly add to the population.

It is unknown if religious factors were a consideration, but no evidence of conflict with the Puritan leadership in Massachusetts has been identified. The family of John Denman III was affiliated with the Reformed Church in Newtown and subsequently with the Presbyterian Church in Westfield, New Jersey. We will consider the circumstances that confronted these families and those of our other colonial individuals, Pieter Claesen Wyckoff, and Mary Gano, in the following sections.

C. THE COLONY OF NEW NETHERLAND / NEW YORK

In the autumn of 1609, Henry Hudson, an English navigator sailing on behalf of the Dutch East India Company, had twice unsuccessfully sought the hoped-for northerly passage to Asia. As he sailed the *Half Moon* into the promising harbor previously mentioned but not explored by Giovanni da Verrazano in 1524, he must have been surprised by the unusual river that would subsequently bear his name. The river could easily be navigated in his small but nimble carrack with the aid of tidal flow and coastal winds that blew steadily upstream. He sailed for days before reaching unnavigable water, when he realized that this voyage would end in disappointment. He described the many natives they encountered who were willing to trade for the beaver pelts that were so highly prized in Europe. He also noted the rich land bordering the river, teeming with wildlife and suitable for settlement as he claimed the area for the newly created Republic of the Seven Provinces of Netherland.

Although fur traders would be frequent visitors, it would be six years before the establishment of a Dutch settlement, and then it would only be a fortified warehouse (Fort Nassau). It, as well as its successor, would be destroyed by the river's spring floods (freshets) before a permanent facility (Fort Orange) would be built in 1624 near the junction with the Mohawk River at the navigable limit of the North River (Hudson's). There was little enthusiasm for Netherland residents to emigrate, and the colony's population showed only slight growth until the West Indies Company (WIC) took steps to incentivize development.

The Dutch had been at war with Hapsburg Spain for years, and their success led to the formation of a republic, which was widely recognized in 1609 at the start of the Twelve-Year Truce. The republic was developing a colonial empire, dominating world trade and becoming the wealthiest and most urban state in Europe. It was the home of the first stock market and modern banking system, and employment was high. It was the home of the most tolerant personal religious environment of Europe and was its academic and artistic center. It is not surprising that few Dutch citizens saw benefit in moving to the colony, especially as information about the hardships experienced by the English in Virginia filtered back to Europe.

The profitable fur trade drew the interest of Dutch merchant investors who obtained in 1614 a charter with a three-year monopoly from the states-general for the New Netherland Company. When the charter expired in 1618, other traders entered the competition, until 1621 when the WIC was chartered. The WIC was similar to the English East India Company, which had been chartered by Elizabeth I in 1600 and led to English domination of world trade by the end of the seventeenth century. The Dutch WIC had political, judicial, military, and administrative authority as well as a commercial monopoly within the Dutch merchant community on trade with West Africa and the Americas. Their initial efforts were directed to the African coastal area (from the kingdoms of Guinea to the Cape of Good Hope), South America (Guyana and northern Brazil), and the Caribbean. It was not until 1624 that the first settlers arrived in New Netherland on a ship captained by Cornelius May.

As the Dutch claim extended from the South River (now named the Delaware) to the Connecticut River, settlers were sent to those destinations as well as up the Hudson River to Fort Orange. Those sent to the Connecticut area may have included the family of Sarah Hollander, mentioned in a previous section of our story.[103] She was left an orphan when her Dutch family was killed in conflicts with the natives of the Connecticut River Valley, and she was raised by a family in the Massachusetts Bay Colony. Information about her origin and childhood is not available, but she married John Denman II in 1643, and her descendants contributed importantly to our story.

May served as the director of the colony for a short time and was replaced by Willem Verhulst, who was succeeded by Peter Minuit in 1626. Minuit has been given credit for obtaining Manhattan from the Lenape natives "for the value of 60 guilders" in traded goods claimed to be worth twenty-four dollars. Most authorities conclude that this occurred during the term of Verhulst, but Minuit did purchase Staten Island from the Lenape. New Netherland grew slowly, and by 1628, only 270 settlers were in the colony.[104] The colony was not thought to be financially successful and further investment not justified, but in 1629, the directors of WIC, at the insistence of Kiliaen van Rensselaer, took steps to enhance colonization. They ruled that an investor who brought fifty colonists would become a *patroon* and receive a land grant of eighteen miles along the Hudson River, with no limitation to its extension inland. The land was to be purchased from the natives, who, as in other colonies, would not understand the concept of land ownership held by the Europeans, who likewise did not understand the native concepts of nature. The patroon would have judicial and administrative authority and receive significant trading benefits. Van Rensselaer's agents actively sought potential colonists throughout the Seven Provinces, and much of their success was from the five rural

---

[103] Part I. B. Reflections on the Lives of Colonial Individuals, John Denman of England.

[104] Kammen, M. Colonial New York, A History. 1975, p.30. Charles Scribner's Sons, New York, 1975, p. 30.

areas, including Friesland, where they would obtain the services of the teenage Pieter Claessen as an indentured servant.

Land ownership in the Netherland provinces was influenced by the patterns set in medieval Europe, and individuals not a part of the land holding class had little opportunity to advance in that agrarian economy. Simon Walischez was such an individual and was willing to risk going to an unknown territory with the expectation of this opportunity. He apparently lacked the personal characteristics needed to succeed in that environment. The Dutch middle class was not attracted to New Netherland, and our character, Cornelis Hendrick van Ness, was an exception to this observation. The rules for land ownership by individuals in the colony were erratically enforced and subject to controversy, which may have been a source of the difficulties that van Ness experienced with the WIC authorities. Attracting immigrants was an ongoing challenge for the colony, and by 1640, there were only about five hundred European settlers. By 1664, when the colony was taken by the British, the population was only about nine thousand, compared to New England and Virginia, which counted forty thousand to fifty thousand respectively.[105]

Leadership of the colony was often ineffective due to the directors reporting to the authorities in Amsterdam and being expected to improve the financial prospects while lacking the authority or resources to achieve such goals. Peter Minuit, director from 1626 to 1631, brought a democratic approach to government and encouraged some industrial-type activity, which increased the colony's trade. He encouraged improved relations with the Lenape tribes of the area, but his policies with the patroons were more liberal than approved by the WIC directors in the Netherlands. He was dismissed in 1631, and the two subsequent leaders of the colony accomplished little to advance its population or profitability.[106]

---

[105] Ibid. p.38.

[106] Sebastien Krol was director from 1632 to 1633 and in 1630 had facilitated the purchase of what was to become Rensselaerwyck. He was followed by Wouten van Twiller (1633–38), who accomplished little for the colony but amassed considerable property for himself. He is credited with beginning construction of

During these years, the Indian natives were experiencing cultural and political changes that were to affect the European settlers. The Mohawk tribe began to expand its territory, which caused their Algonquian adversaries, the Mahicans, to move into areas in Connecticut and the lower Hudson Valley, which were occupied by the Narragansett and other Lenape tribes who were their rivals. These tribes in Connecticut and New Netherlands were eager to accept the Europeans as potential allies in their conflicts. This was a factor in the war in Massachusetts that pitted the Pequot tribe against their enemies who had Anglican allies. Similar issues occurred in the New Netherland colony.

The colony grew significantly with the recruitment efforts for Rensselaerswyck and the attraction of fur traders and others to New Amsterdam, which was the most diverse settlement in North America. About one half of the inhabitants were of Dutch origin, with significant numbers of Walloons, Frisians, English, French, Swedish, Danish, Germans, and Africans. Slaves in New Amsterdam were not significant in numbers until the WIC brought eleven men from the Caribbean in 1626 and three women from Angola in 1628. The numbers of slaves increased after 1637 when the Dutch captured the west African Elmina Castle and assumed control of the Portuguese Gold Coast with the slave trade.[107]

In 1638, the WIC, controlled by the Herren XIX, took steps to encourage immigration to the colony, and van Twiller was replaced by Willem Kieft. Over the next fifteen years, about 2,200 new residents were added, and the total population neared 3,500. It was said that "no fewer than eighteen different languages" were spoken in New Amsterdam. Although only the Dutch Reformed Church was allowed to stage public worship, there were numbers of Roman Catholics, English Puritans, German Lutherans, Anabaptists, and Mennonites in the colony.

---

the house that would later be the home of Pieter Claessen Wyckoff and family in the Amersfoort/Breukelyn area (part I, B).

[107] Burrows, E.G. and Wallace, M. Gotham-A History of New York City to 1898. Oxford University Press, 1999. pp.31–33.

Willem Kieft had little administrative experience and no knowledge of his new Indian neighbors. He significantly enlarged the colony by expanding the Dutch holdings in present-day Brooklyn and Queens. This further aggravated the relations with the tribes, which did not understand the European concept of property ownership. The tribes near New Amsterdam depended on the Dutch for protection from the conflicts with the expansion of the Mahicans into their territory. Kieft tried to tax the tribes for this protection, and he responded to minor conflicts with the Indians with excessive force. Between 1643 and 1645, more than a thousand Indians were killed in such strikes as in the Pavonia and Pound Ridge Massacres in Kieft's War. The natives responded with widespread attacks, such as in the Bronx area, where Anne Hutchinson and her family were victims. Although a truce with the decimated Indian tribes was negotiated, possibly due to the skills of Oratam, the sachem of the Hackensack tribe in the Pavonia area of northeastern New Jersey, suspicion and distrust persisted.

The policies of Kieft, including his autocratic regime, his intransigent personality, and dependence on alcohol, were alarming to many Dutch residents, and in 1647, the WIC recalled him. He died in a shipwreck en route to Amsterdam to answer to the critics for his actions. Kieft was replaced by Petrus Stuyvesant, whose personality and leadership would dominate the story of New Netherland until 1664.[108]

Pieter Stuyvesant was born in 1592 in Friesland, one of the Seven United States of the Netherlands, and his father was a minister of the Reformed Church in the city of Peperga. Pieter attended the University of Franeker in 1612–14[109] but was expelled for seducing his landlord's daughter. The ire of the officials was probably surpassed

---

[108] Bailyn, B. The Barbarous Years- The Peopling of British North America: The Conflict of Civilizations, 1600–1675. Random House, Inc. 2012. pp. 216–241.

[109] The University of Franeker was the second oldest university in the Netherlands and an important part of the intellectual and scientific leadership during the Dutch Golden Age. Its most memorable scholar was Rene Descartes, often described as the preeminent philosopher, mathematician, and scientist of his age.

by that of his strict Calvinist father, who sent him to Amsterdam to determine his own faith and future with fear and trembling. He obtained work with the WIC, used the Latin version of his name, Petrus, to show his university training, and by 1630 was appointed commercial agent at Fernando de Noronha. This was a group of small islands 220 miles offshore from Brazil, which the WIC used as a base for military operations against the mainland in their ongoing struggle with Portugal/Spain for a share of the profitable trade. In 1635, he was promoted to a position in Pernambuco and in 1638 was transferred to the Caribbean island of Curacao, the headquarters of the WIC in the Americas. In 1642, he became acting governor of the island and in 1644 organized an expedition to recapture the island of Sint Maarten from the Spanish. He lost his right leg to an enemy cannonball and soon returned to Amsterdam to a hero's welcome. His peg leg became a proud symbol of his sacrifice and "a sign that God had spared him for great things."

He was named director-general of New Netherland at a salary twenty-three times the wage of a company seaman. In 1646, he and his newly married wife, Judith Bayard, sailed to America, arriving in New Amsterdam in August 1647. They must have been appalled at what they found. Many people had left the colony, and only three hundred were capable of bearing arms. About seven hundred had left their farms out of fear of the vengeful Lenape and were existing in squalor in the disorderly village. He immediately began resurveying the lanes and property lines, prohibited the foraging of livestock in the town, and forbade the disposal of domestic, animal, and human waste in the streets. He would return the settlement to an orderly state of public tidiness, which a typical Dutchman, the broom being one of their national symbols, would be able to call home.[110]

Although Stuyvesant appointed an advisory council of nine representatives, his leadership style was best described by himself: "I shall govern you as a father his children," and he reestablished

---

[110] Burrows and Wallace, Gotham: A History of New York City to 1898. pp.42–44.

the authority of the WIC. Soon he became aware of the conflict between his authority and the freedoms assumed by the most successful patroonship, Rensselaerswijck, and its director, Brant van Slichtenhorst. Fort Orange had been established and was controlled by WIC long before the patroonship was created and was clearly under the company's authority. The area around the fort had always been a center for the exchange of goods with the Mohawk natives for the valuable beaver pelts, which constituted the greatest source of wealth for the colony. Van Slichtenhorst assumed jurisdiction over the area, which was developing into a small village, and in 1649, to establish his authority, he prohibited the workers from Fort Orange from cutting wood or quarrying stone on the patroon's lands. When van Slichtenhorst began building houses near the fort, Stuyvesant ruled that the "freedom of the fort" required a secure perimeter and that no construction within three thousand feet (the distance of a cannon shot) of the fort would be permitted. With the specific approval of the authorities in Holland, troops were sent in 1652 from New Amsterdam, and the authority of the director of New Netherland was verified. Eventually van Slichtenhorst would be jailed and returned to the Netherlands. The town continued to be known as Beverwijck and was the center of the fur trade under the authority of the WIC as long as demand for the prized export, the economic mainstay of the colony, would continue.

The controversy with Director-General Stuyvesant was not the only problem that involved Slichtenhorst. As noted in section IV, B, Pieter Claessen and his father-in-law, Cornelius Hendrick van Ness, were involved in lawsuits, with Slichtenhorst as recorded in court records between 1648 and 1650. Pieter Claessen, his wife, Grietje, and their two young children would move to the New Amsterdam area in about 1650. It is likely that this move was encouraged by Stuyvesant, who shared the Frisian language with Pieter and Cornelius and later would have property on Long Island, which would be managed by Pieter Claessen.

The problem of scant population in New Netherland was eased by two circumstances in the 1640–50s, both of which were vexing for Stuyvesant. The first was the spread of New Englanders to eastern

Long Island and soon to its western areas amid growing Dutch settlements. The English came because of religious beliefs that were contrary to the approved worship in the Bay Colony and for their need of productive land for their growing families. They often came with "fiercely independent" leaders, such as Rev. Francis Doughty who in 1642 received land from Director Willen Kieft in the "Maspeth" area of Long Island, which became the settlement of Newtown. The English retreated to New Amsterdam during the wars with the Indians and soon Doughty moved to churches in Maryland and Virginia. English settlers caused problems for Stuyvesant, as they came to the area with dissenting religious beliefs and with expectations of self-governance of their communities, such as they had experienced in Massachusetts, both being contrary to Stuyvesant's goals.

The second event increasing the population and its diversity was the loss of the New Holland area of Brazil, which had been taken from the Portuguese by the WIC beginning in 1624. This area had provided significant wealth from its sugar production and the slave trade, but when the Dutch were defeated and expelled from Recife in 1654, many of the settlers moved to New Netherland. This not only increased the number of slaves in the colony but would expand the religious diversity, as twenty-three Jews would also call New Amsterdam their home. This and the arrival of many outspoken Quakers would require Petrus Stuyvesant to restrain his religious intolerance at the direction of the Amsterdam authorities. It is estimated that two thousand New Englanders and four thousand immigrants from abroad had arrived by 1664.[111]

Slaves had existed in the colony from its early days and were imported by WIC to work at the direction of the company authorities. Their numbers were small until 1655, when the first loaded ship arrived with three hundred slaves. The black population of New Amsterdam increased from 105 to approximately 375 in 1664, and seventy-five of them were free, reflecting a more liberal policy than that which developed in the southern colonies, where the production

---

[111] 49 Baylin, B. The Barbarous Years, pp. 252–61.

of tobacco and rice were large-scale efforts requiring a greater labor force. Until the last quarter of the seventeenth century, most laborers came as indentured servants from England, but this changed, as the cost of their labor became greater than that of African slaves. The demand for slaves increased greatly, and they were often treated as indentured servants and were granted limited basic and civic rights, families that were kept intact, and the ability to work part-time for wages.[112] Documentation of slave ownership by the Denman and Wyckoff families has not been verified, but it is likely their agricultural activities in Long Island and later in New Jersey required labor that could not be obtained by other means.

These internal conflicts in Stuyvesant's colony were not the only problems he faced, as conflict with the Indians had not been addressed following Kieft's War. This war had decimated the tribes of the lower Hudson Valley, and in 1655, an incident began unexpectedly at New Amsterdam and led to reprisals by the Dutch and Indians, resulting in deaths of many natives and colonists. The fear of ongoing hostilities persisted, and in 1658, conflict erupted in the farming area of Esopus, about halfway between New Amsterdam and Beverwijk. Over the next five years, relations with the Esopus tribe remained tenuous, until 1663 when the Indians launched a surprise attack with many casualties on both sides. By the end of the year, an uneasy peace was established, but the exit of Indians from the lower Hudson and Long Island areas would continue. The changes that were to engulf New Netherland in 1664 were not anticipated and without the colony's preparation.

The Dutch and English had been allies in the sixteenth century when they had a common enemy in Spain and its Hapsburg rulers. The peace with Spain in 1604 allowed the Dutch to expand their mercantile fleet at the expense of the Portuguese colonies in the Far East and South America, which they captured in almost continuous warfare. By the middle of the century, the Dutch were by far the most prosperous European country, while the English, facing economic

---

[112] Hodges, Russel Graham,

and political conflicts, had not maintained as effective a merchant fleet. To strengthen their economic position, the English passed a series of Navigation Acts restricting the access of the Dutch to the English colonies. The relations between the two countries were also affected by the English Civil War and the Dutch sympathies for Charles I. The English had improved their naval forces, while the Dutch had expanded their merchant fleet at the expense of the navy.

When Cromwell ordered aggressive enforcement of the Navigation Acts, conflict between the two navies was a certainty, and minor skirmishes that damaged Dutch shipping occurred during 1652. One result of these engagements was that the Dutch were unable to adequately defend their South American possessions from the Portuguese, who recaptured Brazil, forcing many residents of the Dutch holdings to flee to New Netherland. By the next year, the English had adopted new naval warfare tactics, the line-of-battle formation, which gave them the upper hand, and by 1654, both countries were ready for peace. The Treaty of Westminster included the secret Act of Seclusion, unknown at the time by most of the Dutch leadership, which precluded the four-year-old William III from becoming the monarch of Holland, as his mother was the daughter of Charles I. There was concern that at his maturity, he may become sympathetic for his assassinated grandfather and for the Roman Catholic faith and exert his claim to the English throne.[113]

This First Anglo-Dutch War proved little, and the dominance of the Dutch mercantile efforts continued, leading to one of the high points of their Golden Age. The decade of the 1660s saw the restoration of Charles II to the English throne, and his supporters and former Royalists became a favored group. Although Charles II

---

[113] When the commonwealth ceased to exist and this Act of Seclusion became known, it was nullified, and William III, a devout Protestant, would marry the daughter of his uncle James II, with their becoming coregents of England as William III and Mary II. The mercantile conflict may not have been the sole motivation for the English to begin the First Anglo-Dutch War, as their concern about a strong Roman Catholic with a claim to their throne could be a major threat to the commonwealth leadership.

and the gaiety and hedonism of his court were much in the favor of the populace, he was in almost constant conflict with Parliament. He rewarded his brother James, duke of York, by declaring him the lord high admiral.[114] James and his prominent merchant friends were envious of the Dutch prosperity, and he dispatched ships that captured their settlements on the African coast, giving the English control of the slave trade. The Navigation Acts were extended to block the Dutch from trade with the English colonies, and James was declared the proprietor of all lands between the Connecticut and Delaware Rivers.

There was unrest on Long Island as the increasing number of immigrants from New England chafed at the strict governance of Stuyvesant. James, duke of York, took advantage of these circumstances and dispatched Colonel Richard Nicholls with at least three armed vessels and sufficient soldiers to validate his claimed authority over these lands. In the summer of 1664, English troops landed on Long Island and marched toward New Amsterdam, and on September 8, 1664, Stuyvesant ceded the province to England. The Dutch leadership convinced their bellicose governor that the small number of poorly supplied troops at their service would be no match for the pending bombardment of New Amsterdam.

The authority for the colony, renamed New York in honor of the duke, was assumed by Colonel Nicholls, whose magnanimous terms of surrender allowed the Dutch to retain their properties, their inheritance laws, and the Dutch Reformed Church. The treatment of the Dutch was so benign that Stuyvesant, after defending his management of the colony in Amsterdam and claiming that its loss was due to the failure to adequately supply their military, returned to his home in New York, where he and his family resided throughout his lifetime.[115]

Charles II officially declared war on the Dutch the following

---

[114] James had received this designation at the age of three years and at his maturity fully utilized the authority.

[115] Burrows, EG and Wallace, M. Gotham: A History of New York City to 1898. pp. 72–4.

March 1665, but the English were faced with a rearmed enemy navy, which had become expert in the new battle tactics and delivered them embarrassing defeats. This was the same year in which the Great Plague of London appeared, and by 1666, more than a hundred thousand (one quarter of the city's population) died. In September of that year, the Great Fire destroyed more than thirteen thousand houses and most of the buildings and churches in the city of London, including St. Paul's Cathedral. By 1667, the Second Anglo–Dutch War ended, and the New Netherland colony was officially ceded to the English. The colony had never been an adequate commercial success for the Dutch, and they willingly exchanged it for Suriname (north of Brazil and adjacent to the Dutch colony of Guyana) and the Spice Island of Pulau Run (in present Indonesia), which were sources of great wealth due to sugar and spice production.

The first years of English rule were peaceful, and the people of the colony prospered. Both the size of the family and property of Pieter Claessen and Gretje grew significantly during the 1650s. He served as a leader of the local government and in 1661 was a founding member of the Reformed Church of Flatland. John Denman III, who resided in the Maspeth/Newtown area, obtained significant acreage from the Lenape along with his relatives, and he worshipped at the Newtown Reformed Church. Circumstances in England were more unsettled due to conflicts between Charles II and Parliament, related to the Anglican Church as the only permitted worship. Charles was sympathetic to the Roman Catholic Church and would at the end of life reestablish his affiliation. The financial circumstances of the government were tenuous due to the lifestyle of the monarchy and less income from trade than expected. This prompted Charles II to seek support from his cousin Louis XIV, who also sought military assistance from the English in his desire to claim territory from the Dutch and Spanish.[116] By secret treaties, the English were drawn into further conflict with the Dutch and their navy in concert with the

---

[116] Charles II and James II were sons of Henrietta Maria, who was the wife of Charles I and the daughter of French King Henry IV. As she was the sister of Louis XIII, Louis XIV was her nephew and cousin of the two English kings.

French in land and sea actions. The English had rebuilt their navy following the losses after 1667, and in the spring of 1672, the two nations declared war on the Dutch Republic. The French had some success in their invasion of the southern Netherland states, but the English were defeated in the naval battle of Solebay by the Dutch, led by their brilliant commander, Michiel de Ruyter. After a similar result the next year in the Battle of the Texel, in which the combined fleets of England and France were defeated, his enemies stated that de Ruyter was the greatest of admirals.[117] This Third Anglo-Dutch War concluded, the reputation of Charles II was increasingly circumspect and the finances of the realm in even worse condition.

Charles II sought to improve this by making the American colonies more profitable with the Navigation Acts, but this had been less successful than anticipated and had greatly aggravated the colonists. Although Virginia had been changed from a proprietary to a Crown colony, the other colonies remained with either corporate or proprietary charters. An option to lessen the expense of the colonies and bring them more fully under control of the monarchy was to adopt a model of management similar to that of the Spanish colonies. In 1686, the Dominion of New England was established and included the New England colonies and the Provinces of New York and New Jersey. Edmund Andros was named the governor of the Dominion, as he had been appointed the governor of New York by James, the duke of York, in 1674 and had been an able administrator. He had been able to settle relations with the Indian tribes and mediate some of their intertribal conflicts.

His dealings with the colonies in the Dominion were filled with conflict, as his directives to introduce the Anglican Church to Massachusetts where it had been forbidden and to raise revenues by taxing both the land owners and by increasing tariffs were vigorously resisted. The Anglican Church was established in New York, and although the right to practice other faiths was permitted, tax revenues

---

[117] Roger, N.A.M. The Command of the Ocean: A Naval History of Britain. 1649–1815. Penguin, 2004.

were used to support the official church. The public duties of recording baptisms, marriages, and deaths were officially established in these parish churches. Some of the confusion concerning the identity and date of death of the two Gano citizens may result from both being Reformed Church members and probably not personally known by the Anglican authorities.[118]

Concern among the colonists was increased when James II with his Roman Catholic wife assumed the monarchy in 1685 and his administration began replacing governmental leadership with Roman Catholics. The policy of succession for the monarchy specified that the daughters of his first wife, Anne Hyde, would follow James II, as they and their spouses were Protestant. The birth of a son, James Francis Edward Stuart, in 1688 caused alarm, and William of Orange was encouraged to claim the throne with his wife, Mary II, which led to the Glorious Revolution. After a dramatic interlude in which much of his military chose to support the forces of William, James fled to France, Parliament ruled that he had abandoned the throne, and William III and Mary II were made coregent monarchs.

When word of this spread to Massachusetts Bay, the populace in Boston demanded Andros's resignation, and his arrest marked the demise of the Dominion. Word of this action spread to New York, where Lieutenant Governor Francis Nicholson was deposed by the militia in Leisler's Rebellion. Leisler would serve as governor during the next several years until the new monarchy appointed a replacement. During these years, Leisler was instrumental in assisting the Huguenots from La Rochelle, including the family of Francis Gano, as described in section I, D.

The turmoil of the Dominion years and the land ownership changes imposed by the English were factors in the decision of John Denman III to obtain property in the Colony of New Jersey. His family would move there after his death, and the second generation of the children of the Wyckoff family would see many relocate to the fertile and abundant lands in the Jersey colony.

---

[118] See section I, C and VI, C for further information about this controversy,

D. THE COLONIES OF NEW JERSEY AND PENNSYLVANIA

The 1660 Restoration of the Monarchy in Britain brought many changes to its lands and the people. The atmosphere of harsh piety enforced by the central authorities of the Interregnum had become a burden whose end was gratefully received by the populace. After the civil wars, Charles II escaped to France and the protection of Louis XIV, his cousin, and Royalist friends. On his celebrated return to the English throne, he expressed gratitude to his supporters in ways available to a financially restrained regime. His associates, many of whom had Roman Catholic sympathies or to whom he had debts, were appointed to governmental positions or were given control of large areas of the English colonial claims in America.

Following the ceding of New Netherland to the English in late 1664, Charles II and his brother James, duke of York, named Lord John Berkeley (first Baron Berkeley of Stratton) and Sir George Carteret as coproprietors of what became the Colony of New Jersey. Berkeley was a younger son of a prominent family and had served as ambassador to the Swedish court and briefly in Parliament until being imprisoned for suspicion of association with the Royalist Army Plots in 1641. In the First Civil War, Berkeley was an effective military leader of Royalist forces and aided Charles II in his escape to France, where Berkeley also spent most of the Interregnum. With the restoration, he served Charles II in several appointed positions, was one of the proprietors of the Colony of Carolina, and from 1664 to 1674 was a coproprietor of New Jersey. The other New Jersey proprietor, Carteret, served as a naval officer during the civil wars and made the Isle of Jersey a Royalist stronghold until he was forced to escape to France. Neither had any experience in colonial management or personal interest in the progress of the area.

Eastern New Jersey, adjacent to New Amsterdam, had received settlers since the early days of the Dutch presence, and the western part of the colony abutting the Delaware River had been sparsely settled by New Sweden. From the 1650s, increasing numbers had moved to New Jersey from New Amsterdam and Long Island due to available fertile land, despite the threat of local Indians.

In 1665, the coproprietors, to encourage new settlers, advanced a Concession and Agreement Proclamation that granted religious freedom to the people, unlike New York where only the Anglican Church was condoned. By 1673, Lord Berkeley, having grown tired of the difficulty collecting rents from the settlers and controversies between the proprietors and New York Governor Nicholls, sold his one half interest in the colony to a group of Quakers, which included William Penn. The colony was divided with West Jersey, owned by the Quakers, and East Jersey by Carteret. The colony remained divided until 1702, when East Jersey and the bankrupt West Jersey were reunified under the control of the Crown.

The size of land grants was favorable to the ownership of slaves, and it seems certain that the descendants of the Denman and Wyckoff families who relocated from Long Island around the turn of the century were among those slave owners. As noted in section III, C, the numbers of African slaves in New Netherland increased after 1637, and with the English capture in 1664, the number increased significantly. The slaves mainly worked on large land grants, but many were occupied in domestic or urban work in both skilled and unskilled jobs in the port of New York. By 1700, over one-third of New York households used slave labor.[119]

By 1678, Penn had personally sent eight hundred Quakers from England to West Jersey to escape harassment due to their faith. To appreciate the growth of New Jersey and the subsequent development of the Colony of Pennsylvania, it is important to understand the nature of the Quaker faith and its reception by the authorities in England and the colonies. The Religious Society of Friends, known as Quakers, was the creation of George Fox, born 1624 in Fenny Drayton, a village in central England east of Birmingham. Fox was the son of a successful weaver and lay official in the local Anglican

---

[119] Wood, B. Slavery in Colonial America, 1619–1776. Rowman & Littlefield Publishers, Inc. 2005. pp. 13–15.

church. His father died early in George's life but left him a religious upbringing and a substantial legacy that made possible his early-adult spiritual endeavors. At age nineteen, he became disenchanted by what he saw as superficial religious beliefs in his peers and started on a "soul-distressing search for spiritual reality." At the age of twenty-two, he had a transforming experience with the "firm conviction that each person receives from the Lord a measure of spiritual light ... and if this inner light is followed it leads ... to spiritual truth."[120] By 1647, he began preaching that revelation was not confined to scriptures alone, that the spirit of God speaks directly to individuals, and this was available to any man or woman. This inner light was given by divine will and was a valid ministry. Hence he rejected the need for a professional ministry and for outward sacraments. He rejected the use of artificial titles or servility in speech or behavior as a degradation of true Christian respect between individuals. He strongly opposed warfare and slavery and refused the taking of oaths.

His spiritual earnestness, dislike of formalism, demand for inward experiences, and rejection of a formally trained clergy were teachings that drew many from both Reformed, Anglican, and other Dissenter groups. Quaker communities appeared throughout northern England and in London and other cities. This movement met with fierce opposition from the ecclesiastical and secular leaders, and within the next decade, more than three thousand members, including Fox, had spent time in prison. The missionary zeal of his followers spread widely, and by 1656, their intense antiestablishment preaching had reached the Colony of Massachusetts Bay. The reaction of the Puritan leadership to their extravagant conduct was forceful, and by 1661, four Quakers had been executed because of the disturbances caused by their preaching.

These extravagances appear to have been facilitated by the lack of effective organization and discipline among the Quaker communities. This resulted from the belief in the immediate inspiration of the Spirit, and some felt compelled to vigorously spread their beliefs. Fox

---

[120] Walker, W. et al. Scribner. 1985. pp 561–2.

in the mid–1660s brought a strict organization to his followers with regular meetings and a sense of discipline in their activities. This resulted in a more conservative expression of their beliefs and soon evolved into the present-day ministry based on simplicity, equality, and peace.

During the early years of his spiritual journey, William Penn and others spoke widely about their Quaker faith during visits to the German states between 1671 and 1677. On those visits, the Quaker message was responded to by Peter Schumacher Sr. and four of his children. They would be among the earliest German settlers to move from the electoral Palatinate on the Rhine River with Francis Daniel Pastorius to a new home in Germantown in the Colony of Pennsylvania on the Delaware River. He was soon to be followed by his grandsons, the Kolb brothers (sections I, E and IV, D).

The early history of the Colony of Pennsylvania is the story of one man, William Penn, and his quest to promote and sustain his adopted Quaker religious beliefs. It is a remarkable story of how one brilliant, free-spirited young person could use his own abilities and his inherited resources to create a haven for people from diverse backgrounds and faiths. He created out of a wilderness what would become the most prosperous, diverse, and progressive colony in English North America. Although Penn visualized his colony as a utopia, it took the efforts and determination of settlers such as the Schumachers and the four Kolb brothers and thousands of others from various principalities and with different beliefs to make it a reality.

William Penn was born in 1644 during the first English civil war, when his father, Admiral William Penn, was commanding a ship sailing for the Parliament forces. The admiral's service was rewarded with extensive estates in Ireland that had been confiscated during the war by Cromwell's army. Admiral Penn's politics were not reliable, as he had sympathies for the Royalists, and he was an important figure in English naval history. In 1653, he was involved in developing the new and effective line-of-battle naval tactic and served well in the First Anglo-Dutch War (1652–54). In the Second Anglo-Dutch War (1665–67), he served effectively under James, duke of York, whose friendship had been nurtured when Penn was on the ship returning him and Charles II from France at the restoration (1660).

Young William was classically educated at the Chigwell School in Essex with its Puritan influence. While living in Ireland on his father's new estates, he heard Quaker preaching, which had an influence on his youthful beliefs. In 1660, he began studies at Oxford but preferred religious nonconformity to the Anglican teachings and was expelled in 1662. His mother was a socially prominent daughter of a wealthy Dutch merchant, and she and the admiral must have been dismayed when their eldest son seemingly abandoned his social position and his Oxford education because of his Quaker sympathies. He was sent to Paris to broaden his experiences apart from the Quaker influence but was affected by French protestant theology, which encouraged him to seek his own spiritual direction. On his return to England in 1664, he presented a more aristocratic mien but a growing academic skepticism of long-held beliefs and customs. He became more attracted to the Quaker message, and in 1667, at age twenty-two, he announced his conversion to that faith.

By this time, Quakerism was becoming more moderate and attracted prosperous members who supported their preachers and their publications. During this interval, Penn was estranged from his father and during his intermittent imprisonments wrote some of his most important books concerning the Quaker faith and the importance of religious toleration. In one trial, his skillful testimony led to a landmark principle of the independence of juries from the control of the judge.[121] Due to the influence of his mother, the father Penn and his son were reconciled and the young Penn's inheritance

---

[121] This trial is known as Bushell's Case, and Penn's argument was upheld by Lord Chief Justice John Vaughan, who ruled that a judge "may try to open the eyes of the jurors, but not to lead them by the nose." Penn described this trial in his book, The People's Ancient and Just Liberties Asserted (1670).

restored. His father, knowing that his life was soon to end, had written to Charles II and James, the duke of York, who agreed to protect young William in return for the admiral's service to the Crown.

The success of their relocation of Quakers to the Colony of New Jersey encouraged Penn to seek greater opportunities in the colonies for the persecuted religious sects in England. He had a sympathizer in James, duke of York, who was eager to have his fellow Roman Catholics free of the same suppression experienced by the Protestant Nonconformists. James agreed with Charles II in this matter, and in March 1681, land that was a part of the territory north of the Colony of Maryland and west of the Delaware River was given to Penn and named Pennsylvania in honor of the admiral in exchange for removal of an outstanding debt of £16,000 ($2.5–3 million today). The duke of York retained proprietary control of New York and the counties that would later become the Colony of Delaware, which were ceded to Penn in 1682.

Soon after gaining the territory, Penn sailed to his new land and negotiated the purchase of land from the Lenape natives. This would be a policy of his colony, which allowed it to be unique among the others in having no major conflict with the Indian population. His other priority was to produce a charter for Pennsylvania that would assure free elections, guarantee that despotic rule would never appear, require fair trial by jury, prevent unjust imprisonment, and assure complete freedom of religion. The ideas for his "Framework of Government" drew from those of John Locke, but Penn added the ability of the two houses of his new government to amend this framework, a unique concept of governance.

To encourage immigration, Penn made liberal grants of land to those who could help his recruitment, and in less than a year, he had distributed three hundred thousand acres to prospective settlers. He attracted people from nearly every western and Scandinavian area of Europe and representatives of the spectrum of religions, including Jews, Catholics, Lutherans, Huguenots, Mennonites, Baptists, and Reformed Church members. Among the early individuals and groups to receive such grants was Francis Daniel Pastorius for the area of Germantown and a large Welsh contingent that would occupy the First Welsh Tract to the west of his city of Philadelphia.

The new colony was not without problems, and in 1684, Penn returned to England to try to resolve a boundary dispute with Lord Baltimore and the Colony of Maryland. This was done in favor of Penn in 1685 by James II, when he assumed the Crown following the death of Charles II. The colony was poorly managed in Penn's absence, but on his return in 1699, the population had grown to eighteen thousand, and Philadelphia, with three thousand, was one of the largest cities in the colonies. Penn insisted that Quaker schools be open to all, and Philadelphia was to become the center for science, medicine, and academic thought in the colonies. He suggested in his writings the earliest expression of the idea that all of the English colonies should become a federation.

The lower three counties never completely assimilated into the Quaker-controlled government in Philadelphia, and in 1704, Delaware was allowed an assembly of its own but would share an appointed governor with Pennsylvania until the American Revolution. The issue of slavery would become a major controversy in the eighteenth century, and as noted in section IV, D and E, the Mennonites in Pennsylvania would be the first to protest the morality of slavery, and the Quakers would also become major proponents of abolition.

Penn never received financial gain from his colony, and his children were unable to carry on his vision. He returned to England in 1701, and after the Glorious Revolution, he lacked the political influence of earlier times. In 1689, when hostilities with France prompted the English to require Pennsylvania to supply military aid to their efforts and were refused by the Quaker colonial government, the powers of the governor were given to a royal appointee, Benjamin Fletcher. Pennsylvania remained a proprietary colony until the American Revolution, but William Penn had died penniless at his home in England in 1718.

The history of the Welsh Tracts, either west of Philadelphia (the Main Line communities) or in the southern counties, which later would become the Colony and State of Delaware, is described elsewhere and is an important part of the story of our Welsh Baptist and Mennonite Kolb families.

The consideration of these mid-Atlantic colonies and the New England colonies from which many moved and the southern colonies to which many eventually relocated demonstrate the diversity of the thirteen colonies created between 1607 and 1734. Their unique characteristics and cultures had continued to develop by the time of the War for Independence. A high priority of many delegates that helped create that union, the United States of America, was the preservation of the authority of the government in each colony/state and the rights of individuals. The compromises necessary to balance these rights with the need for a central authority that had the ability to confront problems that faced all of the new states led to the Constitution of the United States.

Early accomplishments of this government were the ability to change or amend this Constitution and to permit the orderly admission of new states to this union with full privileges and responsibilities. This federal system has preserved the identity of our fifty states, and the Tenth Amendment specifies that their authority in many areas of governance is preserved. The extent of this authority has evolved over the subsequent centuries, with increasing power and responsibility drifting to the central authority. There are many advantages to this federal system, as it gives great authority to elected bodies that are closer to the individual communities and families that make up the basic units of our society. This independence is a direct outgrowth of colonial America, and we are wise to carefully protect it from erosion and to ensure that the freedoms guaranteed in our Bill of Rights are protected.

Each of the thirteen colonies created between 1607 and 1734 developed unique characteristics and cultures by the formation of the union in the time of the War for Independence. A high priority of the delegates who helped create that union was the preservation of the authority of the government that had developed in each colony and the rights of the individuals that called them home. The compromises necessary to balance these rights with the need for a central authority that had the ability to confront problems that faced all of the new states led to the Constitution of the United States.

Perhaps one of the difficulties that faces developing nations in the perpetuation of democratic systems is that their form of governance tends to be instituted from the top down rather than beginning in local communities and regional states. We are indeed fortunate to have inherited a system that protects our rights and freedoms close to home.

E. THE CAROLINA COLONIES

The territory south of Virginia had been visited and claimed by England, France, and Spain in the sixteenth century, but no settlements were attempted until 1562, when a futile effort to create a haven for French Huguenots at Charlesfort on the present-day Parris Island ended in disaster.[122] The site was taken by the Spanish, who built Santa Elena on Port Royal Sound in 1566. This served as a secure respite for the ships sailing from Havana and heading north through the Bahama Channel to reach the westerly trade winds carrying them home to Spain. The site was the capital of La Florida until it was abandoned in 1587. No further settlements were attempted north of St. Augustine by the Spanish. This was likely due to hostile Indians and an unhealthy climate with associated diseases, such as dysentery, malaria, and yellow fever, which would also affect future settlers.

The English did not attempt to establish a presence in that area for several reasons, including the above issues. A shortage of manpower available to the English, which significantly limited the development of the established colonies in Virginia and Maryland, and a concern about retaliation from the Spanish garrisons to the

---

[122] Parris Island is now best known as the training site for the US Marine Corps and is across the river from Hilton Head, about halfway between Charlestown, South Carolina, and Savannah, Georgia.

south were prominent issues. War with Spain (1625–30) had been costly for the English, and their enemy was firmly entrenched in the Caribbean. The Anglo–Spanish War resumed (1654–1660), resulting in the English gaining Jamaica and the Cayman Islands but only with heavy economic losses.

Although a small number of English immigrants had drifted to an area on the shores of Albemarle Sound just south of the Virginia border, there was no significant settlement until 1663 when Charles II awarded a charter for Carolina to eight proprietors. This grant extended from the Virginia border to the presumed border of the Spanish Florida territory. Two of the eight, Lord John Berkeley and Sir George Carteret, were also named proprietors of the Colony of New Jersey.[123] Two proprietors who most actively supported the Carolina colony were Anthony Ashley Cooper, first earl of Shaftesbury, and Sir John Colleton. The son of the latter was among one of the first groups of settlers to move to Carolina from Barbados.

Barbados, an island in the eastern Lesser Antilles, had been claimed but abandoned by the Portuguese in the sixteenth century and was settled by the English beginning in 1627. Initially, tobacco was the main export, but by 1640, the market for this product was supplanted by a superior Chesapeake variety and replaced on the island by highly profitable sugarcane production. The initial workforce had been indentured servants from England, but after 1660, the small land holders were replaced by large plantations using slaves. Thousands of people of English origin left the island, and many came to Carolina and Virginia.

Attempts to settle the area south of Albemarle Sound had not been successful, mainly due to hostility from the Indians and Spanish. An exploratory effort was sent to the Port Royal area in 1665 and included as the ship's surgeon Dr. Henry Woodward. When the expedition returned, he elected to remain in the St. Helena Island

---

[123] These two and four others, Edward Hyde, first earl of Clarendon, George Monck, first duke of Albemarle, Wiliam Craven, first earl of Craven, and Sir William Berkeley (brother of John), did not have a prominent role in the subsequent development of the area.

area to live with the local Escamacu Indians to learn of their language and culture.[124] Within six months, he was captured by the Spanish as a spy and was a prisoner at St. Augustine when it was attacked and sacked by the English privateer (pirate) Captain Robert Searle. The released Woodward sailed with Searle until August 1669, when they were shipwrecked in a hurricane on the island of Nevis. While they were waiting to be rescued, the ship *Carolina* put in for water while on the way to the new colony. The one hundred fifty English colonists from Barbados and Dr. Woodward continued to the Carolina colony area near the site of present-day Charlestown, South Carolina. The success of this new settlement in 1670 was in part due to Woodward's knowledge and friendship with the Indians. He became an Indian agent and over the next decade would explore widely, establishing relations with tribes that were undergoing upheavals like those in New York and Massachusetts, creating danger for the new colonists. His influence with the warring tribes was a factor in the survival of the settlements.

Dr. Woodward made an additional contribution to the success of the colony in 1685 when he was gifted with a bag of rice seed brought by a privateer captain, John Thurber, who had sailed his pirate ship to Charleston from the island of Madagascar. This rice seed was the first exposure to the grain in the English colonies and would rapidly become the most important product of the tidewater areas. Within the decade, rice was being used for payments to the proprietors, and by 1700, four hundred thousand pounds were exported annually. This increased to 1.5 million pounds by 1710 and twenty million by 1720. The cultivation of rice, a labor-intensive activity, prompted

---

[124] The Escamacu were a subtribe of the Cusabo Indians, which included groups such as the Edisto, Kiawah, Stono, Wando, and others whose names are associated with towns, islands, and rivers in South Carolina. These Indians were displaced by the Westo, who are thought to be the part of the Erie tribe that was displaced from western New York by war with the Iroquois Confederacy (Beaver Wars) and forced to move south. They were in turn assimilated by the Savannah/Shawnee tribes and in conflict with the other earlier resident tribe, the Yamasee. Warfare with and between these various tribes persisted well into the eighteenth century and were a major threat to the colonists in the Carolinas.

the importation of increased numbers African slaves, who brought their own experience in rice farming. Their methods of planting, harvesting, threshing, and polishing the product greatly improved rice production. The use of tidal flow of coastal rivers to flood rice fields made this an ideal and highly profitable commodity for the South Carolina colony.[125]

Of the eight proprietors of the Colony of Carolina appointed by Charles II, the most active in its development was Anthony Ashley Cooper, known as Lord Shaftesbury after 1672. He arranged in 1670 for ships, including the *Carolina*, to transport the first significant number of settlers from Barbados to what would become Charles Town at the confluence of two rivers named for him, the Ashley and the Cooper. The preceding year, Cooper, with the involvement of John Locke, would produce the *Fundamental Constitutions of Carolina*, approved by the eight proprietors on March 1, 1669. This would attempt to define the governance of the colony and define rights that would make it attractive to prospective colonists and be acceptable to the proprietors and the Crown. Included in the incentives were the toleration of all religious sects but with public support for the Anglican Church; a representative assembly with some powers over taxation but with an outsized degree of control by large landholders; and access to land ownership by settlers with limited means. Many of the settlers came as indentured servants, and the prospect of gaining substantial acreage was a significant enticement. Prior to rice production as a valuable export commodity, the settlers emphasized cattle and sugarcane production and the harvesting of the abundant pine forests for timber and naval stores. In each case, the prosperity of the colony was dependent on the labor of an increasing slave population with continuous tension between the races.

As often noted in our study, the critical shortage of labor in the premechanical agricultural economy made the presence of slaves critical for the success of the colonies. In those colonies able to sustain large-scale commercial agriculture and produce profitable exports,

---

[125] Linscombe, S. The History of U.S. Rice Production—Pr11, LSU AgCenter

slavery as an institution became ingrained in the colony's culture and sustained by their legal systems. There were many colonists from all backgrounds and in all colonies who were aware that slavery was a fundamental moral wrong, but the desire for economic success was clearly a higher trump card. Even colonies with little need for slave labor benefitted greatly from the economic effects of the agricultural wealth, without which the entire colonial venture would not have had the ongoing support of the European homelands so critical for its success in the seventeenth century.

From the distance of several centuries and an awareness of the Civil War disaster that was the ultimate solution to the slavery issue, one can speculate about what might have been done about slavery. Such speculation seems of little value other than realizing that without compromise, the union of states with the Constitution would not have occurred. The issue of what the American culture could or should do about these past wrongs is apparently incompletely resolved and deserves consideration. Some suggestions may be appropriate based on the awareness that the quest for economic success was a motivation for the problem. Wealth in the early days of the colonies and continuing to the past century was significantly associated with the ownership of land. The provision of land to the newly freed slaves at the end of the Civil War was briefly considered, but this was never accepted. The availability of productive public land has greatly changed in recent centuries and is not the unique key to wealth that it had been in earlier days. This source of advancement has been replaced by education, which is now the most reasonable pathway to economic success.

It is my opinion that the consideration of education as an effective pathway to improved economic conditions for a large part of our population requires several changes in political thinking. Just as the availability of land for the initial colonists was a start, the individual had to put a great deal of their own effort and talent into the venture for it to succeed. Just as with all land, "higher education," as it is often currently described, is not equally economically productive. Our society has taken the bait that a college degree is essential for economic success when many college programs, even if they can lead to degrees, are not likely to raise one to a desired economic level alone. It is a reality that not all persons are suited for advanced academic endeavors. Training in skills and crafts in addition to basic academic skills and knowledge may be more likely to lead to productive careers in many cases.

Recent publicity concerning high levels of college debt incurred by students who have no apparent ability to repay must be considered. The commercial loans used to pay tuition charges for student programs that may not be within the students capacity or not leading to productive careers but that yield significant debt are counterproductive. Much more effort should be spent on middle and high school counseling and guiding students into career fields for which they have the appropriate talents and interest. Debt to a public agency could be forgiven or reduced after a period of active employment following completion of their training. It is clear that this would take more than one generation to spread compensation widely, but meaningful social and economic progress in families can rarely be measured in shorter intervals. Similar opportunities should be available to the children of recent legal immigrants and established residents of all races and backgrounds. Such a program could be considered a part of public school systems, and levels of administration could reflect the states' commitments to this and other educational opportunities.

In the seventeenth and early eighteenth centuries, management of the Carolina colony was erratic, and the governance of the growing population in the Albermarle Sound area was difficult due to the distance from Charles Town, the seat of the governor and the assembly. North and South Carolina would not become distinct entities until 1712, but they long had separate assemblies, the north led by a lieutenant governor, while the governor presided in Charles Town.

Distance was not the only hurdle causing conflict in the colony. Issues between the Anglicans and Nonconformists and between the large land owners and the many small land owners and tradesmen were disruptive. Another concern of all residents was the continuous threat of attacks from the Indian tribes, the Spanish with their substantial forces in Florida and the Caribbean, pirates who threatened the coastal settlements, and the danger of a slave rebellion, which was always a threat and became a reality in 1739.[126]

Throughout the proprietorship era, there was never adequate support of a military presence to meaningfully protect the growing population. Wars in the northern colony with the Tuscarora tribe and with the Yamasee in the south in 1712–16 were costly, with the latter being as bloody as King Philip's War had been in New England. Conflicts within the elected assembly and the need for military protection led to a bloodless revolt by the South Carolina assembly against the proprietors in 1719. A delegation was sent to England to urge the Crown to replace the proprietors. What likely was decisive in the ending of the proprietorship in the Carolinas were economic factors that gained the attention of the Crown. First was the inability of the English authorities to impose the Navigation Acts in Carolina and the awareness that enhancement and control of the supply of naval stores could make the English a preeminent naval and mercantile force. An attempt of the Crown to gain support of Parliament for vacating the charters was refused due to an unwillingness to tamper with property rights. It was clear that the proprietors would need compensation for their contracts.

In 1729, the Crown bought out seven of the proprietors and appointed Robert Johnson as the governor—a position he had popularly held during the last years of the proprietorship. One of his first solutions was to establish frontier townships that would increase the immigrant population and establish a militia that would provide for their defense.[127] Governor Johnson's instructions were to establish townships about sixty miles inland on navigable rivers. These were a square about six miles on each side, with about twenty thousand acres, for families that would settle near each other. Each family would receive a town lot and fifty acres of outlying land for

---

[126] Weir, R.M., pp.193-4, Colonial South Carolina—A History, This Stone Rebellion was the largest slave rebellion in the colonial period.

[127] Weir, R.M. pp. 105–116.

each family member. The assembly agreed to provide the necessary survey, transportation for the settlers and the waiving of quitrents for the first ten years.[128]

This was highly successful in expanding the European population of the colony and attracted many non-English settlers, including Scottish, Irish (mainly from Ulster), French, German, and Welsh (about 9 percent). Our immigrant family was among this population in a group of thirty-five families moving from the second Welsh Tract of the Pennsylvania colony, led by James James, Esq., with his sons and an in-law, Johannes Kolb, and their children and livestock (sections I, E and IV, D). As previously noted, the favorable publicity about the prospects for settlers in Carolina expressed in Benjamin Franklin's *Pennsylvania Gazette* may have been a factor in their decision to immigrate. They settled in a township known as the Welsh Neck in the Cheraw District on the Greater Pee Dee River, where Kolb would operate a mill and ferry. The expanding population was mainly occupied with raising livestock and providing naval stores, which were made profitable by new incentives provided by Parliament in 1729. This community would establish the Welsh Neck Baptist Church in 1738, and its first pastor was a son of James James, Esq., the Rev. Philip James, who married Ann Kolb, daughter of Johannes. Over the years, this Cheraw District community would grow, and the need for educational opportunities for their children led to the formation of the St. David Society, which provided a school.[129] As the population increased, the settlement became known as Society Hill, and the town became a commercial center for the area and a circuit court for St. David's Parish.

As religion was of importance to the individuals and the families described in this work, it is significant that the 1730s, the time of the First Great Awakening, was a prominent period in the colonial era and in their story (see section IV, M). It was certain that this spiritual revival

---

[128] Ibid, pp. 105–116.

[129] The name St. David, patron saint of Wales, represented a remnant of their Welsh heritage, which was transient, as by the second generation, there were no apparent speakers of the Welsh language in their area.

had an impact on those who moved from the Pennsylvania colony to the Cheraw District of South Carolina and on their Welsh Neck Baptist Church. The noted historian, now professor emeritus at the University of South Carolina, Robert M. Weir, in his comprehensive history specifically refers to these Welsh Neck Baptists:

"Although the Great Awakening had relatively little effect among blacks in South Carolina, it was more important than historians sometimes realize, perhaps because its permanent effects tended to be localized while its general impact was temporary. Yet among the Baptists from Delaware who settled on the Pee Dee River in 1737, the Awakening was a vital ideal, and, significantly, their church had a substantial number of black members by the 1770s. Tax returns also indicate that this area contained perhaps the largest number of free blacks."[130]

It is uncertain how or when the Great Awakening came to the Welsh Neck Baptist Church, which was established in 1738, and specifically to its first pastor, Rev. Philip James, who was ordained April 4, 1743. According to Weir, "as in so many other places, the Great Awakening came to South Carolina in the person of the most famous itinerant evangelist of the eighteenth century, George Whitefield. A great orator and a shrewd operator, Whitefield concentrated his efforts on cities where he reached the maximum number of people and where his criticism of supposedly unregenerate Anglican clergymen appealed to local dissenters who resented the privileged position of the established church. During several visits to Charles Town in the late 1730s and early 1740s, he preached to large sympathetic audiences."[131]

Whitefield had been closely associated with the Wesleys at

---

[130] Op. cit. Weir, R.M. page 186. The second Welsh Tract created by William Penn in his colony was later a part of the colony and state of Delaware.
[131] Ibid. page 220.

Oxford, and in 1738, he replaced John Wesley as the parish priest at Savannah in the new colony of Georgia. He returned to England in 1739 to raise funds for his Bethesda Orphanage, and on his return in 1740, he began an extensive evangelistic tour by horseback from New York to Charles Town. Whitefield preached nearly daily to large crowds, such as his sermon to two thousand on the grounds of the Pennepack Baptist Church in Germantown (gallery, figure 7). This church was well known to the James/Kolb families, but by then, they had moved to the Welsh Neck in the Cheraw District. Whitefield preached extensively in the Charles Town area, and his influence was certainly felt in the Welsh Neck.

One of the most important effects of the First Great Awakening was the inclusion of the slave population in these evangelistic efforts and their inclusion and subsequent active roles in the congregations. As noted by Weir and confirmed by the records of the Welsh Neck Baptist Church, many blacks were on the roles and were full participants in the activities of the church. The white population was encouraged to provide literacy for the slaves, and the reports of the subsequent generation of the Kolb families indicate that this was the case (section IV, D). Further information concerning the effects of the Great Awakening on the culture of the South Carolina colony, including the impact on the settlers the Welsh Neck area, is discussed in sections IV, D ("Additional Information about the Family of Johannes Kolb") and in V, M ("The Great Awakening").

PART IV

APPENDIX: ADDITIONAL INFORMATION ABOUT THE COLONIAL INDIVIDUALS AND OTHER DOCUMENTATION

A. JOHN DENMAN I AND JUDITH STOUGHTON OF NOTTINGHAMSHIRE, ENGLAND

John Denman II was born in 1621 in West Retford, Nottinghamshire, and came to the Massachusetts Bay Colony in 1635 with his mother and two siblings. They would join his mother's relatives who had preceded them and later welcome others who later made the journey to North America. Their extended family would be significant additions to the English population. His father, John Denman I, born in 1591, died when John II was two years old. His grandfather, Rev. Francis Denman, had been the rector of West Retford Church from 1579 to 1596 and was a son of Rev. Nicholas Denman and Lady Anne Hercy.[132]

John Denman I and his wife, Judith Stoughton, had two children, John II, born January 1621, and a daughter, Mary, born December 1621. After John I died in 1623, Judith married William Smead, having another son, William Smead II, born in 1627. By the next year, Judith was a widow for the second time, and in 1635, she and her three children, ages eight to fourteen, sailed for New England. They would join her two brothers, Thomas Stoughton Jr. and Israel Stoughton, who had sailed in 1630 to the Massachusetts Bay Colony with John Winthrop's first convoy, accompanied by their twelve-year-old nephew, John Scudder II.

Judith and her children sailed from Gravesend on the ship *Dorset*, captained by John Flower, on September 3, 1635. After a stop in Barbados in the West Indies, they arrived in Boston in that year. Other than the needs of a young family without a father, another factor in their move to New England was the upheaval in the religious life in England and Wales. This resulted from conflicts between the Church of England and the Christians who were sympathetic to the Reformed theology of the Puritans and other forms of nonconformity of the Calvinist, Congregationalist, and Baptist traditions. Tumult in the religious climate of England significantly affected the Stoughton

---

[132] Harris, Harriet N., 1913. pp. 1–17. It is reported that p,

family, causing all but one of Judith Stoughton's five siblings to immigrate to the Massachusetts Bay Colony.

Thomas Jr., Judith, Elizabeth, and Israel Stoughton were children of Rev. Thomas Stoughton and his wife, Katherine Montpesson, and are significant figures in our story of the Massachusetts Bay Colony. These children were born between 1586 and 1603 during Rev. Stoughton's service as rector of parishes in Suffolk and Essex. He had been educated at Cambridge and influenced by Reformed teachings. During these Elizabethan years, he became increasingly interested in what would later be known as Congregationalism. In 1600, he was appointed the parish priest of St. Peter ad Vincula Church (St. Peter in Chains) in Coggeshall, Essex. Their last child, Israel, was born in 1603, and two months later, Katherine died.

In 1606, early in his reign, King James I was reasserting the authority of the Anglican Church following the more lenient dealings with religious diversity of Queen Elizabeth I. Rev. Thomas Stoughton was removed from the vicarage in Coggeshall, likely because of his nonconformist teachings. Historical records do not clearly delineate his activities following his dismissal, but in 1610, he married Elizabeth Knight, a widow with five children. Their blended family would become more intertwined as her daughter, also named Elizabeth Knight, would marry his son Israel Stoughton in 1627 before their move to the Massachusetts Bay Colony in 1630. Rev. Thomas Stoughton had financial reverses and treatises written in 1616 and 1622, indicating that he was living at the Hospital of St. Bartholomew, Sandwich, Kent, where he likely served as chaplain. St. Bart's was an ancient hostel for travelers and pilgrims; the name indicated its role of providing hospitality to those in need.

The Rev. John Stoughton was the only surviving child of Rev. Thomas Stoughton who did not move to New England. He had a successful career as an Anglican minister following his education at Emmanuel College, Cambridge. He and his associates were actively involved in the religious and philosophical life of England, and although he was suspected of nonconformity, he avoided serious controversy.

In 1630, the families of two Stoughton sons, Thomas Jr. and Israel, and their young nephew, John Scudder II, sailed to the Massachusetts Bay Colony in the convoy led by Gov. John Winthrop on the first voyage of the ship *Mary and John*. Thomas Jr., whose wife had died prior to the time of the voyage, settled in Dorchester with his three children. He became a leader of the Dorchester community, being named a freeman (full church membership with secular voting rights), served on the General Court and as the constable. In 1635, he married a widow, Margaret Barrett Huntington, the mother of five children. In 1636, they and their eight children moved to Windsor in the Connecticut River Valley, where records indicate that he was a significant landowner. During the next two decades, he wrote at least two theological treatises, which were sent to Gov. John Winthrop.

Israel Stoughton and his wife, Elizabeth Knight, and their children also settled in Dorchester, where he prospered in the mercantile business and represented Dorchester as a deputy to the colony's governing body in Boston. He held military and governmental positions, but his public career would be delayed when he became involved in a controversy with the General Court in Boston. Israel wrote a pamphlet concluding that the General Court should not have the authority to veto rulings of the local Dorchester leadership. In his scholarly study of the times, Emery John Battis describes him as "the strenuously independent deputy from Dorchester," and his "challenging of the primacy of the governor and magistrates" was a greater assault on their authority than was acceptable. Israel was admonished and disabled from holding office for three years at the same time that John Endicott of Salem was punished for insisting that the royal flag of the colony be altered by eliminating the cross from the standard, as it was "a popish symbol."[133] Political controversy was common in the Massachusetts colony and encouraged Rev. Thomas Hooker and one hundred of his Newtown (Cambridge) congregation to move to Windsor in 1635. Israel Stoughton had recanted the ideas that were displeasing to the Puritan authorities, and all copies of his

---

[133] Battis;, E.J. Saints and Sectaries, pp 81-2.

pamphlet were destroyed. Stoughton's punishment was rescinded within a year, as his services were required by the colony to command the Massachusetts contingent in the Pequot War in 1636 (see part III.B. for details).

He later served with John Endicott in settling a boundary dispute with Plymouth Colony and his extended family prospered in the Dorchester community. Israel Stoughton returned to England in 1644 to aid the army of Oliver Cromwell, serving as lieutenant colonel of an artillery company in the regiment of Colonel Thomas Rainsborough.[134] Stoughton never returned to New England, as he died in 1645 in the town of Lincoln, where his father had been ordained as an Anglican deacon and priest in 1582.

Israel Stoughton's extended family that remained in New England contributed to the colony's religious and secular life as well as its population. Notable were his son William[135] and three daughters who married and lived in the Dorchester area, Susanna (married George Starkey), Hannah (married James Minot), and Rebecca (married William Tailer). The siblings of Israel's wife, Elizabeth Knight Stoughton, also had settled in New England and included Ursula Knight, who married David Yale. Their son, Elihu, would become a successful merchant, governor of the East India Company, and benefactor of the Collegiate School of Connecticut, which would be renamed in his honor in 1718.[136]

The third member of the Stoughton family to come to New England was Judith Stoughton Denman Smead with her three

---

[134] Bailyn, B. The Barbarous Years, p. 474.

[135] Israel Stoughton married Elizabeth Knight, the daughter of his stepmother, also named Elizabeth, and Stoughton's wife's family all moved to Massachusetts Bay Colony in 1632–34. His son, William Stoughton, was born in England in 1630, graduated from Harvard, and returned to England, graduating with an MA from New College, Oxford, in 1653. Following the restoration, he was forced to return to New England, where he served in a number of positions, including lieutenant governor, and presided over the court constituted for the trial of the Salem witches. He died unmarried and left his estate to Harvard, founding Stoughton Hall, which continues to bear his name.

[136] Dexter, F.B., Documentary History of Yale University, Press.

children, fourteen, thirteen, and eight years of age. They arrived in 1635 and settled in Dorchester but soon moved to Salem, where she was listed as a church member and property owner. Records indicate that she died in March 1639 in Salem, her estate was administered by her brother, Israel, and bequests were made to each of her three children.

Her oldest son, John Denman II, married Sarah Hollander in 1643 at Dorchester, Suffolk County,[137] and they lived in Salem, raising three sons, John III, William, and Philip. During the last half of the seventeenth century, the family of John II moved permanently to Long Island. It is unknown if they were with other members of their extended family moving in 1651 from Salem to Southold in eastern Long Island, then a part of the Connecticut colony, or if they came directly to New Netherland. By 1660, John Denman II and his family and relatives, John Scudder II and Richard Betts, were located near the Maspeth area in the western part of Long Island in the Dutch colony.

Judith's second child, Mary Denman, married Clement Maxfield in 1639 or 1640, had a son, Samuel Maxfield, and six grandchildren. She died in Dorchester in 1707. Clement Maxfield fought in King Philip's War and lived until 1692. Judith's third child, William Smead II, was twelve years old when she died, and he was apprenticed to John Pope, a weaver in Dorchester who provided for him and taught him his trade. William II would marry Elizabeth Lawrence in 1658, and they had nine children, all of whom married and had families. He served in King Philip's War, as did his eldest son, William III, who died in the Bloody Brook Massacre on September 18, 1675. This war was also known as the First Indian War or Metacom's Rebellion, and it had profound effects on the New England colonies (see section III, B).

Elizabeth Stoughton Scudder Chamberlain was the younger sister of Judith and the last of their clan to come to New England.

---

[137] It is uncertain if her family name was actually Hollander or if that was a description of the origin of her family, which seems more likely, as no other people with that surname in the colony have been identified.

Elizabeth's arrival date is uncertain but was likely 1640, when she brought her daughters Elizabeth Scudder and Joanna Chamberlain and her son Samuel Chamberlain to join her eldest son, John Scudder II, in Massachusetts Bay Colony. He was thought to have come with his uncles, Thomas and Israel Stoughton, in 1630, when he would have been twelve years old. Elizabeth and her first husband, John Scudder I, had married in 1613, having two children, Elizabeth and Thomas, who both died in infancy, a son, John Scudder II, born in 1618, and a daughter, Elizabeth Scudder, born in 1625. Her first husband died in 1625, and she married Robert Chamberlain in 1627, giving birth to Samuel in 1628 and Joanna in 1630. Robert Chamberlain died in 1639, shortly before the family sailed for New England.

The activities of John Scudder II and his sisters are difficult to document and are confused by the given names of John and Elizabeth used in multiple families and generations. Genealogists agree that the children of Elizabeth Stoughton Scudder Chamberlain who survived to adulthood included Elizabeth Scudder (born 1625), who married Samuel Lathrop (November 28, 1644) and died in Norwich, Connecticut, in 1682; Samuel Chamberlain (born 1628), who died in Massachusetts in 1649 without marrying; and Joanna Chamberlain (born 1630), who married Richard Betts in 1649 in Ipswich, Massachusetts. By 1652, Richard and Joanna had moved to Long Island, and he is listed as an original settler of Newtown, New Netherland. Due to controversy with Pieter Stuyvesant, he and others purchased land from the Indian sachems Pomwaukon and Rowerowestco, gaining title to Newtown. He served as magistrate, member of the High Court, and was an extensive land owner in the English Kills area. After the succession of the English, he was a delegate to the Provincial Assembly held in Hempstead in 1665, and at his death in 1713, Rev. Thomas Poyer, the rector of the Episcopal Churches of Newtown, Jamaica, and Flushing, wrote the burial notice: *"Richard Betts of Newtown, age 100 at ye Kills."* It should be noted that survival to age one hundred in the seventeenth century was most unlikely, and confusion of the names of various settlers was likely, as the Anglican hierarchy was responsible for the records. As the Betts, Scudders, and Denman families worshiped at the Reformed Church, they may not have been well known to Rev. Poyer. Similar confusion is described in the ages and names of settlers with the surname of Gano in section I, D and IV, C. Richard Betts and Joanna had seven children and numerous descendants.

Records indicate that the Scudder family had one or more individuals with the surname John in each generation and that there were two such close relatives among the early Puritans of New England. The abovementioned John Scudder II was the son of John Scudder I and Elizabeth Stoughton Scudder Chamberlain and grandson of Henry Scudder and Elizabeth Hale. John II and his wife, Hannah, were married in 1645 and lived at Barnstable until his death in 1690. There is no record of his living in the Long Island area.

His cousin, also John Scudder, the son of Thomas Scudder (brother of Henry), came to Salem in 1635 with his parents and five siblings, where he would own land. He and Mary King married in 1642 and were on the role of the Salem Church in 1647. In 1651, John and Mary, along with two of his brothers and other Puritans from Salem, sailed to Southold on the eastern end of Long Island. This settlement was established as a part of the New Haven Colony in 1640 by Rev. John Youngs, a minister of the Salem Church. Southold is the oldest English town, and their church is the second oldest in what is now New York. John and Mary remained in Southold until 1657, when they moved, and by 1660, they were prominent residents of Newtown. It was this John Scudder who along with John Denman II and Richard Betton (sic. Betts) are mentioned in the *Old Brooklyn Records,* where it is noted that "John Denman [presumed to be John II], with John Scudder [his cousin], John Coe, Richard Betton] sic. Betts—also a relative as the husband of Joanna Chamberlain, daughter of Elizabeth Stoughton Scudder Chamberlain], Samuel Toe, George Sergeant, and Thomas Reede purchased land from the Indian Chiefs, Wamatupa, Wozone and Powatahuman on 3 Oct

1662.[138] This was a neck of meadow land commonly called by the English, 'Plunder's Neck,' and was known as the English Kills. It lay on the south side of Long Island, bounded on the east side by the river Hohosboco, with a small brook on the west, running into the river."

It is thought that this is the same river today known as Newtown Creek, as one of its tributaries is the English Kills. The Denmans lived in the Maspeth area, but both John II and Sarah are reported to have died in Long Island City, a village at the entrance of Newtown Creek into the East River, which included the area of Maspeth. It is known that John II died there in 1691. The locations of the Newtown Creek and Long Island City are indicated on the previous maps of the area. Newtown Creek is still prominent on Long Island, as it marks a part of the boundary between Brooklyn and Queens, New York City. In the mid-seventeenth century, this was likely a pristine stream flowing through virgin forest, but the succeeding centuries have turned it into an industrial waterway, which is one of the most contaminated streams in the country. Figure 1 (gallery) is a view downstream toward East River and Manhattan. Looking upstream, the heavy industrial use of the area is evident. The Newtown Creek has been included as a superfund site by the EPA for possible remediation.

On September 8, 1664, New Amsterdam ceased to exist after the Second Anglo-Dutch War, and the territory became New York. The land titles of the Dutch colony were annulled, and records of what happened to the Denman land have not been located. The next evidence of the Denman family on Long Island is found in the office of the county clerk in Jamaica, Long Island, where it is recorded that "In pursuance of said license, in same year, did in due form of law purchase of and from Indian natives all that tract of land situated between Maspeth Hills and Flushing Creek, on Long Island, to hold unto the said inhabitants of Newtown forever; as by a certain deed or writing under the hand and seal of Powanhon, dated July 9, 1665."

---

[138] More information about the Stoughton extended family is presented in section IV.

This was signed by John Denman and Samuel and John Scudder Jr. It seems likely that this was John Denman III who lived in Newtown, Queens, Long Island, with his wife, Mary Gano (Gaineau), following their marriage in 1690.

Newtown, now known as Elmhurst, located between Maspeth and Flushing Creek in present-day Queens, is evident on local maps. Flushing Creek is now mainly contained in an underground storm sewer but, where evident, is not restored. The adjacent area, however, is part of Flushing Meadows Park, the home of the US Tennis Center and the US Open. John and Mary Denman worshipped at the Reformed Church in Newtown (Gallery, Figure 2). Because of the disputed ownership of these lands and the strict religious laws imposed by the English governor with taxation to support the Anglican Church, John III obtained property in Westfield, Essex County, Colony of New Jersey, in about 1703. He continued living in Newtown, where he was appointed surveyor of highways on April 6, 1708. The English government had seized 1,200 acres of the original property, leaving only 170 acres to the Denmans. John Denman III died in 1713 and was buried in Newtown. His will was recorded in abstracts of early wills of Queens County, New York: "Denman, John of Newtown 13 Dec 1714 [sic. 1713]. Estate to wife Mary during widowhood, with remainder to sons John, William, Phillip & Thomas; personal est. to daus. Martha, mary & Elizabeth; to son John my musket as a birthright. Exrs: wife Mary & my brother-in-law Jeremiah genoung [sic. Gano] of Flushing. Wits: Samuel Schuder [sic. Scudder], Jacob reeder, & John Gunnell. Pro. 1 March 1714." Jeremiah Gano, Mary's brother and an executor of the estate, lived in Newtown his entire life but never married.

The property was sold in 1717 by his heirs to Richard Hallett, and Denman's family moved permanently to New Jersey. Their sons, John IV (born 1700), William (born 1702), Philip (born 1704), and Thomas (born 1706 or '07), and daughters, Martha, Mary, and Elizabeth (dates of birth not available), all settled and raised families in the Elizabeth, Westfield, and Springfield areas of Essex County,

Colony of New Jersey.[139] Each had large families, and most were living in that area at the time of the American Revolution. A number of their family members were involved in the War for American Independence, and after the war, many moved to the Midwest (Ohio) and the South (Georgia).[140]

B. PIETER CLAESSEN WYCKOFF AND GRIETJE VAN NESS OF THE NETHERLANDS

Pieter Claessen arrived in the Dutch colony of New Netherlands in 1637 as a youth unaccompanied by any family. His date of birth is unknown, but he is thought to have been in his midteen years when he made this life-changing journey. The identity and fate of his parents and the location of his birth are also uncertain, but it is likely that both parents died in the plague epidemic that swept the Low Country, killing many thousands in 1635–36. His father's name was Claes, and the name Pieter Claessen indicates that he was Claes's son. The name Wyckoff was adopted later in his life and was consistently used in deeds and other documents and by his offspring after the English assumed control of New York and required the former New Netherland residents to use a family name in public documents. Careful research by Professor M. William Wykoff has shown that Pieter chose the family name of Wyckoff due to his coming from an area known as the Wyckhof estate, near the town of Norden in the province of Ostfriesland (East Frisia) in Lower Saxony, now a part of Germany.[141] Earlier genealogists had suggested that he assumed the name of Wyckoff from the Dutch words "wijk" (parish) and "hof" (court) when he was named the magistrate of the town court of Flatlands, and this is stated on a plaque in the Flatlands Reformed Church (Gallery, Figure 4). That conclusion had always been questionable, as he held that position only for several years,

---

[139] See appendix VI, C for information about the children of Mary Gano Denman.
[140] Harris, Harriet N. p.11–13.
[141] Wykoff, M.W. What's in a Name? History and Meaning of Wyckoff, 2014.

as did others from their community, and Pieter Claessen's family members are the only ones using the name Wyckoff.

Pieter Claessen's journey to New Netherland and his activities during the years that he lived in Beverwiick are much more certain. We know that he sailed on the ship *Rennselarwich* from the log records, which state that they "sailed from Amsterdam, Holland on 25 Sept 1636 and on Tuesday, 7 April 1637, about three o'clock in the morning came to anchor ferore foort acranien (the end of our journey upward)." This was a very difficult voyage, as noted in the introductory section, which is described in detail in the log record.

Pieter was assigned to Simone Waischez for a six-year term of indenture, to receive fifty guilders per year for the first three and seventy-five guilders for the last three years. After his arrival in New Amsterdam, Pieter continued up the Hudson River to area of Fort Orange and the frontier town of Beverwijck, a fur-trading community to its north, near the present city of Albany, New York. He worked for Simone Waischez until 1643, when he would have completed his term of service. Pieter would rent property in his own name and likely took over the tract on which he had worked for Simone Waischez, who was dismissed for not being an adequate manager. Pieter must have learned farming skills and a sense of responsibility and within two years married Grietje van Ness. Grietje was the daughter of Cornelis Hendrick van Ness and his wife, Maycke Hendrick van Der Burchgraeff. Although Pieter was of a lower social strata than the van Ness family, he and Cornelis both were native speakers of the Frisian language and developed close ties as Pieter became the manager of farming activities for both families.

Cornelis was well educated and a brewer by occupation who was often involved in public matters. The court records of Rensselaerwyck between 1648 and 1650 list numerous conflicts between the director of Rensselearwyck, Brant van Slichtenhorst, and both Pieter and Cornelis. Some of these issues were related to business transactions, but many seem to be the result of personal conflicts with the contentious director.[142] Van Slichtenhorst exceeded political boundaries when he proceeded to develop the town of Beverwyck closer to Fort Orange than had been the requirement of the general director, Pieter Stuyvesant. The directors of the individual patroonships in the colony had acquired a sense of independence from the colony director since the lenient approach of Peter Minuit, the director from 1626 to 1631. The colony general director had full political authority and was appointed by the Dutch West India Company. Stuyvesant, who happened to also be a native speaker of Frisian, was supported by van Ness and Pieter Claessen and eventually would arrest and deport van Slichtenhorst. In the midst of these controversies, Pieter and Grietje (June 5, 1649) permanently leave Rensselaerwyck with their two children and move to New Amsterdam.

Two children were born while the family was living in Rensselaerwyck, Claes Pieterse (Nicholas) and Margarietje.[143] By 1650, their family had relocated to the New Amsterdam area of Long Island and the community of Flatlands then known as Nieuw Amersfoort. Nine other children were born there between 1650 and 1665. Pieter signed a contract to superintend the farm and cattle of Peter Stuyvesant. In 1652, Pieter and Grietje obtained their own farm, which had a building begun by the former owner, Wouter van Twiller, the colony director from 1633 to 1638. On this farm, they would have raised beans, corn, and tobacco, skills that the Dutch had learned from the indigenous Lenape tribesmen. The home was occupied by their descendants for many generations and still exists today as the Fidler-Wyckoff House in Brooklyn, New York, the oldest surviving structure in New York City (Gallery, Figure 3).

The Wyckoff home is located at 5816 Clarendon Road in Brooklyn. The name *Canarsie* is derived from the language of the Lenape Indians, who were the native inhabitants of that part of western Long Island. The Lenape natives were part of the Algonquian

---

[142] – translated and edited by A.J.F. van Lear, University of the State of New York, Albany 1922 and quoted in the WikiTree website –

[143] The records of their marriage and the christening of these two children were lost to a fire in the Beverwyck church.

language group and were called the Delaware by the Europeans. The word *canarsie* is the Lenape word for fenced land or fort. The Lenape clans that were indigenous to the forests and fields of Long Island were well known to the Europeans who had located to the area in the early to mid-seventeenth century.

Pieter was one of the founders of the Dutch Reformed Church of Flatlands in 1654, which was formed by the outreach efforts of the Collegiate Church in Manhattan to the rural population living in the countryside of Flatlands (Nieuw Amersfoort) and Brooklyn (Breuckelen) (Gallery, Figure 5).

This mother church has had several names and locations over the years and is now known as the Collegiate Reformed Protestant Dutch Church or the Marble Collegiate Church located on Fifth Avenue at Twenty-Ninth Street. In recent times, the church has been well known as the church of Dr. Norman Vincent Peale, author of *The Power of Positive Thinking.*

Pieter became a significant landowner in New Amersfoort and served terms as the magistrate of the town court. As previously noted, he and his sons signed an oath of allegiance when the colony became New York, and that document was the first record of the use of the surname Wyckoff, which was consistently used by descendants in subsequent years. The children of Pieter and Grietje married spouses from the Dutch community and were prominent members of the colonial era. The next generations were often found in the Colony of New Jersey as well as New York. Pieter died on June 30, 1694, and Grietje died around 1701, and both are buried in the church cemetery in a plot now covered by the sanctuary building.

For additional information concerning the immediate descendants of Pieter and Grietje and the large numbers of members of subsequent generations, one should consult the book by W. F. Wyckoff and M. B. Streeter, *The Wyckoff Family in America. A Genealogy.*

C. MARIE GAINEAU (GANO) OF LA ROCHELLE, FRANCE

Marie Gaineau and her brother Jeremie came from La Rochelle, France, to the English Colony of New York with their father, Francis Gaineau, after the revocation of the Edict of Nantes in 1686. The events that directly affected the Gaineau family are known only by tradition, but as a prosperous merchant, Francis Gaineau would have been in peril in the France of Louis XIV. The story of their escape and their journey via London to the Colony of New York is described in section I, D. Many Huguenot families arrived in New York in 1686–87. Although there had been Protestant Christians fleeing France over several decades when the regime of Louis XIV had intensified the persecution of those not adhering to the beliefs of the Roman Church, these increasing numbers gained the attention of Jacob Leisler. As a leader in the New York colony who shared their Reformed faith and their concern about the potential effects of the reign of King James II on their freedom to worship, Leisler was instrumental in obtaining the land that would become New Rochelle and the home for Huguenots arriving in this post-revocation time.[144]

Among the names of these early residents seen on the plaque of Huguenot Family Names in Hudson Park is *Gaineau*, although the identity of the persons so represented has been questioned (Gallery, Figure 6). Francis Gaineau and his children, Marie and Jeremie, are the only individuals in that immediate family, according to reliable records, to have settled in New Rochelle at the founding of the community. There is confusion with another family from La Rochelle, France, with the *Gaineau* surname that sailed to America in 1661 and settled in Staten Island. This family included Etienne (Stephen) Gaineau, his wife, Lydia Mestereau, and three children, Stephen II (born 1654), Lidie (born 1657/58), and Marie (born 1660). They would have at least four more children born in New York, and

---

[144] See part I, D for information about King James II and the Dominion of New England, which represented significant changes in the structure of these English colonies and the concerns about his sympathy for the Roman Church.

they remained in Staten Island for the next generation and beyond. One of the grandchildren of Etienne and Lydia named Francis, born in 1688 in Staten Island, lived in New Rochelle later in his life. He was not of the family of Marie Gano, who would marry John Denman III and live in the Newtown (Elmhurst) area of Long Island with their seven children, as described in part I, B. Jeremie Gano, the brother of Marie (Mary) Gano, would also live in that area but would never marry, and no subsequent descendants of this family would carry the Gano name.

Among the descendants of Etienne Gaineau and Lydia Mestereau were a number of well-known citizens of the colony, including the Rev. John Gano, who would serve as the founding pastor of the First Baptist Church in New York, a chaplain for the Continental Army, and an original trustee of what later was known as Brown University in Rhode Island. As an evangelist, he traveled widely throughout the colonies and late in life lived in Kentucky, where he and Daniel Boone are buried in Frankfort. Other notable descendants include generals in the Civil War serving both the Confederacy and the Union armies. Richard M. Gano (1830–1913), the grandson of a War of 1812 general, was a physician who would serve as a Confederate brigadier general after serving in the Texas legislature when he was a rancher in the Dallas/Fort Worth area. His granddaughter was the mother of Howard Hughes, a billionaire industrialist, aviation entrepreneur, and motion picture tycoon. Another descendant was Vice-Admiral Roy A. Gano (1902–1971), whose US Navy career spanned forty years with numerous honors. Another factor that confuses the identity of these Huguenot families is the various spellings of the name *Gaineau* in colonial records and the frequent use of the Anglicized name *Gano*.

The surviving descendants of Francis Gaineau were children of his daughter Marie Gaineau, who married John Denman III in 1690 when she was twenty-seven years old. John was forty-seven years old when they married, and the family lived in the Newtown/Elmhurst area of Long Island, where they worshiped at the Newtown Reformed Church. We know from sections II, B and IV, A that the

Denmans and their close relatives had lived in Long Island since the 1650s and had purchased property from the Lenape. When the English gained control from the Dutch, this property was lost, and John Denman III obtained property in the new Colony of New Jersey. He and his family remained in New York, where he had responsibilities for road construction and where he died in 1713.

Mary Gano Denman moved her family of six children to Elizabethtown, Essex County, in New Jersey in 1717 after his estate was settled and the remaining 170 acres sold to Richard Hallett for "the sum of three hundred and fifty pounds current money of the Colony of New York, well and truly paid."[145] The family included three daughters, Martha, Mary, and Elizabeth. The dates of their births are not known, but Martha married John Cory in 1733, and they lived in the community of Westfield only a few miles from Elizabethtown. They raised seven children, worshiped at the Presbyterian Church where he was an elder, and are buried in its churchyard. The other daughters of Mary Gano and John Denman III married and lived in Elizabethtown.

Their four sons were John IV (born 1700), William (born 1702), Philip (born 1704), and Thomas (born 1706/7). John IV obtained a farm in Westfield in 1720, and within a year, he married Mary Williams, whose family had come from Wales. They had two daughters, Mary and Jennie, and four sons, John V, Joseph, Daniel, and Christopher. William lived in Elizabethtown and died in 1751, leaving no record of family. Philip and Thomas lived in Springfield in western Essex County and over the next two generations had numerous descendants. Some of these men served in the American War for Independence and afterward joined the great westward movement, especially to Ohio and Georgia.

Details of the occupations of these families is undocumented, but they had sizable properties and were certainly involved in farming and cattle raising. It is probable that some of them had slaves, as this had been introduced by the Dutch West India Company in 1625 and

---

[145] Harris, H.N., 1913.

was especially prevalent in areas such as the New Jersey colony with their predominant agricultural economy. It was not until 1804 that the state of New Jersey adopted laws gradually abolishing slavery.

An interesting part of the story of these American colonists is the large numbers of children born to these families and who survived to adulthood. Although the immigration of Europeans continued, the percentage of native born people greatly increased during the early eighteenth century.

D. JOHANNES KOLB OF THE ELECTORAL PALATINATE, GERMANY

The story of the immigration of Johannes Kolb and his brothers to the Colony of Pennsylvania in 1707 begins with their maternal grandfather, Peter Schumacher. He had been a Mennonite living in the Palatinate village of Kriegsheim, a short distance north of the Kolb home in Wolfsheim. Peter and his wife, Sarah Hendricks, had a daughter Agnes, born in 1652 who was their fifth child, and she married Dielman Kolb in 1670. The children of Agnes and Dielman included Johannes and his brothers, Martin, Jacob, and Heinrich Kolb, who sailed to Pennsylvania in 1707 after the death of their mother in 1705. Peter Schumacher preceded his grandsons to Penn's Colony by twenty years, arriving in Philadelphia in August 1685, sailing from London on the ship *Francis and Dorothy* with his son Peter Jr. and daughters Mary, Frances, and Gertrude and his niece Sarah, the daughter of his brother George.

The Schumacher family had been Mennonites until Peter and George converted to the Quaker faith in 1659 when William Ames and George Rolfe came to Kriegsheim preaching the Quaker doctrines of George Fox, the English founder of the sect. In 1663, the brothers' cows were taken in payment of fines imposed for their refusal to support the established church, as the Quakers, unlike the Mennonites, refused all payment of taxes to the church or state. These two Protestant sects had much in common, including belief in strict pacifism, in the separation of spiritual and secular duties, and that outward behavior of the believers was evidence of their salvation. William Penn visited Kriegsheim in 1682 to encourage them to join his new colony in the province of Pennsylvania. Peter and his family sailed from London with a group of thirty-three Germans, mostly Quakers from the Rhineland city of Krefeld, and would be joined by his brothers George and Jacob.[146]

Another German who converted to the Quaker faith was Francis Daniel Pastorius, a wealthy and well connected young man with a legal and academic background. He had traveled to Philadelphia representing a group of Frankfurt Quakers and obtained from William Penn a warrant for a fifteen-thousand-acre tract at a time when the Krefeld group had obtained a similar warrant.

On their arrival in the colony and with the awareness that the Frankfurt Quakers would not be emigrating, Pastorius negotiated an agreement with William Penn to designate a suitable tract for the German-speaking arrivals. As the Welsh Tract was a precedent for this, they agreed on a six-thousand-acre tract four miles north of Philadelphia. This was level ground suitable for their agricultural efforts and with access by two navigable creeks, the Wissahickon and Wingohocking. Most of the thirteen families were skilled tradesmen with little farming experience. The first winter, they lived in the city while clearing their land in preparation for planting. The spring of 1686 saw them build log structures that would be their homes in the new village of Germantown.

In 1691, sixty-four Germantown residents were declared to be Freemen (full citizens of England and the colony) when they pledged allegiance to William and Mary, king and queen of England. Among those listed were Francis Daniel Pastorius, Peter Schumacher Sr., Peter Schumacher Jr., Jacob Schumacher, and several with the surname of Op de Graef. In 1697, Peter Schumacher Jr. and Margaret Op de Graeff were married, and among the witnesses were Peter Sr., George and Jacob Schumacher, Francis Daniel Pastorius, and others.

---

[146] Jordan John W. p. 435, 1911, reprinted 1994 Genealogical Publishing C.., Baltimore.

The Kolb family members were Mennonites who had lived in the electoral Palatinate prior to the devastating Thirty Years' War (1618–1648). During the war, they had escaped, likely to the Transylvania area of Hungary, where religious freedom had been protected since the Treaty of Vienna in 1606. Their family name appears on a list of refugees who returned from that eastern area to the Palatinate after the Peace of Westphalia in 1648, when the elector, Karl Ludwig,[147] was seeking people to restore and repopulate his domain. One of those was Heinrich Kolb, born in 1615 in Wolfsheim, who returned to the town of his birth. His oldest son, Dielman, was born there in 1648.

Dielman Kolb married Agnes Schumacher, whose family name also appears on a list of those returning from Transylvania. Agnes was the daughter of Peter Schumacher Sr., who lived in Kriegsheim, a center of Mennonite activity, where he was born in 1622. Dielman and Agnes were twenty-two and eighteen years old at their marriage in 1670, and they raised nine children at their home in Wolfsheim. Census reports indicate that he was a successful farmer and wine maker, served as a Mennonite preacher in Mannheim, and assisted Swiss Anabaptist refugees fleeing to the Palatinate in the early 1700s. Dielman died in Mannheim at sixty-four years in 1712, and he had apparently become a Quaker late in life. During his lifetime, the Palatinate would endure repeated invasion and destruction from the French armies, as Louis XIV was hostile to all non–Roman Catholic Christians and eager to extend his territory and reputation in Europe. These conflicts included the War of the Grand Alliance (1688–97) and the War of Spanish Succession (1701–14), both of which wreaked havoc on the Palatinate. The awareness of the opportunities for land and the freedom to worship according to their conscience in Pennsylvania that had been enjoyed by their Schumacher relatives must have been an encouragement for the Kolb brothers to emigrate.

Four of Dielman Kolb's sons left the Palatinate in 1707, seeking safety with others of their continuously harassed Mennonite faith and

---

[147] Also known as Charles I Louis, he followed his father, Frederick V. His mother was Elizabeth Stuart, daughter of James I of England.

to avoid the threats of warfare that had marked their youth. These young men, Heinrich, Martin, Johannes, and Jacob Kolb (born between 1679 and 1683), initially settled in Germantown, Colony of Pennsylvania. Their oldest brother, Peter Kolb (1671–1727), did not emigrate and was an elder in the Kriegsheim Mennonite congregation, where he remained until his death in 1727.

The Mennonite records indicate that the first meeting of their congregation in America was held in conjunction with a Quaker meeting at the house of Thones Kunders in 1683. The Mennonites worshipped in private homes or outdoors when appropriate or shared services with the Quakers, until the arrival in 1688 of their first minister, William Rittenhouse. By 1686, a Quaker meetinghouse was built in Germantown. The first Mennonite congregation in America was officially organized in 1708 by Bishop Jacob Godshalk with Minister Rittenhouse and included the four Kolb brothers with forty-three members. Martin Kolb was ordained to the ministry in the Mennonite Church in Germantown, and his signature along with Dirk Keyser's appears on the deed dated September 6, 1714, for the meetinghouse property, which was also used as a schoolhouse. In 1709, Martin Kolb moved to Skippack with his wife, Magdelena Van Sintern, where they would raise seven children. He served as minister and trustee of the Mennonite Church in Skippack, where he lived until his death in 1761 at eighty-one years.

By 1709, Johannes had moved to Skippack (now in Montgomery County), where by a deed dated December 15, 1709, he purchased one hundred and fifty acres, and he also had property in Chester County. Johannes and thirty others signed a petition presented on June 2, 1713, to the Court of Quarter Sessions in Philadelphia requesting the building of a road connecting Skippack and Germantown. This road still exists as Route 73 and is known as the Skippack Pike. The petition stated that the route would pass through Gwynedd and near Pennepack, both Welsh communities.

The first child of Johannes and his wife, Sarah, was born in 1720, and by 1736, their family included nine children. Sarah's family name and their origin have not been found, but it is likely that she was of

Welsh descent, probably living in the Pennepec area of Pennsylvania and a relative of James James, Esq.[148] While in Pennsylvania, Johannes and his brothers owned property in the area of the first Welsh Tract west of Philadelphia near the settlement of Skippack. We can only speculate about their use of the land, but it is likely that they raised livestock and grew flax to provide the fiber used by weavers, such as their brother Heinrich, to make linen cloth and linseed meal as feed for their cattle. Records suggest that Johannes visited South Carolina as early as 1732 or 1733, when he may have traveled with James James, Esq., to assess the proposed tract in the Cheraw area on the Pee Dee River. A survey of a 650-acre plot dated about 1732 is preserved, and this location would be the site of his ferry and mill as well as acreage where his family would live for several generations. He may have recognized that the wealth of this land was in the long-leaf pines that would supply naval stores.[149]

This activity would require much more labor than was needed for his agricultural venture in Pennsylvania. It is unknown if he owned slaves then, but they would be essential for his efforts in Carolina.[150] Slave ownership was common in Penn's Colony, as about half of British Quakers, including William Penn, were owners. The Mennonite settlers were much opposed to this activity and in February 1688 had presented a Petition Against Slavery that was signed by four German residents, Garret Henderich, Derick and Abram Op de Graeff, and Francis Daniel Pretorius, only the latter being a Quaker. The petition was presented to the monthly,

---

[148] It is an unfortunate reality that the maiden names and dates of birth of the wives were often omitted from colonial marriage records, and establishing the identity of these women with certainty is problematic. As noted in part II, E, Sarah Kolb was certainly a member of the Welsh community in Pennsylvania and likely a member of at least the extended family of James, Esq.

[149] Pine lumber, ship masts, pine tar, pitch, and turpentine for use by the British navy and commercial sailing vessels were profitable due to the bonus from Britain encouraging their colonial production.

[150] The story of slavery in the various colonies is described in the parts of section III and was very different in the several colonies, mainly due to the differences in their economies and needs for laborers.

quarterly, and finally the annual meeting of the Quaker governing body without a decision or action due to the significant effect that a ban on slavery would have on the economy of the colony. Even William Penn had expressed satisfaction about the prosperity of the colony, which was such, he stated, that in a year ten slave ships had called at the Philadelphia port.

This petition, in an original copy kept by the Lillian Goldman Law Library of Yale Law School, presents its arguments with such subtle but indisputable logic that it is certainly a classic, and a transcript is found in section IV.E. The petition appeals first to the golden rule in such a way as to be beyond debate. It also states that participating in slavery is supportive of theft and adultery, which would be anathema to the pious Quakers. It concludes with a rhetorical question about how their Quaker pacifism would react to a slave revolt in which their belief could result in their becoming slaves rather than owners. The petition was tabled and forgotten for many decades, as slavery was not prohibited for Quakers until 1776.

This moral and economic conflict must have been a concern for Johannes and a factor in his willingness to remove his family to South Carolina and to later join the Welch Neck Baptist Church in place of his Mennonite roots. The conflicts of the issue of slavery were a problem in each of the colonies and, from our perspective centuries later, we know would not be resolved peacefully. Although we cannot know with certainty the thoughts and actions of Johannes Kolb, we can use the parts of the puzzle that are available to come to some reasonable conclusions. In 1736, the ninth child of Sarah and Johannes was born, and in the following year, they joined thirty-five members of the Welsh Baptist community and moved with their children, ages one to fourteen years, to their new home in the Cheraw District of South Carolina. They likely sailed from the Chesapeake Bay area to the Carolinas and the port town of Georgetown at the mouth of the Pee Dee River. This group of Welsh Baptists was led by James James, Esq., and included his three sons, Philip, Daniel, and Abel James, and their families. Johannes Kolb, on arriving from Pennsylvania, settled at his grant in a neck of the

Pee Dee River of between 650 and 1300 acres on differing surveys near the subsequent town of Society Hill. He operated a mill and the Cashaway Ferry at Kolb's Neck, and these activities would have required labor that could only have been supplied by slaves. James James died within a year of their move to the Cheraw District, but his sons and their families remained in the area. On April 4, 1743, his son Philip was ordained and served as the first minister of the Welsh Neck Baptist Church.

The years from the mid-1730s to the 1740s experienced a significant religious transformation in both Britain and her American colonies known as the Great Awakening. This is often dated in the colonies from 1734 with the ministry of Jonathan Edwards and the evangelical revival at his Congregational Church in Northampton, Massachusetts. The roots of the movement began in the preceding decades in other colonies and in Europe and were greatly stimulated in America by the visits of George Whitefield, who came from Britain to preach widely throughout the colonies. During that interval, he preached to two thousand on the grounds of the Pennepack Church in Pennsylvania. He had particular influence in South Carolina on his visits from 1738 to 1741. It seems certain that Rev. Philip James was influenced by this Great Awakening evangelical movement and the effect of the preaching of Whitefield that the gospel must be made available to the slaves.[151] An abstract of the records of the Welsh Neck Baptist Church, Society Hill, South Carolina, indicates that many slaves were admitted to full membership in the congregation, and in 1797, the number of white and black members of the church were equivalent. Whitefield also preached that the slaves should be taught to read and be prepared to teach the gospel to other slaves. This movement did not encourage the elimination of slavery but did foster a paternalistic attitude on the part of some owners and perhaps improved the living conditions for some of the slaves. This situation in the James and Kolb families likely improved the outlook

---

[151] Gallway, Alan. In Masters & Slaves in the House of the Lord, John B. Boles, Editor, The University Press of Kentucky, 1988.

for some of the slaves, as suggested by the experience in the family of Col. Abel Kolb, the grandson of Rev. Philip James and his wife, Elizabeth Thomas. Col. Kolb was the son of Peter Kolb and Ann James Kolb and commanded the regiment of the South Carolina Militia in the Upper Pee Dee River area, reporting to Brigadier General Francis Marion. During the war, the British took one of the Kolb slaves, Abraham, who was assigned duties in the British camp that likely would have required literacy. Later in the war, Col. Kolb was surprised by a band of Tories and killed at his home. The Tories burned his home, leaving his wife, Anne Kolb, and her two young daughters in a desperate situation. The slaves of the family could have easily escaped but chose to remain with the family and help them reestablish their lives.[152] In no way is this information intended to diminish the tragedy of slavery, but some slaves and their owners, due to their spiritual beliefs, were able to heal some of the effects of an institution that was a disaster for individuals, families, and the nation.

The Kolb brothers and their families contributed significantly to the religious life, economy, and population of the Pennsylvania and South Carolina colonies. Over the decade after their arrival in America, they were joined by family members and others seeking respite from the devastation of war and persecution for their faith and establishing homes in the New World with its freedoms and opportunities.

It is worthwhile to consider seventeenth-century Europe and the conditions and circumstances that led to the movement of so many to North America and the establishment of their lives in what initially was a wilderness that always posed challenges. Individuals who contributed to the early decades of our nation's history often demonstrated a deeply held commitment to their religious values and to their families, which elevate them to the highest level of our admiration. The details of their lives must often be left to our imagination, but they were surely eventful and filled with great uncertainty, making their dependence on God and their loved ones

---

[152] Gregg, Alexander. 1867, reprinted 2012. pp. 334–382.

even more critical to their success. It is important to consider the beliefs that these forbearers held and to consider our own beliefs as being influenced and perhaps reflecting those of so long ago. The experiences and decisions made by these initial colonists were major factors in the later formation of the government and culture of the United States. Much is to be learned from their experiences and the outcome of their lives.

Information about the early descendants of the brothers of Johannes Kolb (Heinrich, Martin, and Jacob) can begin with a publication *A Genealogical History of the Kolb, Bulb or Cup Family, and Its Branches in America,* Morgan Wells, Morristown, Pennsylvania, 1895 as reprinted.

E. ANTISLAVERY RESOLUTION OF THE GERMANTOWN MENNONITES, FEBRUARY 18, 1688

This is to the monthly meeting held at Richard Worrell's:

These are the reasons why we are against the traffic of men-body, as followeth: Is there any that would be done or handled in this manner? viz., to be sold or made a slave for all the time of his life? How fearful and faint-hearted are many at sea, when they see a strange vessel, being afraid it should be a Turk, and they should be taken, and sold for slaves in Turkey. Now, what is this better done, than Turks do? Yea, rather it is worse for them, which say they are Christians, for we hear that the most part of such (negroes, sic.) are brought hither against their will and consent, and that many of them are stolen. Now, though they are black, we cannot conceive there is more liberty to have them slaves, as it is to have other white ones. There is a saying, that we should do to all men like as we will be done ourselves; making no difference of what generation, descent, or colour they are. And those who steal or rob men, and those who buy or purchase them, are they not all alike? Here is liberty of conscience which is right and reasonable; here ought to be likewise liberty of the body, except of evil-doers, which is another case. But to bring men hither; or to rob and sell them against their will, we stand against. In Europe there are many oppressed for conscience sake; and here there are those oppressed which are of a black colour. And we who know that men must not commit adultery some do commit adultery in others, separating wives from their husbands, and giving them to others: and some sell the children of these poor creatures to other men. Ah! do consider well this thing, you who do it, if you would be done at this manner and if it is done according to Christianity! You surpass Holland and Germany in this thing. This makes an ill report in all those countries of Europe, where they hear of [it], that the Quakers do here handel men as they handel there the cattle. And for that reason some have no mind or inclination to come hither. And who shall maintain this your cause, or plead for it? Truly, we cannot do so, except you shall inform us better here of, viz.: that Christians have liberty to practice these things. Pray, what thing in the world can be done worse towards us, than if men should rob or steal us away, and sell us for slaves to strange countries; separating husbands from their wives and children. Being now this is not done in the manner we would be done at; therefore, we contradict, and are against this traffic of men-body. And we who profess that it is not lawful to steal, must, likewise, avoid to purchase such things as are stolen, but rather help to stop this robbing and stealing, if possible. And such men ought to be delivered out of the hands of the robbers, and set free as in Europe. Then is Pennsylvania to have a good report, instead, it hath now a bad one, for this sake, in other countries; Especially whereas the Europeans are desirous to know in what manner the Quakers do rule in their province; and most of them do look upon us with an envious eye. But if this is done well, what shall we say is done evil?

If once these slaves (which they say are so wicked and stubborn men,) should join themselves fight for their freedom, and (handel, sic.) their masters and mistresses, as they did handel them before; will these masters and mistresses take the sword at hand and war against these poor slaves, like, as we are able to believe, some will not refuse to do? Or, have these poor (negroes, sic.) not as much right to fight for their freedom, as you have to keep them slaves?

Now consider well this thing, if it is good or bad. And in case you find it to be good to handel these blacks in that manner, we desire and require you hereby lovingly, that you may inform us herein, which at this time never was done, viz., that Christians have such a liberty to do so. To the end we shall be satisfied on this point, and satisfy likewise our good friends and acquaintances in our native country, to whom it is a terror, or fearful thing, that men should be (handelled, sic.) so in Pennsylvania.

This is from our meeting at Germantown, held ye 18th of the 2d month, 1688, to be delivered to the monthly meeting at Richard Worrell's.

Garret Henderich

Derick op de Graeff

Francis Daniel Pretorius

Abram op de Graeff

From the Yale Law School, Lillian Goodman Law Library, the Avalon Project—*Documents in Law, History and Diplomacy.*

F. WRITTEN PRECEDENTS OF THE SEPARATION OF CHURCH AND STATE AS DESCRIBED IN THE FIRST AMENDMENT OF THE US CONSTITUTION

When they have opened a gap in the hedge or wall of Separation between the Garden of the Church and the Wilderness of the world, God hathe ever broke down the wall it selfe, removed the Candlestick, &c. and made his Garden a Wildernesse, as at this day. (Roger Williams)

Quotation is from Williams's pamphlet titled *Mr. Cotton's Letter Examined and Answered.* Although these sentiments were not popularly accepted in London, the pamphlet was widely read, and with his charisma and persuasive logic, Roger Williams was able to obtain a Parliamentary Charter for his colony. Williams believed that the affiliation of the church with the secular government resulted in corrupting influences for the church and that a colony separate from the Massachusetts/Anglican influence would be necessary for him and his fellow believers to achieve what he considered the fundamental human right of "Soul Libertie." After intense efforts to persuade Parliament and with his scholarly reputation and the high opinion in which he was held by prominent political leaders in England, Williams received his charter on March 14, 1644.[153]

Virginia's Act for Establishing Religious Freedom, January 16, 1786

The following was written by Thomas Jefferson in 1777 and introduced to the Virginia General Assembly in 1779 but was

---

[153] Barry, John M., Roger Williams and the Creation of the American Soul: Church, State, and the Birth of Liberty. Penguin Books, 2012. Pages 299–314.

opposed by the powers of the established Church of England and did not receive a vote at that time. The prior year (1776), the Fifth Virginia Convention had adopted a Declaration of Rights, which had an influence on the subsequent Declaration of Independence and Bill of Rights. Section 16 stated "That religion, or the duty which we owe to our Creator, and the manner of discharging it, can be directed only by reason and conviction, not by force or violence; and therefore all men are equally entitled to the free exercise of religion, according to the dictates of conscience; and that it is the mutual duty of all to practice Christian forbearance, love and charity toward each other."

There were other issues that this Declaration did not address, including the support of the Anglican clergy by taxation and the deeding of property to the church for support of needy colonists, as directed by a minister. Hence in January, 1786, the assembly approved the much more strongly worded statute written by Jefferson. He felt very intensely about this accomplishment, as he directed that it be included on his tombstone along with "author of the Declaration of Independence and father of the University of Virginia":

> An Act for establishing religious Freedom.
>
> Whereas, Almighty God hath created the mind free;
>
> That all attempts to influence it by temporal punishments or burthens, or by civil incapacitations tend only to beget habits of hypocrisy and meanness, and therefore are a departure from the plan of the holy author of our religion, who being Lord, both of body and mind yet chose not to propagate it by coercions on either, as was in his Almighty power to do,
>
> That the impious presumption of legislators and rulers, civil as well as ecclesiastical, who, being themselves but fallible and uninspired men have assumed dominion over the faith of others, setting up their own opinions and modes of thinking as the only

true and infallible, and as such endeavoring to impose them on others, hath established and maintained false religions over the greatest part of the world and through all time;

That to compel a man to furnish contributions of money for the propagation of opinions, which he disbelieves is sinful and tyrannical;

That even the forcing him to support this or that teacher of his own religious persuasion is depriving him of the comfortable liberty of giving his contributions to the particular pastor, whose morals he would make his pattern, and whose powers he feels most persuasive to righteousness, and is withdrawing from the Ministry those temporary rewards, which, proceeding from an approbation of their personal conduct are an additional incitement to earnest and unremitting labors for the instruction of mankind;

That our civil rights have no dependence on our religious opinions any more than our opinions in physics or geometry,

That therefore the proscribing any citizen as unworthy the public confidence, by laying capacity of being called to offices of trust and emolument, unless he profess or renounce this or that religious opinion, is depriving him injuriously of those privileges and advantages, to which, in common with his fellow citizens, he has a natural right,

That it tends only to corrupt the principles of that very Religion it is meant to encourage, by bribing with a monopoly of worldly honors and emoluments those who will externally profess and conform to it;

That though indeed, these are criminal who do not withstand such temptation, yet neither are those innocent who lay the bait in their way;

That to suffer the civil magistrate to intrude his powers into the field of opinion and to restrain the profession or propagation of principles on supposition of their ill tendency is a dangerous fallacy which at once destroys all religious liberty because he being of course judge of that tendency will make his opinions the rule of judgement and approve or condemn the sentiments of others only as they shall square with or differ from his own;

That it is time enough for the rightful purposes of civil government, for its officers to interfere when principles break out into overt acts against peace and good order;

And finally, that Truth is great, and will prevail if left to herself, that she is the proper and sufficient antagonist to error, and has nothing to fear from the conflict, unless by human interposition disarmed of her natural weapons free argument and debate, errors ceasing to be dangerous when it is permitted freely to contradict them,:

Be it enacted by General Assembly that no man shall be compelled to frequent or support any religious worship, place, or ministry whatsoever, nor shall be enforced, restrained, molested, or burthened in his body or goods, nor shall otherwise suffer on account of his religious opinions or belief, but that all men shall be free to profess, and by argument to maintain, their opinions in matters of Religion, and that the same shall in no wise diminish, enlarge or affect their civil capacities. And though we well know that this Assembly elected by the people for the ordinary purposes of Legislation only, have no power to restrain the acts of succeeding Assemblies constituted with powers equal to our own, and that therefor to declare this act irrevocable would be of no effect in law; yet we are free to declare, and do declare that the rights hereby asserted, are of the natural rights of mankind, and that if any act shall be hereafter passed to repeal the present or to narrow its operation, such act will be an infringement of natural right.[154]

Enacted by the Virginia Assembly, January 16, 1786.

Jefferson's Letter to the Danbury Baptists[155]

To messers. Nehemiah Dodge, Ephraim Robbins, & Stephen S. Nelson, a committee of the Danbury Baptist Association in the state of Connecticut.

Gentlemen
The affectionate sentiments of esteem and approbation which you are so good as to express towards me, on behalf of the Danbury Baptist association, give me the highest satisfaction. My duties dictate a faithful and zealous pursuit of the interests of my constituents, & in proportion as they are persuaded of my fidelity to those duties, the discharge of them becomes more and more pleasing.

Believing with you that religion is a matter which lies solely between Man & his God, that he owes account to none other for his faith or his worship, that the legitimate powers of government reach action only, & not opinions, I contemplate with sovereign reverence that act of the whole American people which declared that their legislature should "make no law respecting an establishment of religion, or prohibiting the free

---

[154] "Act for Establishing Religious Freedom, January 16, 1786" (http://www.virginiamemory.com/docs/ReligiousFree.pdf)
[155] The Library of Congress, Information Bulletin, June 1998, Vol. 57, No. 6.

exercise thereof," thus building a wall of separation between Church & State. Adhering to this expression of the supreme will of the nation in behalf of the rights of conscience, I shall see with sincere satisfaction the progress of those sentiments which tend to restore to man all his natural rights, convinced he has no natural right in opposition to his social duties.

I reciprocate your kind prayers for the protection & blessing of the common father and creator of man, and tender you for yourselves & your religious association, assurances of my high respect & esteem.

Th Jefferson
Jan. 1. 1802

G. TEXT OF A MARKER PLACED BY THE BAPTIST HISTORY SOCIETY MAY 8, 2007 (FIGURE 7)

Pennepack Baptist Church
In the latter half of the seventeenth century, Baptists from England and Wales settled in the County of Philadelphia. Their gathering as baptized believers led to the formation of the Pennepack Baptist Church.

In 1686, Elias Keach, son of the famed English Pastor, Benjamin Keach arrived in America. Though unconverted, he presented himself as a minister of the gospel. His name secured him the opportunity to preach and the aforementioned group of believers, in need of a pastor were among those who gave ear to his message.

Baptist historian Morgan Edwards records the details of this event.
"He performed well enough till he had advanced prety far in the sermon.
Then stopping short, looked like a man astonished. The audience
concluded he had been seized with a sudden disorder; but on asking
what the matter was, received from him the confession of the imposture
with tears in his eyes and much trembling."

The deceiver became the first convert of his own preaching
for from this time he dated his conversion!
Keach repaired to Elder Thomas Dungan who, at Cold Spring in 1684,
founded the first Baptist Church in the colony of
Pennsylvania. Dungan administered the
ordinance of baptism to Keach and
the young preacher returned to Pennepack.

The Pennepack Baptist Church was constituted in 1688.
It is recorded that "by the advice of Elias Keach and
with the consent of the following named persons viz:
John Eatton, George Eatton, John Baker, Samuel Vaus,
Joseph Watts, and Elias Keach, a day was set apart
to seek God by fasting and prayer in order to form
ourselves into a church. Whereupon Elias Keach was
accepted and received as our pastor and we sat down
in communion at the Lord's table."

The same year, 1688, Elder Dungan died, and in 1703,
the Church at Cold Spring was absorbed into the Pennepack Church.
Though not the first established, to "Ye Olde Pennepack"
belongs the distinction of being the oldest Baptist Church in Pennsylvania.
It is also one of the oldest Baptist Churches in America.

In 1707, Pennepack, with four other Baptist Churches,
Middletown, Piscataway and Cohensay in New Jersey,
and Welsh Tract in Delaware, became constituent members of the
Philadelphia Association, the first Baptist Association in America.

*Pennepack is mother to Baptist Churches in Pennsylvania,
New Jersey, Delaware and beyond. Her influence extended
throughout the colonies and her early pastors traveled far and wide
preaching the gospel and organizing churches.*

*The great evangelist, George Whitfeield, preached
on these grounds to about two thousand people May 10, 1740.*

*Elias Keach returned to England in 1692.
John Watts, second Pastor of the Church is buried here.
Other early pastors include:
Evan Morgan, Samuel Jones, Joseph Wood,
Abel Morgan, Jenkin Jones and Peter Van horn.*

*The present rock building was constructed in 1805
during the ministry of Dr. Samuel Jones and his remains are
buried behind the meetinghouse in which he preached
for over fifty years. Other pastors and many of the faithful
saints of God rest in these hallowed grounds.*

*W.T. Brently wrote the following words after visiting here in 1829:
"We always look with feelings of veneration upon the habitations
which may be regard ed as the cradle of greatness or goodness,
and on which antiquity has marked its deep impressions.
In passing over such scenes, we seem to hold communion with
the reposing spirits that once enlivened that solitude, and to
identify them with the names and incidents which gladden and
diversify the present moment. We look back upon the generous
anxiety with which their bosoms throbbed, when they laid those
foundations on which others have built. We call to mind their
mingled feelings of hope and fear, when they stretched the cords
and planted the stakes of their tents; and fixed a habitation for their God.
Will the generations which are to come after us build up,
or demolish those feeble beginnings?"*

Therefore, my beloved brethren, be ye steadfast, unmovable,
always abounding in the work of the Lord, forasmuch as ye know
that your labor is not in vain in the Lord. I Corinthians 15:58

Text of a marker placed at the Pennepack Church by the
Baptist History Preservation Society May
8, 2007. The church is the
oldest in Philadelphia and the seventh oldest in the English colonies
(picture of the church building in gallery).

H. THE CHURCH OF ST. PETER UPON CORNHILL AND CELTIC/WELSH CHURCH HISTORY

As noted in section II, C, some Welsh Christians claim by tradition
that their religious forbears date from the second century AD in
Roman Britain. References to their history often point to a book
written in 1778 by Rev. Joshua Thomas of Wales, *The History of the
Welsh Baptists, from the Year Sixty-Three to the Year One Thousand Seven
Hundred and Seventy.* This was translated from the Welsh language
by the Rev. J. Davis, published in the late nineteenth century by
D.M. Hogan in Pittsburgh, and is now available in electronic format.
Historical writings on Britain between the Roman occupation and
the fourteenth century must be received with a degree of skepticism,
as much information about the era is dependent not on primary
sources but on tradition and rare archeological findings interpreted
centuries after the events. The difficulty in documenting the record
of the Celtic-Romano-Saxon centuries should not completely render
available information unbelievable. It may be surprising that one of
the most eminent scholars of the Anglo-Saxon language and culture
argues that information passed down by oral tradition over centuries
is likely based on facts that carry significant germs of truth. This
scholar was the late J. R. R. Tolkien, professor of Anglo-Saxon
Studies at Oxford and the author of such popular works as *The Hobbit*
and *The Lord of the Rings.*

The reference to an ancient Celtic King Lucius, said to be the first monarch to embrace Christianity, is an example of such uncertain historical claims. It was suggested that supportive evidence for this could be found at a church, St. Peter upon Cornhill, in the city of London. If such evidence exists, it is reasonable that it would be found in London, the historical center of the English-speaking world and the principal city of Roman Britannia. The origin of the city dates to the coming of the Romans, first under Julius Caesar in 55 BC and more definitively under Emperor Claudius in AD 43. The Romans built a fortified town, Londinium, at an area on the Thames River that had been the site of an established settlement whose origins will likely remain uncertain. When the Romans came to Britannia, they encountered a well-developed and long-existing Celtic iron-age culture. This culture had been preceded for millennia by earlier cultures about which little is understood. These early Britons, however, were capable of sophisticated activities, such as the creation of Stonehenge and other structural wonders and significant mining activities that produced flint and metallic ores. Evidence indicates that they had been engaged in active trade with mainland Europe for centuries.

The remnants of Roman influence in Britain are clearly visible today in much of the English countryside, but most evidence of their presence in London has been covered by two thousand years of successive construction. Excavations in the city of London area clearly document the previous Roman presence and may contribute to an understanding of subsequent activities in the city and of these early Christians.

St. Peter upon Cornhill now is a component of the Anglican Parish of St. Helen's Bishopsgate in the city of London amid the present financial district. The church dates to 1210 when a nunnery of the Benedictine order was established on this site. This was during the reign of King John, whose reputation has suffered due to comparison with his brother, Richard I (Lionheart), his parents, Henry II and Eleanor of Aquitaine, and the legends of Robin Hood. The nuns at St. Helen's had the later support of Edward I (1272–1307), and their activities in this location persisted until 1538. It was during the reign of Henry VIII that the nunnery was suppressed by the efforts of Sir Richard Wyllyams, better known by his assumed name of Cromwell, the nephew of Thomas Cromwell, first earl of Essex, the chief minister to Henry VIII from 1532 to 1540. Richard was the great-grandfather of Oliver Cromwell.

St. Helen's has been an active parish for centuries. One of its unique features is a divided apse, one side originally for the nuns and the other for the public. It had been the church of William Shakespeare, whose name was on their role in 1597, and the memory of his membership is sustained by a large stained glass window in his honor. The church survived the Great Fire of London (1666), the Bishopsgate fire of 1765, and the Battle of Britain in World War II but was severely damaged by terrorist bombs in 1992 and 1993. It has now been authentically restored and is actively used for ministry in the surrounding Financial District of the city of London. St. Helen's is the central church for a parish that includes several smaller facilities, including St. Peter upon Cornhill (figure 9a and b).

Cornhill is a thoroughfare in the city of London, and the church site is on a hill by that name, equidistant from the Tower of London and St. Paul's Cathedral, which are on similar hills. These geographic features of Roman Londinium are now obscured by urban construction. The site of the church had been occupied by a Roman basilica, a term referring to a public or governmental building, which was considerably larger than the present church building. Lucius may have cooperated with the occupying Roman authorities, as they may have given him permission to build his church on this site and to use existing stone foundation piers from the previous structure for his construction. Those supports of the present structure are obscured by the building, but similar piers of the original Roman basilica are readily viewed below a building across the street from the church. It is of interest that the Roman authorities may have not been hostile to the worship customs of the Celtic natives as long as they cooperated with the ruling secular governance. The actual date of the first church construction is not documented.

What remained of the original church structure was largely

destroyed by the Great Fire (1666), and only the lower parts of the outer wall are the original construction. The church was rebuilt by Sir Christopher Wren in 1672, the tower added in 1722 by Nicholas Hawksmoor, and further restoration occurred in 1860 by Sir George Gilbert Scott. A brass plaque dating from the thirteenth or fourteenth centuries survived the passage of time and is preserved in an office near the altar of the church.[156] The text of this plaque relates much of the traditional story of the church and Christian history of the succeeding centuries (figure 10).

> Bee it knowne to all men that in the years of our Lord God 179 Lucius the first Christian King of this land, then called Britaine, Founded ye first Church in London, that is to say, ye church of St. Peter Upon Cornehill, and hee founded there an Archbishops See, and made that Church ye Metropolitane and cheife Church of this Kingdom, and so it indured ye space 400 years and more, unto the coming of St. Austin the Apostle of England, the which was sent into this Land by St. Gregorie, ye Doctor of ye Church in the time of King Ethelbert and then was the Archbishop's See & Pall removed from ye foresaid Church of St. Peter upon Cornehill unto Dorobernia, that now is called Canterburie & there it remaineth to this day, and Millet a monke which came into this land with St. Austin, hee was made the first Bishop of London and his See was made in Paul's Church and this LUCIUS King was the first founder of St. Peters Church upon Cornehill & he reigned King in this land after Brute 1245 yeares And in the yeare of our Lord God 124 LUCIUS was crowned King and his reigne were 77 yeares and hee was buried (after some Chronicles) at London and after some Chronicles hee

---

[156] See gallery #2 for a picture of the plaque.

was buried at Gloucester in that place where ye Order
of St. Francis standeth now.

Certain historical references in this transcript deserve clarification.
The language (and the spelling) of the thirteenth century contains
terminology that is unfamiliar to twenty-first-century readers, and
explanation is appropriate. The identity and role of Lucius is obscure,
and the extent of his realm is unknown. The sixth-century *Liber
Pontificalis* (*Book of the Popes*) notes that Lucius wrote Pope Eleutherius
(papacy from c. 174 to c. 189) requesting to become a Christian,
but this was apparently added to a revised edition in the fifth or
sixth century and not previously reported. The Venerable Bede,
an Anglo-Saxon saint, reported this event in his *Historia ecclesiastica
gentis Anglorum* in 731. Lucius was said to be a Celtic ruler of a tribal
area, and the church was built on the remains of a previous Roman
basilica that may have been destroyed in one of the frequent serious
fires that occurred in ancient Londinium.

The reference to the archbishop's see is to the seat from which
a bishop or archbishop would exercise their jurisdiction and would
be represented by a heraldic pall or altar cloth that would have
accompanied the archbishop when he relocated to Canterbury. The
plaque refers to the bringing of Roman Christianity to Britain by
Augustine (also called Austin), who had been sent by Pope Gregory
I in the 590s. By 597, he had baptized thousands of the subjects of
King Ethelbert, an Anglo-Saxon monarch who eventually moved the
archbishop's see to Canterbury, the capital from which he ruled his
kingdom of Kent. St. Augustine, the apostle of the English (Austin), is
not to be confused with St. Augustine of Hippo, the great theologian
and philosopher who lived in what is now Algeria and is widely
regarded as one of the greatest of all Christian thinkers. The King
Ethelbert (c. 560–616) mentioned in the plaque refers to the king
of Kent who married Bertha, the Christian daughter of the king of
Paris, and this Ethelbert was converted to Christianity during St.
Austin's ministry. King Ethelbert (sic. Ethelberht of Kent) mentioned
on the plaque is not the much later Anglo-Saxon King Ethelbert

(860–866), the son of King Egbert and brother of Alfred "The Great" (871–899) who played an important role in holding back the Viking invasions during his reign.

The phrase *"after Brute 1245 yeares"* would have been familiar to a reader in the thirteenth century, as it refers to the legendary king of Britain, Brute, said to be the great-grandson of Aeneas of Troy, who came to Britain and founded a New Troy or Trinovantum, which became London. This legend is told in Nennius's *Historia Britonum* (ninth century), in Geoffrey of Monmouth's *Historia Regum Britanniae* (c. 1135), in Wace's French *Brut* (c. 1155), and in Layamon's English *Brut* (c. 1200). (Brute would have been pronounced bru-TAY, as in Julius Caesar's quote "Et tu Brute"). The language on the plaque is so similar to these sources that it is likely that it was taken directly from them, which casts question on its greater antiquity.

Several other features of St. Peter upon Cornhill deserve mention, especially the organ, which dates from 1681 and was played by Felix Mendelssohn, whose autograph, dated September 1840, is in the gallery. Numerous stained glass windows depict scenes from the life of Christ and St. Peter, and one is a memorial to the Royal Tank Regiment. St. Peter upon Cornhill is the historic church of the regiment that saw extensive service in World War I in the Battles of the Somme and Cambrai[157] and in WWII at Dunkirk, El Alamein, and Normandy.

One question that remains incompletely answered is by what path did the Celtic Christians of the early centuries of the Christian era possibly lead to a group of Welsh Baptists who made their homes in colonial America. The original Celtic natives would not have referred to themselves as *Welsh* but as *Britons*. The term *Welsh* was used to describe them as foreigners *(Walkaz)* by invading Anglo-Saxons in their Proto-Germanic language. Later, Celtic residents of Wales would refer to themselves as *Cymry* and their land as *Cymru* (Latinized version is Cambria).

---

[157] The Royal Tank Regiment led the Battle of Cambrai on November 20, 1917, with the first effective use of tanks in combat. Mechanized warfare had first appeared in the Battle of the Somme in Summer, 1916.

The history of the post-Roman era is further confused by the uncertainty of proper names of both Anglo-Saxon and Celtic leaders. In an important battle, the Anglo-Saxons were said to have been led by *Hengest* and his brother *Horsa*, but it is suspected that these names may have referred to their transportation, as their translation from the ancient language is stallion and horse. A supposed leader of the Celtic forces, *Vortigern*, requested Saxon support for his efforts in defending against invading Picts. The later Saxons settled on the "eastern side of the island," and their involvement would be a future detriment to the Britons. Vortigern may be a generic term for "great king" rather than a proper name.

As the names of the leaders during this age are uncertain, so are the dates and locations of notable events. One of the many examples of this is the important Battle of Badon. The site of the battle has never been determined, and it is dated sometime between AD 430 and 520. It was one of the infrequent decisive victories over the invaders by the Britons, whose leader was said to have been King Arthur. His persona is shrouded in legend, and there is no evidence to support this involvement.

The dates that are more certain relate to the diminishing influence of the Romans in Britannia. After AD 360, gaps in the legions of Roman troops were filled with Germanic recruits, and the number of tribesmen became a significant factor. Dissension among the Roman troops, tribal invasions, civil unrest in Rome, and upheavals throughout the empire diminished the ability of Rome to maintain control of their possessions in Britannia. The attempts of the newcomers to take over Roman-fortified towns led to an appeal for assistance to Roman Emperor Honorius in AD 410, which was refused. Britons in the fifth century saw repeated defeats by Germanic forces, and mass migration of the Celtic natives to the west occurred, especially to the protection of the mountainous area of Wales. By the middle of the century, the Britons had abandoned Kent and other southeastern areas. During the era of Anglo-Saxon dominance and the later Viking incursions, the Celtic descendants would be primarily located in what is now Wales. We can refer to them as Welsh Christians. They would not have been aware of the designation as "Baptists," as that term was not used in Britain until the early 1600s. As described in section II, C, the Baptists have historically been defined by 1) their quest for separation of their ecclesiastical organization and its governance from that of the civil or secular authority and 2) their interpretation of the sacrament of baptism as being reserved for individuals of an age of accountability rather than in infancy.

There is evidence of an active Christian community in Britain prior to the fifth century and the coming of Austin, but their specific interpretation of their faith can only be assumed, as documentation does not apparently exist. Some have contended that there were some who shared the Baptist beliefs, although they were not specifically identified. The Britons were mentioned in Christian writings in the early third century, and their representatives (bishops) were present at church councils in the fourth century. Britain produced a number of prominent figures in the Christian faith, including Pelagius, who was born in the midfourth century and became an influential scholar and proponent of asceticism. He engaged in theological controversies with St. Augustine of Hippo and Jerome of Palestine. Pelagius's teachings were opposed by an early Welsh Christian, Dewi Sant (Saint David), whose mother, St. Non, had introduced him to the faith.

These Celtic believers may have been at odds with the Roman Church brought by Augustine, which became the official state religion after the baptism of King Ethelbert of Kent and the relocation of the archbishop to Canterbury, the capital of his realm. This would reflect the official establishment of the Roman Church as had developed in other parts of the empire after the rule of Constantine the Great with his Edict of Milan in 313 and the First Council of Nicaea in 325. The relocation of the bishop of London to St. Paul's Church first built in 604 also suggests some antagonism between the Celtic Christians of St. Peter upon Cornhill and the official Roman Church. These differences may have been related to ethnic distinctions rather than for ecclesiastical reasons.

There were other conflicts between adherents of Celtic Christianity (often identified as the Ionan church from their monastery on the Isle of Iona) and the Roman Church. These conflicts, as described by the Venerable Bede, led to the Synod of Whitby called by the Anglo-Saxon king of Northumbria in 664. Two of these issues were conflicting methods of calculating the date for the observance of Easter and variations in hairstyles for the clergy (clerical tonsure). A third issue mentioned by Bede was some variance in the rite of baptism that Augustine had not approved, but the nature of this is unknown. Various scholars have concluded that this was not a primary concern, and it is not mentioned in writings other than by the Venerable Bede. The dissenters who wished to maintain their usual traditions withdrew to Iona and contributed to an ongoing Celtic Christian community. Definitive evidence of the practices of this non-Roman Christian worship prior to the reformation is difficult to document but is now accepted as tradition. There is no evidence to suggest that ancient worshipers had any theological issues that would relate to the much later variations in interpretation or that they had access to any written scripture.

The coming of the pagan Vikings in the tenth century and the victory of the Normans in 1066 would have reinforced the official antagonism to these Celtic Christians and increased their interest in separating their ecclesiastical organization from that controlled by the secular hierarchy, the second defining characteristic of the Baptist tradition and of a possible Welsh component.

A final word about the Christian church in the Romano-Anglo-Saxon eras is in order. Although much is dependent on tradition and medieval texts whose documentation is suspect, many of these misconceptions have been rectified by modern scholarship. One of the glaring errors that persisted until the nineteenth century was the confusion of the identities of Saint Helen of Caernarfon and Saint Helen of Constantinople. Both of these women greatly advanced the Christian faith, lived in the early centuries AD, and had sons named Constantine who had presences in Britannia. They were, however, not the same person, and Helen of Constantinople preceded her namesake by at least fifty years. This confusion stemmed from the twelfth-century *Historia Regnum Britanniae* by Geoffrey of Monmouth and was perpetuated by the writings of G. K. Chesterton in the nineteenth century.

It is possible that Welsh Baptists who came to the Massachusetts Bay and Pennsylvania colonies may have been influenced by traditions passed from a millennium of their forbears. It seems more likely that their existence as a Baptist religious entity grew from the Anabaptist influence coming from Holland in the early 1600s.

I. ROGER WILLIAMS—MINISTER, SEPARATIST THEOLOGIAN, AND FOUNDER OF THE COLONY OF PROVIDENCE PLANTATION AND RHODE ISLAND

Providence may be defined as "circumstances ascribable to divine interposition" and was the name chosen by Roger Williams for his new settlement in the colonies and the first child to be born there (their third, a daughter).[158] It is also a description that seems to apply to many of the episodes of his life. Roger Williams was an extraordinary man of great intellect, faith, and insight who rose from modest origins to become a widely recognized spiritual leader respected by the highest levels of the English political leadership. His most enduring contribution to colonial America in the seventeenth century and to the succeeding generations of humanity was the establishment of the separation of church and state. The incorporation of this concept in his Colony of Providence and Rhode Island and eventually the First Amendment of our Constitution would establish the relationship between religious freedom and individual liberty of conscience. It was perhaps the most unique feature of the political experiment that was the United States of America. The story of his life describing many of these circumstances with exceptional clarity is the publication *Roger Williams and the Creation of the American Soul,*

---

[158] Funk & Wagnalls New College Standard Dictionary, New York.

written by John M. Barry and published by the Penguin Group (USA) in 2012.

Roger's father was a merchant tailor, and their middle-class family lived in the London district of Smithfield near the Newgate Prison and St. Sepulchre's Church, where they worshiped. The prison was the site of public executions, including some prisoners whose crime was to disparage the Church of England. St. Sepulchre's was the church of Captain John Smith of Virginia fame and of Sir Edward Coke. The latter must have noticed Roger recording sermons by shorthand, a skill much admired by those in the legal profession. Coke, thought by many to be the preeminent jurist in English history, must have recognized the potential in this intelligent and enthusiastic young teen.[159] Coke requested that he be his apprentice and became a surrogate father for Roger. Williams was brought into the daily world of a man who was one of the most influential individuals in the land and observed him in his dealings with Parliament and its conflicts with James I and Charles I, who actively supported their divine rights in opposition to the common law.

Williams was educated at Charterhouse with Coke's influence and received a BA from Pembroke College, Cambridge, in 1627. The Puritan affiliations gained at Cambridge prevented his receiving a position in the Anglican Church, but Williams served as chaplain for Sir William Masham, a distinguished English politician and member of Parliament. Williams was a trusted aide and became well known to the Puritan members of Parliament. His scholarly achievements became widely recognized. His legal and governmental experiences likely exposed him to the controversies created by conflicts between

---

[159] Sir Edward Coke was the first to be called lord chief justice of England and was said to be the embodiment of the common law. He ruled from the Court of the King's Bench that the common law was supreme over all persons and institutions except Parliament. He ruled "the house of every man is to him as his castle." Among the precedents set by his rulings were the prohibition of double jeopardy, the right of a court to void a legislative act, and the use of writs of habeas corpus to limit royal power and protect individual rights. Coke wrote the later Petition of Right, limiting royal power.

the secular government and those with religious views deviating from the established church. Before 1630, his views, which were of a strict Calvinist interpretation, were becoming increasingly Separatist. He also became associated with John Murton, who, when returning to England from Holland, had brought Baptist beliefs that were intensely opposed by the Anglican hierarchy.

Williams was not with the original 1630 convoy of John Winthrop that sailed with a thousand Puritan colonists to settle the Massachusetts Bay Colony. When Williams and his new bride, Mary Barnard, arrived in Boston on the *Lyon* in December 1630, he was warmly received and offered the post of teacher at the church. As the Boston congregation was still officially a part of the Anglican Church and therefore not "separated" sufficiently to suit him, Williams declined the offer. His views that had developed over the previous months were unwelcome in Boston, and Williams accepted the offer to assist Rev. Samuel Skelton in Salem.

The antagonism created with the Boston leadership would grow and led to his leaving the Massachusetts Bay jurisdiction for the more welcome environment of the Separatist Plymouth Colony. By 1633, Williams concluded that their degree of separation from the Anglican influence was not sufficient, and he returned to Salem as the assistant to Rev. Skelton. In August 1634, Skelton died, and Williams served as acting pastor of the Salem church until his controversial teachings led to his removal by the General Court of the colony. He was convicted of sedition and heresy and banished from the Bay Colony in late 1635.

After a desperate one-hundred-mile trek through a New England blizzard, he gained shelter from the Wampanoag Indians and their chief, Massasoit. In the spring of 1636, Williams bought land from the tribe and created a settlement, Providence, where he was joined by his wife and their three children and twelve other sympathetic families from Salem. This became the first jurisdiction in modern history to provide religious liberty, at least for protestant Christians, with a degree of separation of church and state.

By 1638, Williams had adopted the beliefs of the Particular

Baptists, including the practice of baptism only for believing adults. This caused anxiety for the Boston leadership, who were influenced by the awareness of the political and social disruption attributed to a violent fringe group of Anabaptists in the German city of Munster one hundred years earlier. Over the next several years, Providence and other nearby settlements on Rhode Island attracted a number of dissidents, including pacifist Anabaptists who had been banished from the Massachusetts Bay Colony. Massachusetts claimed authority over the Narragansett Bay area, and the armed force of the United Colonies of New England invaded the Rhode Island territory in 1643.[160] This prompted Williams to return to England to seek legal protection for Rhode Island and Providence Plantation from the Cromwell government.

On his arrival in England, he became a consultant to the Commonwealth government, drawing on his friendship with Oliver Cromwell and John Milton, who both held him in high regard. Despite his seemingly heretical views, including the full liberty of conscience and the free practice of religion, and despite the opposition of the Massachusetts Bay agents, Williams was able to secure a charter from Parliament for his Providence Plantation in 1644. In that year, Williams published a pamphlet in which he used a phrase that would be often repeated and eventually become established as an inviolable feature of the United States. "When they have opened a gap in the hedge or wall of Separation between the Garden of the Church and the Wildernesse of the world ... God hathe ever broke down the wall it selfe, removed the Candlestick &c and made his Garden a Wildernesse."[161] He meant by this that the affiliation of church and state corrupts the church and that religion and politics, when mixed, can only diminish the church. He used the term "Soule Libertie" to indicate the goal of his new colony, which he would pursue with his relentless charm and reason. On March

---

[160] The United Colonies of New England was an alliance between Massachusetts Bay, Plymouth, Connecticut, and New Haven colonies for mutual defense. It excluded the Rhode Island jurisdiction.

[161] Quoted in Barry, John M. p. 307–8.

14, 1644, he would obtain his charter, which gave the colony "full Powre & Authority to Governe & rule themselves, and such others as shall hereafter Inhabite within any part of the said Tract of land, by such a form of Civil Government, as by voluntary consent of all, or the greater Part of them shall find most suteable to their Estates & Conditions." Williams had succeeded in creating the freest society in the Western world.[162] The significance of these ideas, first articulated by Roger Williams, has reverberated throughout the history of our land, culminating in the First Amendment of the Bill of Rights with its Establishment and Free Exercise Clauses for the freedom of religion. The evolution of the interpretations and implications of this amendment has played an important role in the societal history of the United States.

A reading of our Constitution and Bill of Rights indicates that the writers of those documents were confronted by a number of issues that had affected settlers from the earliest colonial days and were important issues to the subjects of our stories. Commentary on constitutional law is beyond the scope of this writing and its author, but it is interesting to consider the circumstances of colonial times that were reflected in the Declaration of Independence and the Constitution. The latter was a unique document when first composed, as it defined for a new nation the structure and responsibilities of the central authority and the role of the states that comprised the republic. The Bill of Rights specified certain rights of the individual citizens that were considered granted by their Creator and could not be abridged by legitimate government. Diverse beliefs in such a Creator/God with different styles of worship were integral parts of the lives of the people in this new nation and its preceding colonies.

The issue that was the first to be addressed in our Bill of Rights was a written definition of the respective role of churches and the state in the new nation. The initial phrase of that amendment, "Congress shall make no law respecting an establishment of religion or prohibiting the free exercise there

---

[162] Ibid., p. 309–10.

of ..." has produced as much controversy and interpretation as almost any in our language. The writers seemingly wanted to assure that the new nation would never have an official religion and that one's ability to worship according to their conscience would never be prohibited by law. Words of Roger Williams and Thomas Jefferson, although not a part of the amendment, have contributed greatly to its interpretation, which may have expanded in subsequent years beyond the original intent.

An often-quoted phrase is from a pamphlet published in February, 1644, written by Roger Williams when he returned to London to lobby the Commonwealth Parliament for a charter to his Providence Plantation and Rhode Island colony separate from Massachusetts Bay. The pamphlet was a response to a letter to Williams from Rev. John Cotton, the preeminent minister in Massachusetts, which had supported the prior banishment of Williams from the colony because of his disagreements with the official church. Williams argued that as this secular punishment was due to his spiritual beliefs, it confirmed the concept that the church and state were acting as one entity, which he found unacceptable. Williams described what he felt was the true church as a magnificent garden with the purity of Eden and the secular world as "the Wilderness,"[163] using the description of a "wall of Separation," which he felt had been breached by the policies of his native England and the Massachusetts Bay Colony.[164]

Considering seventeenth-century England, its colonies, and most of Europe shows that they had overlapping ecclesiastical and secular authorities. In England, the monarch was the head of the Anglican Church, and the local church ministers were paid from taxes as public employees. Attendance in the Anglican services was mandatory, and membership was required for admission to universities and membership in the learned professions. The church, through its own courts, was the source of what would now be considered family law

---

[163] From Barry, John M.. Roger Williams and the Creation of the American Soul: Church, State, and the Birth of Liberty. Penguin Books, 2012. Pages 306–310.

[164] See appendix section IV, F, for wording of the statements of Roger Williams and Thomas Jefferson.

issues, such as marriage, divorce, adoption, child custody, and estate resolutions. It was this legal entanglement, punishment for failure of participation and direct tax support, that was deplored by Williams and Jefferson and the large majority of American citizens.

The principal objection of Roger Williams to the church-state relations in 1640 was what he perceived as the harmful effects of the state involvement on the beliefs and commitment of the communicants. He viewed the state's regulations and secular leadership as contaminants for what could otherwise be a degree of spiritual purity of one's worship. Jefferson objected to the state's imposition on the freedom of individuals to choose if and in what manner to worship. Neither would have imagined a true separation of religious belief from the secular society. In fact, judicial scholars agree that complete separation of religious institutions and secular activity has never been a consideration. One only need realize that churches and their affiliates benefit from public services, and their exemption from many taxes confirms this association.

The predictions of Roger Williams may well have been validated, as the political activities and scriptural interpretations of many churches in the twenty-first century are thought to have alienated large segments of the population. The continuing affiliation of national governments with religious worship in Europe may be in part a cause of the drastic decrease in religious participation by the public, at least since World War II. Truly secular politics and the attempt to legislate issues of religious significance to some, but not accepted by many, may have reduced the importance of religion in the American culture.

The opinions of Thomas Jefferson are best described in the Act for Establishing Religious Freedom written in 1777, which was not confirmed by the General Assembly until 1786.[165] The text clearly shows that he had no intention of eliminating the religious element of the culture but strongly supported one's individual right to develop their own beliefs without governmental interference.

---

[165] See appendix IV, F for texts of these documents.

The phrase in his Letter to the Danbury Baptists in 1802 suggests that the "wall of separation between Church & State" could imply a more stringent separation than his other writings about religious freedom would support. It is likely that this letter was to reassure the Baptists that he would oppose the wishes of the New England Congregationalists who wanted much closer relationships with the state. Incidentally, these non-Baptists were generally strong Federalist supporters and therefore antagonistic toward the Jeffersonian politics. The significance and interpretation of this simple phrase continues to be an issue for our society.

J. ANNE HUTCHINSON—MASSACHUSETTS BAY COLONY SPIRITUAL LEADER AND CREATOR OF THE ANTINOMIAN CONTROVERSY

The Antinomian Controversy, although seemingly misnamed, has been known by that designation since the seventeenth century and was a conflict between what is known as the covenant of works and the covenant of grace. These are two approaches to the Calvinist idea that an individual's realization of salvation by the atonement of sin through Christ is limited and available only to individuals elected by God from the time of creation. The anxiety created by one's attempt to identify if they were one of the elected few was the basis for much of the controversy. The Puritan leadership and most of the congregations accepted that one's behavior was the hallmark of the elect (i.e., their works would be evidence of their election). Conflict between one's outward behavior and inner thoughts left many individuals with uncertainty concerning their prospects for eternal life. Some of the women of the colony shared their anxieties with Anne Hutchinson, who began to counsel with them and held "conventicles" or midweek meetings in her home to discuss the sermons heard from the pulpit on Sunday.

The covenant of grace, espoused by Rev. Cotton and his followers, including Anne, held that one's works could never be totally acceptable to God and that the promises of atonement of sin through Christ could only be perceived as a gift from God resulting from His grace. Furthermore, one's personal certainty of this grace and salvation was made evident to an individual by the presence of the Holy Spirit, which became an awareness for the believer at the time of conversion and grew with the maturity of their faith. Also at issue was the question of the ability of pious behavior, as directed by the church and its leaders, to advance one nearer to the realization of one's justification and salvation. These controversies reached a peak in the activities of Anne Hutchinson and contributed to disputes between prominent ministers such as Joseph Cotton and Thomas Hooker. The schism with the Puritan leadership created by Anne Hutchinson in the summer of 1636 was primarily the result of Anne's accusations that those ministers who failed to preach the covenant of grace did not possess the gift and authority of the Holy Spirit and therefore were not preaching what, to her, was an authentic gospel. While few of the population were as polarized in their assessments as was Anne, the association of many with her group and the defense of her from the attacks of the secular leadership were sufficient to result in their banishment from the Bay Colony.

The first to be punished was Rev. John Wheelwright, an effective preacher in the community of Wollaston, married to the sister of Anne Hutchinson's husband. On his banishment from Massachusetts Bay Colony, he and his supporters resettled in Exeter, which would be in the Province and later the Colony of New Hampshire. Soon, two other supporters of Anne's, John Coggeshall and William Aspinwall, would be similarly charged, who after their banishment eventually created the communities of Newport and Portsmouth in Rhode Island. Left without her strongest supporters, Anne Hutchinson was banished in November 1637 "as being a woman not fit for our society."[166]

For a woman to openly criticize the ecclesiastical and secular leadership was so far beyond the limits of seventeenth-century English

---

[166] Battis, E.J., Saints and Sectaries, page 208, quote of John Winthrop.

culture that it resulted in severe reprisals. To be banished from the security of the community and its habitations was a dangerous and serious penalty. As we will see, the Indian natives were very much in control of the vast wilderness beyond the confines of the Puritan communities. Relations between Indians and English settlers were rapidly deteriorating in many areas and added to the uncertainty of survival away from the population centers. This danger was realized by Anne Hutchinson and a number of her many children who perished at the hands of Indians in Kieft's War in 1643 while they were living in an area of New Netherland now known as the Bronx.

K. THE SALEM WITCHCRAFT TRIALS

Perhaps as much shelf space could be occupied by writings concerning the tragic frenzy that constituted the Salem witchcraft episode as any event in colonial history. Belief in witchcraft was common in Europe and colonial North America and had grown over the previous several centuries. It was widely held that the world was a battleground between the forces of God and of Satan and that possession of individuals was a device whereby the devil could incite evil actions. There were few who denied the reality of witchcraft, but much controversy existed concerning the identification of possessed persons. Beginning in the winter of 1691–92 and lasting until May 1693, there were hundreds of people in Massachusetts Bay Colony accused and jailed under suspicion of satanic possession. A much smaller number were actually tried, and twenty were executed.[167]

One of the markers of witchcraft that was allowed in the trials was known as *spectral evidence*, where the person who had been affected by the accused claimed to have seen an apparition with the likeness of the accused that caused harm or fright. Deputy Governor William Stoughton had been appointed chief magistrate over the court of inquiry, and he ruled this testimony permissible and an

---

[167] Ibid. pp.120–124.

indication that the accused had consented to the demonic possession. The Puritan hierarchy was actively involved in these trials, as Rev. Cotton Mather sent a letter encouraging the court to vigorously pursue their mission. His father, Rev. Increase Mather, with twelve other Puritan ministers, wrote a negative response to the acceptance of spectral evidence, with the conclusion that it was "better to let ten witches go free than to condemn one innocent person."

Modern writers have suggested factors that may have contributed to the hysteria that attended the trials, including differences between the accused and their accusers, such as psychological issues, age, economic and social status, personal jealousies, conflicts between religious conservatives and liberals, and even the possible ingestion of rye bread contaminated by a fungus producing an ergot-like hallucinogen similar to LSD. A less specific explanation could be that this was an example of mass hysteria, based on beliefs long held by a population whose views of themselves and the world in which they lived had become increasingly circumscribed and unquestioned. In his comprehensive study of the Salem trials, Emerson Baker analyzes the political and personal aspects of the accused and the key figures in the proceedings that led to convictions. He elaborates on the religious factors that motivated the trials and the effects on the Puritan church, which was greatly affected by the resulting twenty executions.[168] After the trials ceased, the Puritan community soon began to express remorse and sought to compensate for the accusations and executions, one writer suggesting that "Salem witchcraft was the rock on which the theocracy shattered." Members of other religious sects expressed opposition to the trials, including a Baptist minister, Rev. William Milbourne, and a Quaker, Thomas Maule, who were severely punished by fine or imprisonment for their beliefs.

Of particular interest to our story of the Stoughton-Denman extended families is the role of William Stoughton (the son of Israel Stoughton, nephew of Judith Stoughton Denman Smead, and

---

[168] Baker, Emerson W., A Storm of Witchcraft: The Salem Trials and the American Experience. pp. 161–93.

cousin of John Denman II) in presiding over the trial–permitted testimony, which, as described, would not have been allowed in the seventeenth century or in subsequent eras. Spectral evidence referred to individuals seeing an apparition of a suspected witch and could only be seen by the affected accuser. The admission of evidence that was not observed by two witnesses was not permitted in trial testimony in the English law, and such would not have been considered under customary legal proceedings.[169] Baker analyzes the details of the aftermath of these trials and the attempted coverup of the event by Governor Sir Wiliam Phips, who tried to dissociate himself from the proceedings and to prevent publicity after the trials were ended. Baker concludes that "the trials changed people's views of their government and helped bring an end to the Puritan theocracy ... and the witch trials would trigger political, social and religious changes that would transform the Bay Colony."[170] The result of these trials was a decline in the importance of religious institutions in their culture, which would persist until the First Great Awakening forty years later. That event would start from the Puritan pulpit (then known as the Congregational Church) of Jonathan Edwards in Northampton, Massachusetts, and have profound influences on Christian worship throughout the colonies.

L. THE PRAYING INDIANS IN COLONIAL NEW ENGLAND

Each of the European states claiming parts of the New World devoted efforts to spreading the Christian faith to the native inhabitants. Both the Spanish and French sent with their explorations Roman Catholic priests whose work was instrumental in the colonial establishments. These activities by the Spanish in the Caribbean area, Mexico, and South America and by the French in the northern area of Canada are well referenced in the classic writing and bibliography

---

[169] Ibid. p. 173.
[170] Ibid. p. 195.

of Thomas S. Kidd, which is suggested for those wanting more information about the nature and results of those missionary efforts.[171] There was similar interest in evangelical work by the English colonists in Virginia and Massachusetts, but in both situations, these religious efforts would be overshadowed by military and cultural conflicts between the settlers and the indigenous population.

The European presence in North America had profoundly affected the native population beginning at least seventy years before the appearance of the Jamestown colony. The expedition of Hernando De Soto exposed the Indians to diseases against which they had no immunity. The pandemic of small pox and measles that spread through the population of the southeastern part of the continent devastated the large and complex Mississippian culture that had existed for centuries. This civilization is often referred to as the "Mound Builders" because of the large earthen mounds throughout the area that are presumed to have religious significance.

It has been estimated that the mortality among the native population was as high as 90 percent as a result of this disaster, similar to the effects of the coming of Europeans to the Caribbean and Mexico. This depopulation of the eastern area of North America prompted an expansion of the Algonquian and Iroquoian tribes into new areas. The conflicts between these populations and the remaining indigenous tribesmen led to disruptions in the native cultures. Intertribal conflict was later intensified with the competition for the trade of beaver pelts, other animal hides, and food for metallic objects and weapons with the Europeans in the sixteenth and seventeenth centuries, resulting in the decades-long Beaver Wars. The newcomers in some situations were seen as desirable military allies by the Indians, which was an important factor in the Pequot War in Massachusetts Bay Colony and Kieft's War in New Netherland. Even if the Native Americans had no awareness of the effects of the Europeans on their health, their relations with the newcomers soon deteriorated from

---

[171] Kidd, T.S. America's Religious History: Faith, Politics and the Shaping of a Nation, pp 9-31.

what have been considered by some as inevitable cultural conflicts. The Indians' initial amicable interactions diminished as they realized that the English wanted to obtain land that they would control indefinitely, which conflicted with the ethic of the Indian culture.

To appreciate the nature of this cultural impasse and the challenges that would face the Puritan and Separatist religious communities in New England and the Reformed/Anglican missionary efforts in Virginia, one needs an awareness of the spiritual and social structure that had developed in the native culture over thousands of years. This is described by Professor Bernard Baylin in the first part of his classic text.[172] In it, he describes the "purposeful, powerful spiritual forces" of the Indians' world that included "every aspect of nature and which demanded conformity to an ethic upon which their survival depended." The universe and the land that sustained them was "suffused with spiritual potency … that embraced all of life's diversity in an ultimately unified and comprehensive state of being." As their survival depended on the bounty of nature, which in their beliefs required adherence to strict protocols and demonstrations of respect, the ownership of land was no more understandable to the natives than would be the ownership of the air, rain, or animal life that inhabited the lakes and forests.

Kidd estimates that there were perhaps five hundred different tribes that shared some common religious themes about which little specific information is now available. The dominant theme, however, was the "pervasive spirituality of their world view." Superficially, it may appear that the religion of the Indians was similar enough to the Judeo-Christian beliefs of a creator and sustainer God of nature and a direct spiritual presence (i.e., the Holy Spirit), with values (commandments) whose violation (sin) would be offensive to God. The reality of the interactions between native Indians and European immigrants soon became anything but cordial and was further complicated by the language barrier. Whatever common

---

[172] Baylin, B. The Peopling of British North America—The Barbarous Years. The Conflict of Civilizations 1600-1675, pp 3-31.

ground may have existed was dissipated by the events of the early years of colonial settlement.

Part III, A of this book describes the events of the Virginia colony in the years following Jamestown's founding in 1607. The expectations of Rev. Robert Hunt and Rev. Richard Buck and the missionary interests of laymen George Thorpe and Alexander Whitaker produced only limited interest from the natives. The newly arriving settlers brought with them an unshakable sense of superiority to all other cultures and races, and it was without hesitation that the Jamestown arrivals used military force to obtain food from the Indians in 1609 when a drought had reduced all agricultural production in eastern Virginia. This produced aggressive retaliation by the Indians, which nearly eliminated the Jamestown settlement during the "starving time" of 1609–10 and began the First Anglo-Powhatan War (August 1609 to April 1614). These early interactions with the natives were followed by a decade of apparent calm following the marriage of Pocahontas to John Rolfe and her acceptance of Christianity. During this time, the Powhatan tribe and allies planned a surprise attack on the English settlements along the James River, expecting to permanently limit their presence. A few Indians were sympathetic toward the English and may have been influenced by Christian teachings. The devastation on March 22, 1622, would have been even greater were it not for their warnings that came before the onset of the attack. Thus began the Second Anglo-Powhatan War, lasting a decade, which decimated the tribal population and ended any subsequent chance for meaningful religious interaction. After 1632 and the end of the war, the remaining Indians began the westward relocation that would continue for the next century, during which there would be no significant missionary efforts in Virginia.

Circumstances in New England took a somewhat different path, but hostility between the natives and the English was still significant. The Pilgrims in Plymouth Colony may not have survived had it not been for the assistance provided by the Wampanoag Indians due to the influence of Squanto. The military strength of the settlers, as demonstrated by Myles Standish, made the newcomers welcome allies for the Wampanoag in the intertribal conflicts with the Narragansetts, Pequots, and others. There is little evidence of Christian conversion by the Indians in the Plymouth and Providence Plantation colonies. In Massachusetts Bay, there were significant effects of the missionary activities of Rev. John Eliot, who has been called the "apostle to the Indians."

Rev. Eliot attended Cambridge University, where he secured his Reformed faith, and in 1631, he arrived in Massachusetts Bay as the chaplain of a ship. He soon was named the minister and teaching elder of the First Church in Roxbury, a position he would hold for sixty years. He also preached occasionally in Dorchester and was the founder of the Roxbury Grammar School. His zeal for spreading Christianity to the Indians was never exceeded but was stifled by the language barrier. He began to learn the language of the Wampanoag (Massachusett) tribe from an Indian in 1637 during the Pequot War. Although there may be some uncertainty about the identity of this individual, the Natick Historical Society and Museum describes him as a youth born around 1620 who may have been orphaned by a small pox epidemic in 1633 and was sheltered in the family of Richard Callicott of Dorchester. Wassausmon, known to the English as John Sassamon, learned to speak and write English and in 1637 served with Callicott as a soldier and interpreter for the colonial troops in the Pequot War (1636–38).[173]

Eliot learned to speak the language well enough to preach and to translate scripture, prayers, and sermons into a phonetic rendering of the language. This was thought to be the first example of a written Indian language and facilitated the bringing of the Christian faith to the native population by other preachers. By 1663, Eliot had translated and published the Bible into the Massachusett language, and in 1670, he ordained the first Indian pastor in New England.[174] By 1675, 20 percent of the Indian population in the area was affiliated with the fourteen Christian communities known as Praying Towns. The best

---

[173] The Natick Historical Society, https://www. natickhistoricalsociety.org/faqs.
[174] Kidd, T.S. America's Religious History, Page 14.

documented example is Natick, in which the Indians expressed the greatest degree of adoption of English culture. This was certainly disruptive of their traditional culture, and the nature and extent of that conflict has been the subject of much research and speculation. The promotion of these towns, which were inhabited solely by the Indian population, were developed due to the belief of the English that the Reformed faith, their culture, and social structure were thoroughly intertwined. Hence, the Indians adopting the Reformed faith would be required to adopt the English culture and work habits. The possible motivation for the Indians to adopt this way of life may not have included an understanding or adoption of the new religious beliefs.

Harold W. Van Lonkhuyzen in his thoughtful publication describes several reasons why numbers of Indians were willing to adopt English customs.[175] As previously noted, the association with the English was seen as strategically useful with the ongoing hostility between tribes, and trade for English goods was both materially and socially beneficial. Certain aspects of English life were attractive to the Indians; for example, women wished to learn to spin and create fabrics. Farming and woodworking techniques and domestic animals, such as hogs and cattle, were of value to the Indians. The Praying Towns flourished, and by King Philip's War in 1675, nearly one-fourth of the Indians in southeastern New England considered themselves Christian. These influences greatly changed a number of cultural issues and led to a dependence by the Indians, which created the irreversible environment leading to that war (see section III, B). It was precipitated by the murder of John Sassamon, who had been a close associate of Rev. Eliot for decades, and the war was devastating to all Indians as well as the English. The attitude of the English toward the Indians was profoundly changed, and any sense of trust by the Indians toward the English was irreparably damaged.[176]

"The continuing processes of internal and external change in the post-war period rapidly dissolved the social organization underpinning

---

[175] Van Lonkhuyzen, Harold. The New England Quarterly, Vol. 63, No. 3 (Sep., 1990), pp. 396–428.

[176] Ibid. page 421.

Indian identity … the story of Natick offers some sobering insights into a world increasingly characterized by the confrontation and commingling of cultures. Contact with Europeans did not drastically alter traditional Indian goals; it simply made their realization through traditional means more difficult and finally impossible."[177]

M. THE FIRST GREAT AWAKENING

At the close of the seventeenth century, the Puritan society in New England was very different from what had begun eighty years earlier. The population had grown from a few hundred in the early 1620s to nearly fourteen thousand by 1640 with the great migration begun by John Winthrop. With the beginning of the English Civil Wars, this flood of Puritans ceased, and emigration from the English homeland was insignificant during the rest of the century. The population, however, expanded to over ninety thousand by 1700, due to the usual birth rate and a lower than expected death rate, growing the population at a rate of 2.7 percent annually, doubling every twenty-seven years.[178] The population growth and other factors affected the economy and politics of the area, but the experiences of the Pequot and King Philip's Wars and the religious disruptions from the Antinomian Controversy and the Salem witchcraft trials certainly had major effects. The changes in Puritan New England during the seventeenth century are beautifully described by Bernard Baylin in his introductory book published in 1986.

> [The] Puritan world whose inner spirit, once powerfully creative and fearless, had survived into a third generation in a faded and defensive form. The fierce religious intensity, the sense of daring and risky enterprise in the service of a demanding God—an enterprise of great relevance to the whole informed

[177] Ibid. page 424 and 427.
[178] Colonial and Pre-Federal Statistics, United States Census Bureau, 2004.

Protestant world—all of that had passed. The first generation's accomplishments had been products of passionate striving in an atmosphere of fear and desperation; but to their children the founders' world was an inheritance they were born into—respected but familiar and routine. And to *their* children, adults at the end of the century, what had once been rebellious, liberating and challenging had become a problematic anachronism.[179]

Although the church organizations remained important parts of the colonial culture, by the beginning of the eighteenth century, there was an apparent ebbing of enthusiasm for the spiritual aspects of the Puritan faith. This would change significantly in the 1730s with what has been known as the Great Awakening (or the Evangelical Revival). This movement had begun in the 1720s in the Moravian church in continental Europe and soon involved the Lutheran, Reformed, and Anabaptist sects. At this time, similar changes in worship style and emphasis were developing in Scotland, with protests against the attempts of James I and Charles I to extend control over the Church of Scotland with its Reformed (Presbyterian) emphasis. Immigrants from Scotland brought this new worship style to the Middle Atlantic colonies, where their faith coexisted with others such as Dutch Reformed, Quakers, Lutheran, Anglican, Baptists, and Congregational (Puritan).

The Reformed churches that had grown from the early Puritan influence stressed behavioral aspects of their faith, and their worship was characterized by formal rituals rather than the spiritual emphasis that had been suppressed, possibly as a result of the earlier Antinomian conflicts. This began to change gradually but did not gain wide awareness until 1734 when Jonathan Edwards, preaching at his Congregational church in Massachusetts, began an evangelical revival

---

[179] Baylin, Bernard. The Peopling of British North America: An Introduction. p. 91.

that would spread throughout the colonies. Edwards published his experiences in *A Faithful Narrative*, which was a stimulus to a spiritual revival similar to what was developing in England.

The evangelical enthusiasm developing in England would be brought to the colonies in the person of George Whitefield, who on his return to New England preached to tens of thousands in churches and public venues. He would travel throughout the colonies, spreading the gospel of the awakening in large cities and the smallest of towns. The effects of his campaign would not be limited to the spiritual aspects of colonial life. His message would be disruptive to many individual churches, as the emotional expressions of the Holy Spirit were disparaged by the more conservative members, and thus began the growth of the many denominations of Protestant Christianity that has since characterized the church in North America. The contact between Whitefield's preaching in Pennsylvania and South Carolina would be important in the lives of the original colonial subjects of our story. The important role that Whitefield played in the formation of the spiritual aspects of the American colonies is well described in *America's Religious History* by Thomas S. Kidd. For the effects of the Awakening on the Welsh Neck Baptist Church and Kolb/James families, see III, E.

BIBLIOGRAPHY

Bailyn, Bernard. *The Barbarous Years: The Peopling of British North America—The Conflict of Civilizations, 1600–1675*. New York: Random House, Inc., 2012.

Baker, Emerson W. *A Storm of Witchcraft: The Salem Trials and the American Experience*. New York: Oxford University Press, 2015.

Barry, John M. *Roger Williams and the Creation of the American Soul*. New York: Penguin Books, 2012.

Battis, Emery J. *Saints and Sectaries: Anne Hutchinson and the Antinomian Controversy in the Massachusetts Bay Colony*. Chapel Hill: University of North Carolina Press, 1962.

Brown, DeNeen L. "Slavery's Bitter Roots." *Washington Post*, August 24, 2018.

Burrows, E.G. and Wallace, M. Gotham: A History of New York City to 1898, Oxford University Press, New York, 1999.

Cassel, Daniel Kolb. A Genealogical History of the Kolb, Kulb or Culp Family, and its Branches in America. Morgan Wells, Morristown, PA. 1895.

Drake, James D. King Philip's War: Civil War in New England, 1675–76. University of Massachusetts Press, Amherst, 1999.

Foner, Philip. History of Black America: From Africa to the Emergence of the Cotton Kingdom. Oxford University Press, 1980.

Gallway, Alan. Planters and Slaves in the Great Awakening, in Masters & Slaves in the House of the Lord, John B. Boles, Editor, The University Press of Kentucky, 1988.

Gausted, Edwin S. Roger Williams. Oxford University Press, 2005,

Gregg, Alexander. History of the Old Cheraws. Richardson and Company, New York, 1845. (reprinted by Forgotten Books, 2012)

Halbrook, Stephen P. The Founders' Second Amendment. Origin of the Right to Bear Arms. Ivan R. Dee, Chicago, 2008.

Hamburger, Philip. Separation of Church and State. Harvard University Press, Cambridge, MA, 2002.

Harris, Harriet N. Denman Family History. From the Earliest Authentic Records to the Present Time. The Glendale News, 1913.

Hodges, R.G. Root and Branch: African Americans in New York and East Jersey 1613–1823. 1999.

Illick, Joseph E. Colonial Pennsylvania, A History. Charles Scribner's Sons, New York, 1976.

Johnson, L. The Welsh in the Carolinas in the Eighteenth Century. North American Journal of Welsh Studies, Vol. 4.1 (Winter, 2004)

Jordan, John W. Colonial and Revolutionary Families of Pennsylvania. Volumes 1 and 2, 1911.

Kammen, Michael. Colonial New York, A History. Charles Scribner's Sons, New York, 1975.

Kidd, Thomas S. The Great Awakening. The Roots of Evangelical Christianity in Colonial America. Yale University Press, New Haven, 2007.

Kidd, Thomas S. American Colonial History: Clashing Cultures and Faiths. Yale University Press, New Haven, 2016.

Kidd, Thomas S. America's Religious History: Faith, Politics, and the Shaping of a Nation. Zondervan Academic, 2019.

Kraft, Herbert C. The Lenape: Archeology, History, and Ethnography. New Jersey Historical Society, Newark, 1982.

LaBaree, Benjamin W. Colonial Massachusetts. A History. KTO Press, Millwood, New York, 1979.

LaPlante, Eve. American Jezebel. The Uncommon Life of Anne Hutchinson, The Woman Who Defied the Puritans. Harper San Francisco, 2004.

Linscombe, S. The History of U.S. Rice Production—PRT 1, LSU Ag Center.

Malcolm, Joyce Lee. To Keep and Bear Arms. The Origins of an Anglo-American Right. Harvard University Press, Cambridge, MA, 1994.

McBeth, H. Leon. The Baptist Heritage. Four Centuries of Baptist Witness. Broadman Press, Nashville, TN, 1987.

M'Crie, Thomas. Life of John Knox. W. Blackwood, Edinburgh, 1831. (Reprinted 2018)

Morgan, Edmund S. Roger Williams, The Church and the State. W.N. Norton & Co., New York, 1967.

Natick Historical Society, The. https://www.natickhistoricalsociety. org/faq.

Orcutt, S. and Beardsley, A. The History of Old Town Derby 1642–1800, 1880.

Philip, Robert. The Life and Times of George Whitefield, 1837. Reprinted by The Banner of Truth Trust, Carlisle, PA, 2007.

Prime, Nathaniel Scuddder. A History of Long Island, from its first settlement by Europeans, to the year 1845. Robert Carter, New York, 1845.

Roger, N.A.M. The Command of the Ocean. A Naval History of Britain: 1649–1815. Penguin Books, 2004.

Scharf, Thomas J. History of Delaware, 1609–1888, Vol. Two.

Taylor, Alan. American Colonies. The Settling of North America. Penguin Books, New York, 2001.

Vaughan, Alden T. New England Frontier. Puritans and Indians 1620–1675. The University of Oklahoma Press, Norman, OK, 1965.

Van Lonkhuyzen, Harold W. *A Reappraisal of the Praying Indians: Acculturation, Conversion, and Identity at Natick, Massachusetts, 1646–1730.* The New England Quarterly, Vol 63, No. 3, pp. 396–428. Published by The New England Quarterly, Inc.

Walker, W. et al. A History of the Christian Church. Scribner, 1985.

Warren, James A. God, War, and Providence, Scribner, 2018.

Weir, Robert M. Colonial South Carolina, A History. KTO Press, 1983.

Winship, Michael P. The Times & Trials of Anne Hutchinson. Puritans Divided. University Press of Kansas, Lawrence, Kansas, 2005.

Wood, Betty. Slavery in Colonial America 1619–1776. Rowman & Littlefield Publishers, Inc. Lanham, MD, 2005.

Wyckoff, W.F. and Streeter, M.B. The Wyckoff Family in America. A Genealogy. The

Tuttle Group, Rutland, VT, 1934.

Wykoff, M. William. What's in a Name? History and Meaning of Wyckoff. Rochester, NY, 2014.

GALLERY

Figure 1. Newtown Creek, looking downstream toward
Manhattan from an area near the colonial site of Maspeth

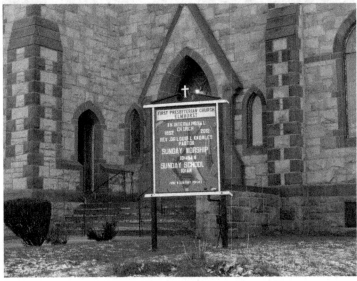

Figure 2. The picture below (L) is thee rear facade of the Newtown Reformed Church, whose name was changed to Elmhurst when New Netherland became New York. The other side of the building has the current name as the First Presbyterian Church of Elmhurst (R)'

Figure 3. Pieter Claesen Wyckoff House, 5816 Clarenden
Road at Ralph Avenue Brooklyn, New York 11230

Revolutionary War Heritage Trail Plaque

PIETER CLAESEN WYCKOFF HOUSE

*Originally the enter of a Dutch West India Company bowery, or farm, the
original portion of the Pieter Claesen Wyckoff House was built c. 1652 by
Pieter and his wife, Grietje Van Ness and is the oldest surviving structure
in New York City. The house was enlarged c. 1740 and again in 1819
in a pattern typical of the Dutch-American farmhouse. The house was
built along Canarsie Lane, which linked the settlement of Canarsie with
Kings Highway. During the Revolutionary War, Pieter and Grietje's
great grandson, Peter A. Wyckoff, and his wife, Heyltie Remsen lived
here with three small children and several slaves. The Wyckoff House
is an excellent example of the Dutch Colonial vernacular style with its
H-frame structure, shingled walls, split doors, and deep, flared "spring"
eaves. Today it is one of the few surviving examples of the many hundreds
of such buildings that doted the landscape of Kings County when British
and American forces clashed in the Battle of Brooklyn on August 27, 1776.
The Pieter Claesen Wyckoff House is owned by the New York City
Department of Parks & Recreation, is operated by the Wyckoff House &
Association and his a member of the Historic Trust of New York City.*

221

Figure 4. Brass plaque in the foyer of the Dutch
Reformed Church of Flatlands, which helped perpetuate
the incorrect origin of the Wyckoff name.

In grateful memory of
PIETER CLAESEN
Arrived in the new world from Holland
March 4, 1637 at twelve years of age found work on
a farm at Fort Orange and after marrying
GRIETJE VAN NESS
Moved to New Amstooriwhere
by native worth he became a leading citizen.
In 1664 he assumed the surname of
WYCKOFF
signifying his public service as a magistrate of
of the town court
thus becoming the progenitor of
the Wyckoff family in America.
One of the founders of this
Flatlands Dutch Reformed Church
and honorably buried in the plot covered
by the primeni edifice.

Figure 5. Flatlands Dutch Reformed Church.

Text of a plaque at he Dutch Reformed Church in Flatlands

Landmarks of New York—Dutch Reformed Church of Flatlands—Constructed in 1846 in late Federal style this edifice occupies the site of the original octagonal shingled church built in 1665 and rebuilt in 1794. The congregation was formed in 1654 by the Rev. Johannes Megapolensis, Pastor of the Collegiate Church in Manhattan.

HUGUENOT FAMILY NAMES
IDENTIFIED WITH THE HISTORY OF NEW ROCHELLE
DURING THE COLONIAL PERIOD

ALLAIRE	BOUTEILLIER	Du BOIS	JAMAIN	MARTIN	RAMBERT
ALLE	BOULEMAN	Du PRE	JANDRON	MEMBRUT	RAVAUX
ANGEVIN	BOUYER	DeTUFFEAU	JOUNEAU	MERCIER	RAYMON
ARNAUD	CAILLAUD	EROUARD	JUIN	MERGINE	RESSEGUIER
ASSIRE	CAMBY	FANEUIL	LADOU	MESNARD	RICHE
BADEAU	CARRE	FEURT	LAMBERT	MINVIELLE	RINEURE
BAIGNOUX	CHADAINE	FLANDREAU	LAMOUREUX	MOREAU	ROGHAR
BARTOW	CHAMPENOIS	FORESTIER	LANDRIN	MORIN	SANSON
BASSET	CHAPERON	FOUCAULT	LASTY	MOULINARS	SICARD
BAYEUX	CLEMENT	FREHEL	LAURAN	MOYNOT	SIMON
BERRIAU	GLERAMBEAU	FRESNEAU	LAVIGNE	NAUDAIN	SORIN
BERNARD	CONTESSE	GAINEAU	LEAR	NEUFVILLE	SOULICE
BERTAIN	COQUILLET	GALLAUDET	Le BOITEUX	NIGOLLE	STOUPPE
BESLY	COTHONNEAU	GARNIER	Le CONTE	NOLLEAU	STREING
BOISSEAU	GOUJANT	GILLOT	Le REAN	PAQUINET	SUIRE
BONDEE	DAS	GIRAUD	Le ROUX	PARGOT	THAUVET
BONGRAND	DASSERLX	GOMBAUD	LeVILAIN	PELLETREAU	THEROUIDE
BONNEAU	DE BANE	GOUGEON	LILUKE	PERIORD	TOULON
BONNEFOY	DI BLEZ	GUERIN	LISPENARD	PEROT	TOURNEUR
BONNET	DE BONREPOS	GUERINEAU	LUMPREY	PETIT	TIESE
BONNIN	DE ROESSBEL	GUION	MABILLE	PILLION	TREHEL
BONLEGOU	DESCHAMPS	HASTIER	MAGHET	PINTARD	VALLADE
BONYOT	DELMARESI	HONORI	MAGNY	POIRIER	VALLEAU
BOREE	DESTECROIX	HOUDIN	MAGNON	QUANTIN	VERGERAU
BOURGUTI	DEVEAUX	JABOUIN	MAQUEINON	RAINEAU	VILLEPONTEUX
					VINCENT

NAMES FURNISHED BY HUGUENOT & HISTORICAL ASSOCIATION

THIS TABLET ERECTED BY
THE NEW ROCHELLE TWO HUNDRED-FIFTIETH ANNIVERSARY COMMITTEE
1938

Figure 6. Plaque in Hudson Park, New Rochelle, New York, listing names of Huguenot families living there in the colonial period, including the family name of Gaineau.

Figure 7. Pennepack Baptist Church, Krewestown Road, Philadelphia, Pennsylvania.

Figure 8. Welsh Tract Baptist Church--originally in the
"second Welsh Tract of the Colony of Pennsylvania",
later renamed New Castle County, Delaware.

Figures 9 a and b. Exterior and Interior of the St. Helen's Church building, including the window honoring William Shakespeare.

Figure 10. Plaque from Church of St. Peter upon Cornell in London. See section V, H for a transcription of the plaque.